BY EVAN THOMAS

Road to Surrender

First: Sandra Day O'Connor

Being Nixon

Ike's Bluff

The War Lovers

Sea of Thunder

John Paul Jones

Robert Kennedy

The Very Best Men

The Man to See

The Wise Men (with Walter Isaacson)

ROAD TO SURRENDER

ROAD TO SURRENDER

Three Men and the Countdown
to the End of World War II

Evan Thomas

RANDOM HOUSE
NEW YORK

Published in the United States by Random House, an imprint and division of
Penguin Random House LLC, New York.

RANDOM HOUSE and the HOUSE colophon are registered trademarks of
Penguin Random House LLC.

LIBRARY OF CONGRESS CATALOGING-IN-PUBLICATION DATA

Names: Thomas, Evan, author.
Title: Road to surrender : three men and the countdown to the end of
World War II / by Evan Thomas.
Other titles: Three men and the countdown to the end of World War II
Description: New York : Random House, [2023] | Includes bibliographical
references and index.
Identifiers: LCCN 2022023935 (print) | LCCN 2022023936 (ebook) |
ISBN 9780399589256 (hardcover) | ISBN 9780399589263 (ebook)
Subjects: LCSH: Capitulations, Military—Japan—History—20th century. |
United States—Military policy—Decision making. | Atomic bomb. | World War,
1939–1945—Japan. | World War, 1939–1945—United States. | Tōgō, Shigenori,
1882–1950. | Stimson, Henry L. (Henry Lewis), 1867–1950. | Spaatz, Carl,
1891–1974.
Classification: LCC D813.J3 T46 2023 (print) | LCC D813.J3 (ebook) |
DDC 940.53/12—dc23/eng/20220711
LC record available at https://lccn.loc.gov/2022023935
LC ebook record available at https://lccn.loc.gov/2022023936

Printed in the United States of America on acid-free paper

randomhousebooks.com

9 8 7 6 5

Overleaf: Surrender ceremony in Tokyo Bay on the battleship USS *Missouri,*
September 2, 1945.

To Joanna and Noah

Contents

Introduction: The Dilemma   xi

Part One

1. Sleepless   3
"The terrible," "the awful," "the diabolical"

2. Target Practice   27
"May [be] *Frankenstein or* means for World Peace"

3. The Stomach Art   60
"THERE ARE NO CIVILIANS IN JAPAN"

4. The Patient Progresses   87
"You judge it; I can't"

5. Prompt and Utter   104
"Shall the worst occur"

6. A Bucket of Tar   111
"What the hell, let's take a chance"

Part Two

7. Terrible Responsibility   129
"I had a rather sharp little attack"

8. Denial   141
"Fire every damn flare in the airplane!"

9. Sacred Decision   152
"There is life in death"

10. **Gambits** 167
"The Superforts are not flying today"

11. **Plots** 178
"What are you thinking of?"

12. **Is Tokyo Next?** 190
"This man is tottering"

13. **To Bear the Unbearable** 198
"Like a mid-summer's night dream"

14. **No High Ground** 211
"The only way you can make a man trustworthy"

Epilogue: Reckonings 221
Acknowledgments 235
Bibliography 239
Notes 251
Photograph Credits 297
Index 299

Introduction
The Dilemma

B-29s fly past Mount Fuji on their way to Tokyo.

I N AUGUST 1945, AFTER THE UNITED STATES DROPPED atomic bombs on Hiroshima and Nagasaki and Japan surrendered, the soldiers, sailors, and airmen scheduled to participate in the invasion of Japan reacted as you might expect. They cheered, they danced. Some of them wept with relief. Others sat in quiet disbelief. One infantry officer, who had been wounded in action in Europe and was slated to lead a rifle platoon up a defended beach near Tokyo, recalled thinking, "We were going to live. We were going to grow into adulthood after all."

In more recent years, scholars of World War II have argued

that it was not necessary to drop the atomic bombs on Japan, or that it was not necessary to drop more than one, or that the Japanese might have been moved to surrender if the United States had staged a demonstration of the bomb's power on a deserted island. That argument has gained popular currency. When I was writing this book, friends would ask, was it really necessary to drop *two* atomic bombs? In school and college, many had been exposed to books and scholarship that argued that, by August 1945, Japan was ready to surrender, and that America's real motivation in dropping the A-bomb was to intimidate Russia in the earliest days of the Cold War.

The facts are otherwise. On the morning of August 9, 1945, *after* the United States dropped two atomic bombs *and* Russia declared war on Japan, the Supreme Council for the Direction of the War, the group of six leaders who ran Japan, deadlocked on whether to surrender. The vote was a tie, three to three. The most powerful leaders, the ones who ran the army, wanted to keep on fighting. For five more days, Japan teetered on the edge of a coup d'état by the military that would have plunged Japan into chaos and extended the war for many bloody months. On the last night, coup plotters seized control of the Imperial Palace, running through the halls looking for a recording of the emperor's voice, to be broadcast the next day at noon, announcing Japan's surrender. (The recording, fortunately, was tucked away in a room reserved for ladies-in-waiting.) Hot and dark, largely burned out by American firebombs, Tokyo roiled with intrigue and deception, including large doses of self-deception on the part of the leaders responsible for deciding.

In Washington, meanwhile, decision makers were not, for the most part, thinking about the bombs' effect on the Soviet Union. They were praying that the bombs would bring Japan to its senses. Indeed, they were seriously considering dropping another. The Washington leaders were not free of their own illusions as they struggled over what to do, but they faced a hard reality. They were actors caught in a dilemma as old as war but never more grotesquely distended: that to save lives it was necessary to take lives—possibly hundreds of thousands of them.

This book is a narrative of how the most destructive war in history ended—and very nearly did not. It asks what it was like to be one of the decent, imperfect people who made the decision to use a frighteningly powerful new weapon. How did they choose how many bombs to drop, when, where, and to what end? I learned that the word *decision* does not accurately describe the fraught, inexorable process that they went through. Were they somehow subject to "psychic numbing," as scholars have suggested? A few, like Maj. Gen. Curtis LeMay, the chief of the XXI Bomber Command, seemed to be (or pretended to be) unfeeling or at least matter-of-fact. "If you kill enough of them, they stop fighting," said LeMay, whose B-29s burned to death at least 85,000 residents of Tokyo on one night in March 1945. But others were troubled, even tormented, though they, too, tried not to show it. Duty, mercy, expediency, and ending a four-year war all pulled at them.

The problem for these men—the looming, intractable, seemingly unsurpassable obstacle—was that Japan was unwilling to surrender. By the summer of 1945, the empire appeared to be defeated. Japan's ships had been sunk, its cities burned, and its people were on the verge of starvation. But its military leaders, who commanded 5 million soldiers under arms, as well as greater citizen armies equipped with pitchforks and scythes, seemed bent on mass suicide. To attempt to defeat them by invading and seizing territory seemed sure to produce the greatest bloodbath of all time—and the Japanese, or at least their military leaders, beckoned the Americans to it.

The Allied forces assembled a vast invasion armada, including at least a dozen hospital ships, but the projected casualty estimates were so ghastly that even the most upright of men, Gen. George C. Marshall, the chief of staff of the army, invited his subordinates to fudge the numbers. Dropping the A-bomb on Japan was a foregone conclusion. That Japan would surrender was not. The atomic bombs would kill roughly 200,000 people. Had Japan fought on, likely many more people would have died, possibly millions more, in Asia as well as Japan.

Two weeks after the bombs fell, the Allied armed services staged a magnificent surrender ceremony on a battleship in Tokyo Bay, with wave after wave of American warplanes flying overhead. But I wondered: How did they feel, the decision makers, when the celebration ended and the cheering stopped? What were the complicated emotions of these men, most of them never-complain, never-explain stoics of their generation, practiced in the art of denial?

Occasionally true feelings, or something like them, would slip out. In November 1945 J. Robert Oppenheimer, the chief scientist in charge of developing the bomb at the secret laboratories of Los Alamos, appeared in the Oval Office and cried out to President Truman, "Mr. President, I feel I have blood on my hands!" According to the president's account, Truman coolly dismissed Oppenheimer and instructed that "the cry-baby scientist" never be brought around to him again. Telling the story later, Truman would imitate Oppenheimer wringing his hands. "I told him the blood was on my hands—to let me worry about that," said Truman.

In later years, Truman liked to say that the decision to drop the atomic bombs was his and his alone. The reality was not so straightforward. Maj. Gen. Leslie Groves, who ran the Manhattan Project that built the bomb, once scoffed that Truman was "like a little boy on a toboggan" careening downhill—that he had little or no control over a process that was already well along when Truman took office and essentially unstoppable. Groves's jibe about Truman is not fair; as commander in chief, Truman did take responsibility, and if he was sometimes opaque or chose to look the other way, that does not distinguish him from other great presidents who were also politicians, notably his predecessor, Franklin D. Roosevelt. Still, Truman was not the main actor in the story of how America (and its allies) and Japan came to end World War II.

Our story begins and ends with the man who oversaw the building of the atomic bomb and authorized the order to deliver it, FDR's and Truman's secretary of war, Henry L. Stimson. Stimson is today a largely forgotten figure. He was, in 1945, a rather antique Victorian with the blind spots and racial prejudices of his time and class. He was old and sick and sometimes absent or seemingly out of the loop as the war ground to its bloody end. And yet in the last act of a long career of public service, he found a way to face up to the conflicting demands of great power. He embodied and preached a philosophy that would make the United States, for all its flaws, the world's essential nation: the belief that American foreign policy should be a blend of *realism* and *idealism*. It should balance humanitarian and ethical values with cold-eyed power used in the national interest.

This balance is hard to achieve and maintain. At times, it is impossible. The effort almost killed Stimson in the summer of 1945. On the morning he brought Truman the first photos of Hiroshima, or what was left of it, after the first bomb fell, Stimson had a small heart attack. After he presented the president a month later with the first-ever plan to control nuclear weapons, he had a major heart attack. He was physically frail, to be sure, but his diaries show that he was also suffering from existential anguish.

Stimson signed off on the order to deliver the atomic bombs, and it was sent to Gen. Carl "Tooey" Spaatz, the army air forces commander assigned to lead the strategic bombing campaign in Operation Downfall, the final assault on the Japanese home islands. The low-key, almost diffident Spaatz was described by Gen. Dwight Eisenhower as "the best air commander I know." In Europe, Spaatz had been responsible for orders to drop thousands of tons of bombs at the cost not only of tens of thousands of civilians but also of thousands of soldiers and airmen, including many Americans. He quietly, dutifully, and expeditiously gave and carried out death-dealing orders. But that did not mean that he was not affected by what he was doing. On August 11, 1945, after Hiroshima and Nagasaki had been destroyed by atomic bombs—at his command—Spaatz wrote in his diary (self-consciously, awkwardly, as if he were testifying for the historical record—or before his Maker), "When the atomic bomb was first discussed with me in Washington, I was not in favor of it just as I have never favored the destruction of cities as such with all inhabitants being killed." Yet faced with the continued refusal of the Japanese to surrender, he recommended dropping a third atomic bomb on Tokyo, on an area already burned out by firebombs. And indeed, President Truman told America's British allies that he was resigned to dropping a third bomb—on Tokyo—just hours before he learned of Japan's surrender on the late afternoon of August 14 (August 15 in Japan).

Both Stimson and Spaatz followed a rigid code of duty; both agonized over the brutal means to what they saw as a just end. In this book, I draw on their diaries and papers, some given me by family members, to help tell what happened, as closely as possible and as it happened—in real time and in the present tense. I do not pretend that these records are precise road maps to the psyches of the people who kept them. Diaries, after all, are often written for posterity—as a record of the way people *wish* to be remembered. (Spaatz's diary for August 11, quoted above, may be a case in point.) But at important moments, the diaries and letters of Stimson and Spaatz are remarkably candid about the kinds of inner conflicts that can pull at men who are, outwardly at least, sure of themselves.

Of course, the American side is only half the story, and perhaps not even the most important half. What of the Japanese? What made them finally surrender even after two atomic bombs did not? More than seventy-five years later, Emperor Hirohito remains an enigmatic figure, wrapped in veils by palace courtiers who venerated him as a deity. He revered his ancestors, but he was, in truth, a very mortal being who was not sure which frightened him more—the American B-29 bombers or his own rebellious army officers.

Fortunately for history, a proud, brave, stubborn man, Foreign Minister Shigenori Togo, did more than any other person to bring Japan's ruling Supreme War Council to accept surrender in the apocalyptic spring and summer of 1945. I draw on unpublished diary entries provided by his grandsons to tell his story here as well.

Though Stimson and Spaatz never met Togo—and probably knew very little, if anything, about him—these three men became unlikely partners in averting a cataclysm of death beyond anything the world has ever seen or, one hopes, will ever experience. It was a close-run thing.

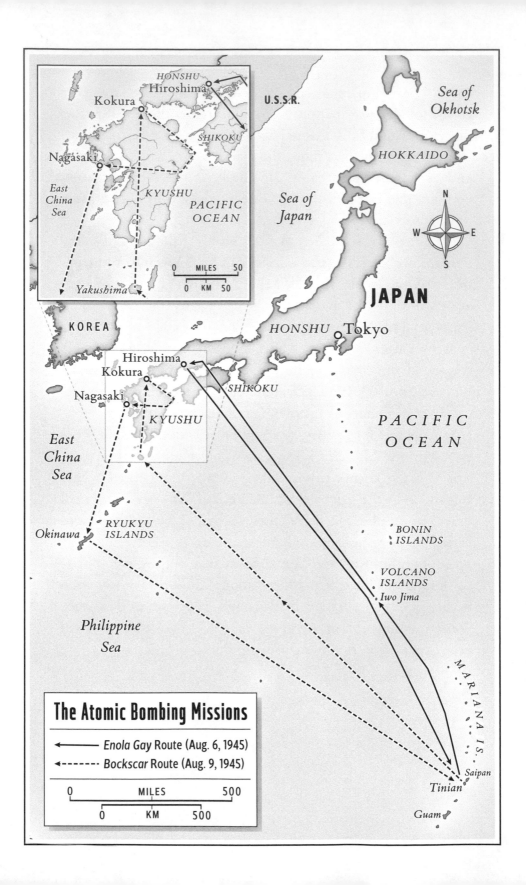

HONSHU
Hiroshima
Kokura
Nagasaki
East
China
Sea
KYUSHU
PACIFIC
OCEAN
SHIKOKU
U.S.S.R.

MILES   50
KM   50

Yakushima

Sea of
Okhotsk

HOKKAIDO

Sea of
Japan

JAPAN

KOREA

Hiroshima
Kokura
Nagasaki
KYUSHU

HONSHU   Tokyo

SHIKOKU

PACIFIC
OCEAN

East
China
Sea

Okinawa   RYUKYU
ISLANDS

BONIN
ISLANDS

VOLCANO
ISLANDS
Iwo Jima

Philippine
Sea

MARIANA IS.

The Atomic Bombing Missions

— *Enola Gay* Route (Aug. 6, 1945)

---- *Bockscar* Route (Aug. 9, 1945)

0   MILES   500

0   KM   500

Saipan

Tinian

Guam

Part One

1.

Sleepless

"The terrible," "the awful," "the diabolical"

Secretary of War Henry Stimson adored Mabel, his wife of more than fifty years.

Washington, D.C.
March 1945

H ENRY STIMSON, THE SECRETARY OF WAR, IS KNOWN for his resolute personal integrity. As a New York lawyer in the early 1900s, he had "stood outside the Wall Street group," as he once explained it, and "did not adopt the methods of the others." He could, and did, turn down clients he thought were likely to be found culpable, no matter how large their potential fees. "I can just hear the gates of the jail clanking shut behind you," he told one group of corporate investors who had come with a scheme to evade the antitrust laws. Stimson has always cared more about his own probity and public service than about amassing wealth. Nonetheless, he is wealthy.

Stimson is a nineteenth-century gentleman contending with the forces of twentieth-century global warfare. He is not lacking in confidence. He is a devout Christian and an equally ardent practitioner of power politics. When the contradictions gnaw at him, he is determined not to show it. Though rich from representing clients with private wealth, he served as a trust-busting prosecutor for President Theodore Roosevelt, as an unapologetic colonial administrator and negotiator for President Coolidge, as secretary of state to President Hoover, and as secretary of war twice—first for President Taft, and now for Franklin Roosevelt.

In Washington, Stimson lives in a spacious, airy, architecturally unremarkable house called Woodley, set on eighteen acres of grass and woods, high on a hill above Rock Creek Park, a couple of miles from the White House. In 1929, newly appointed to be secretary of state in the Hoover administration, Stimson bought Woodley for $800,000, a small fortune at the time.* He was able to afford the house because, on the advice of a shrewd cousin, he had sold his overvalued shares before the stock market crashed in October of that year.

Stimson enjoys Woodley in part because the house comes with a stable for horses. Once he had mounted chargers with hard mouths and ridden to the hounds. Now, at the age of seventy-seven, he guides a Tennessee walking horse into the park, trotting along for ten or twenty miles some evenings, "refreshing rides," he writes in his diary.

In his high-ceilinged bedroom at Woodley on this, the first night of March 1945, Stimson cannot sleep. He takes a sedative, though he does not want to. He does not drink al-

---

* About $13 to $14 million in 2022 dollars.

cohol, and he prefers treating his various ailments, real and imagined—a bum leg, a sore hip, a nervous stomach, an aching tooth—with regular exercise. In addition to a riding stable, Woodley has a platform for deck tennis and, for those evenings when Stimson is truly worn out, a clipped green for tossing lawn bowls.

Stimson has not slept well for many years. He is habitually an insomniac. He was sleepy on the day of Pearl Harbor and sometimes struggles not to doze off at councils of war at the Pentagon. Now, after four years of willing himself to build and oversee the most powerful military force in the history of mankind, his eyes are pools of fatigue.

With short bangs parted in the middle and old-fashioned suits buttoned to the top, Stimson looks like a frumpy schoolmaster. His posture is always erect, as if he is standing at attention, on alert. He has been, in a manner of speaking, on guard almost all his life.

His mother died when Stimson was only eight years old. Grief-stricken, his father had taken refuge in his work, as a doctor at a New York hospital. Stimson was sent to live nearby with his grandparents and a maiden aunt. At the age of thirteen, he was dispatched to boarding school at Phillips Academy in Andover, Massachusetts.

The school known as Andover was, in the 1880s, anything but posh. Boys were charged with removing their own wastewater, and the dormitories stank. Football was the newly popular sport, but Stimson was narrow-shouldered and slight. He preferred to hunt small animals with a shotgun in the surrounding woods. He chased ever bigger game as a young man, sometimes hunting grizzly bears alone.

It is the dreary season between winter and spring in Washington. The sleeping potion taken by Stimson does not work, and he tosses fitfully in his bed at Woodley. "A bad night last night, which required a sedative and consequently made me rather touchy and dull during the day," Stimson records in his diary late on the next day, March 2. "I took up with McCloy the problem of getting up a set of short statements of the points which I wanted to bring up with the President and the things which I wanted to get done, but I was so dull that it was hard work to do it."

"McCloy" is John "Jack" McCloy, one of Stimson's assistants. Stimson likes to hire bright young men from Harvard Law School. (One of his early assistants was Felix Frankfurter, the Supreme Court justice, still a close friend.) Jack McCloy seems to know everything that is happening in Washington, all written down on a yellow legal pad. Stimson is very fond of McCloy and his wife, Ellen. They often take tea or dine with Stimson and his wife, Mabel, in the evening, after a game of deck tennis or lawn bowls.

Stimson is to meet with President Roosevelt the next noontime to talk about Russia. He wants to trust the Russians but is wary of them. They are America's allies in this war, and he does not want them to be America's foes in the next.* Stimson has a maxim, which he says he learned as a member of his Yale secret society, that "the only way you can make a man trustworthy is to trust him." But the reality of world war has tested his faith in this credo. As Hoover's secretary of state in the early 1930s, he shut down America's foreign code-breaking operation because he disapproved of

---

* Russia has been fighting Germany since Hitler broke a peace pact with Moscow and invaded Russia in June 1941. The Kremlin and Japan have a neutrality pact, signed in April 1941, but in April 1945 Russia will announce that it will let the pact lapse in a year's time. At the Yalta Conference in February, discussing the postwar international order, Russia promised the Allies that it would go to war against Japan even sooner, within three months of Germany's surrender.

"reading other gentlemen's mail." Now, a decade later, the secretary of war receives a daily summary of broken Japanese and German coded messages, known as MAGIC and ULTRA.* At an arms control conference at St. James's Palace in London in 1930, Stimson urged the great powers to ban submarines as a cruelly underhanded tool of war; instead, they became vital weapons in America's arsenal.

Now Stimson wonders, can America trust the Russians? If postwar Europe is going to be rebuilt along the lines he imagines—as a place of freedom and the rule of law, open markets, and free trade—the Russians will have to cooperate. But Stimson has been discouraged to learn, especially from the American ambassador to Moscow, Averell Harriman, that Russia is a stubbornly paranoid police state. Stimson is torn between his realism—his intuitive grasp of power as a tool— and his idealism—his wish, however tenuous, that the Russians can be made trustworthy.

As the Red Army smashes into German-occupied eastern Europe in the late winter of 1945, the Russians are moving into German prisoner of war camps full of captured American soldiers and fliers. These men need to be rescued and returned to America. But for no apparent reason, the Russians have banned American planes with medicine and supplies from landing in the "liberated" Soviet domain. Stimson wants President Roosevelt to send the Kremlin leader, Joseph Stalin, a sharply worded telegram demanding immediate redress.

Escorted into the Oval Office at twelve-thirty P.M. on Saturday, March 3, Stimson hands FDR his proposed cable to

---

* MAGIC is the code word for decrypted Japanese diplomatic cables. ULTRA is the code word for all decrypted communications coming out of Europe and the Pacific—the coded messages of at least thirty other governments, including those of America's allies.

Stalin and an underlying batch of papers. Stimson is pleas-
antly surprised when the president actually reads the documents. "He read them both through in detail, every paper,
something that he very rarely does," he recalls as he dictates to
his recording machine that night. In their frequent meetings
over the past four years, the secretary of war has had difficulty
pinning down President Roosevelt, who likes to skip—or
dodge—from topic to topic. Getting FDR to make a decision, Stimson laments, is like "chasing a vagrant sunbeam
around an empty room." He may be the only cabinet officer
to have told the president, face to face, to stop lying to him.
At least once Stimson has hung up on him.

At the same time, Stimson appreciates Roosevelt's broader
vision, his determination to make a world free of tyranny, as
well as his playful humor. "Why, you old Republican lawyer,"
FDR teased Stimson when the secretary of war once suggested an action that, while apparently necessary for the war
effort, was not necessarily legal. It involved circumventing
Congress to aid embattled Britain against the Nazis.

That night Stimson worries in his diary about his old
friend: "The President looked rather thin and a little tired.
He didn't seem to me to be quite as lively as he usually was. I
have been a little bit troubled because the expression on his
face has changed somewhat and he looks older." Roosevelt
has less than six weeks to live.

"Mabel has a little cold, so we didn't go to church and she
stayed in bed all morning," Stimson writes the next day, Sun-
day, March 4. In the afternoon, he sets off on a two-mile walk
"up around the Cathedral," the Washington National Cathedral, with its lush formal gardens and its Anglican neo-Gothic
nave, which is visible for miles across the city. "I found the

long pull up the hill was harder than I had ever had it before and I realized that I am overweight and overage." (He is also suffering, though he does not yet know it, from heart disease.) "When I got back to Woodley, Ellen McCloy and the two children were there and pretty soon Jack came in and we had tea together. This evening I shall be alone with Mabel."

Stimson often ends his diary entries with "I dined alone with Mabel." He avoids most Washington dinner parties and never goes on a whiskey-and-poker night toot with the boys. He is devoted to his wife of more than a half century. As a student at Yale, he was smitten by the pretty, innocent, loving Mabel White at a whist party and courted her in the back pew of a New Haven church. She returns his devotion, accompanying him on long gallops (she rides sidesaddle), on hunting trips, and on lengthy diplomatic missions to Nicaragua and the Philippines. At night, the two often read poetry to each other.

But Mabel is, to use the nineteenth-century term, "neurasthenic," subject to nervousness and vague maladies that can send her to bed for days at a time. She was wounded when Stimson promised his father to keep their engagement a secret for more than five years. Stimson's ambitious father deemed Mabel to be insufficiently grand; she had no place in New York society, and no dowry.

Duty has always weighed heavily on Stimson. In 1910, when his friend Theodore Roosevelt persuaded him to run for governor of New York (his candidacy was ill-considered and unsuccessful), reporters began referring to Stimson as "the icicle." Even his friends joke that he is a "New England conscience on legs." He learned emotional reticence from his father. "I am going out of town for a few days," his father would mumble, without telling his son that he was going to visit the grave of his wife, the mother for whom Stimson still mourned. Stimson, who hates to be physically touched, is not one to ask for a comforting hug. But with one friend of forty years, he let down his guard ever so slightly and revealed that he was laboring under the impression that his father, in some awful way, blamed him for his mother's death.

From suffering can come empathy. Well concealed beneath the erect posture—"he never slumped," recalled a niece—is compassion for the suffering of others, even those who might seem undeserving of pity. When Treasury secretary Henry Morgenthau recommended that Germany be "pastoralized"— its industry plowed under—Stimson vigorously protested, not just because it would weaken postwar Europe's recovery but because Germany might become a wasteland of starving peasants. In his diary, he noted that "it is very singular that I, the man who had charge of the Department which did all the killing in the war, should be the only one to have any mercy for that other side." He said as much to his friend and colleague Gen. George C. Marshall, the chief of staff of the army. "Marshall and I laughed over this circumstance together," Stimson recorded.

The laugh was most likely a dry, rather mirthless chuckle between two congenitally reserved men, but there is, nonetheless, affection between them. Marshall and Stimson have a true bond—fortunately for the war effort, for it would be chaos if the uniformed and civilian chiefs let their egos clash.* By mutual agreement, the door between their adjoining offices at the Pentagon is always kept open. Stimson enormously admires Marshall's legendary self-restraint. ("I have no feelings," Marshall says, "except those for Mrs. Marshall.")

---

* Stimson had served in the military, first as a sergeant in the national guard. (He enlisted partly because he regretted missing the Spanish-American War.) When America entered World War I, he sought—at age fifty—a commission in the U.S. Army. He commanded an artillery unit in France, got a glimpse of action, and quietly relished being called "Colonel" in later life.

Stimson and Marshall do not quarrel and bicker—or posture or strut—but neither do they anguish or vituperate. True, Stimson can be too persistent. Marshall feels obliged to warn him not to lecture the president, whose eyes begin to glaze over when the secretary of war bears down on a point. But neither man, when intent on matters of life and death, shows much emotion. Given their jobs, they cannot afford to.

Some regard a conversation with Stimson as an audience with the Almighty. Still, he has a sweeter, more vulnerable side. Stimson and Mabel had tried but were unable to have children, apparently because Stimson had been made sterile by a case of the mumps a month before they married. They compensated by their devotion to various nieces and nephews and to the young men, like Jack McCloy, who worked closely with Stimson. He welcomes them to his home, plays with their children, gives them freedom and responsibility, and trusts them.

Stimson's charges are a confident lot. They are unintimidated by his moral certainty and laugh off his periodic fits of temper over minor matters, which can pop up at odd moments, often when the secretary of war cannot figure out how to operate his "squawk box," the speaker for his telephone. In the evenings at dinner, McCloy and Bob Lovett, whom Stimson sometimes refers to as "the Imps of Satan," will re-enact Stimson's unsuccessful attempts to conquer his temper over trivial nuisances. Mabel pretends to look surprised. Stimson gives his dry guffaw, then finally laughs until his eyes well up. Stimson has given McCloy and Lovett great authority, which they exceed.

On the morning of Monday, March 5, a still weary Henry Stimson steps into General Marshall's office to attend the daily meeting of the Operations and Intelligence staff. The news from the European front is good. Eisenhower's forces are close to crossing the Rhine, while the Russian army is pushing toward Berlin from the east. Stimson usually just listens to these situation reports; lately, he is so swamped with work that he can attend the morning meeting only every two or three days. But this morning, at the mention of Dresden, a city on the line of the Russian advance into eastern Germany, the secretary of war interrupts. He has read in *The New York Times* this morning an article about the Allied firebombing of this ancient and beautiful city ("Florence on the Elbe") in mid-February, taking thousands of German lives. A German news source is quoted as saying, "Today we can only speak of what was Dresden in the past tense."

Stimson wants an investigation. At the Operations and Intelligence meeting, he points out that Dresden is the capital of Saxony, and that Saxony is "the least Prussianized part of Germany." In his diary later that night, Stimson records that "the account out of Germany" makes the destruction "even on its face terrible and probably unnecessary." According to his diary entry, he goes on to say, "We ought to be careful to see that it is not destroyed so that it can be a portion of the country which can be used to be the center of the new Germany."

His questioning touches on issues about civilian bombing that the U.S. Army Air Forces have struggled with.

In the early days of the war, when politicians were condemning the German bombing of European cities as fascist barbarism, the army air forces promised "precision" bombing of military and industrial targets. Fairly quickly, the British, eager for revenge after their own cities had been extensively bombed by the Luftwaffe, gave up on precision bombing as essentially futile. Instead, RAF Bomber Command, under the leadership of Gen. Arthur Harris, also known as "Bomber"

Harris, opted for "area bombing"—bombing city centers. The hope was to break German morale by "dehousing" the population, a euphemism coined without apparent irony.

But the Americans, idealistic about their moral values and technical knowhow, forged ahead with precision bombing. The idea was that an American bombardier peering through a Norden bombsight should be able to put a bomb "into a pickle barrel," as the manufacturers claimed, or at least within the vicinity of the target. Or so it was demonstrated on clear, windless days, flying over a bombing range in Kansas. In cloudy, stormy Europe, with the skies full of German flak and fighters, the bombs rarely land where they are supposed to— on railway yards and munitions factories. They do land on the civilians living nearby. "Precision bombing" is really a misnomer for what amounted to area bombing. Still, the Americans can say, truthfully, that they intend to hit military or industrial targets, not civilian targets.*

The day after Stimson asks for an investigation into the bombing of Dresden, General Marshall sends the army air forces' response. It is basically a nonresponse. Dresden was an important target, the "center of a railway network and a great industrial town." The British began bombing the city on February 13 "on accurate markers starting fires." The next day a smaller number of U.S. planes bombed it, going after rail-

---

* The British were not wrong that precision bombing was technologically impossible in the early 1940s; their motive for area bombing was not simply revenge. As Tami Biddle, a longtime expert on strategic bombing at the U.S. Army War College explains, *precision bombing* is a misleading term the Americans used—with the best of intentions—to describe area bombing in a reasonably circumscribed area when the conditions (clear weather, no flak, etc.) were just right.

way marshaling yards but unable to aim accurately. Using the "Pathfinder method," the British dropped flares and burning red pyrotechnic candles as target indicators; waves of bombers followed, dropping high explosives and incendiaries. The skies were undefended, and the tight bombing patterns of the Pathfinders created a vast conflagration in a city packed with refugees. Results were "unobserved" in Dresden because there was so much smoke from the massive, wind-whipped firestorm.

Stimson replies with a handwritten note: "I doubt this report makes the case any better—on the face of it the British on Feb 13 bombed the city. While our bombing was said to be aimed at military objectives the results were practically unobserved. I think the city should be photographed carefully and the actual facts made known."

It will take three weeks to receive an inconclusive report from U.S. Strategic Air Forces Headquarters in Europe. Both the Royal Air Force and the U.S. Eighth Air Force dropped incendiary bombs, along with high explosives, Stimson is told, but the British dropped roughly five times as many. "Due to the proximity of these two attacks and the absence of intervening photographic coverage, it has been impossible to allocate damage to attacking air forces."

Once, before exhaustion set in, Stimson might have pressed a little harder to find out exactly what happened in Dresden during those two days and nights in February. As a prosecuting attorney, he was noted for his single-minded pursuit of the facts. As secretary of war, at least in the early days, he was known within the Pentagon for "dipping down," for consulting with a trusted adviser to cut through bureaucratic obfuscation and stay on top of events on the ground.

But his trusted adviser for airpower, Robert Lovett, while devoted and highly capable, is perhaps not entirely forthcoming with his boss. Lovett is assistant secretary of war for air.

Balding, with heavy-lidded eyes and a handsome, chiseled face, sardonically funny, he had been a Wall Street investment banker and urbane sophisticate who socialized with *New Yorker* wits and Broadway producers. He is also an ardent champion of airpower. His Yale secret society tap came while he was training to be a naval aviator in World War I. Commanding a bombing group known as "the Yale Unit," Lovett was one of the first to understand the value of strategic bombing—to bomb not the submarines at sea but the many submarines in port in their pens. In the days before Pearl Harbor, he took the lead in persuading his friends running the automobile industry to begin converting their assembly lines to make warplanes, tens of thousands of them. "My business was banking. Now it's airplanes," he explained.

Stimson depends on Lovett to keep him abreast of the air force. On May 3, 1944, he noted that Lovett gave him his usual "very fair and intelligent analysis." A month later he observed that Lovett was "judicious and fair minded." But as the war has dragged on and problems have multiplied and the weary secretary of war has been forced to delegate more and more to his aides, he can't always remember what Lovett has told him. "Talked to Lovett, whom I had not seen in a long time," he recorded in late November 1944. "He gave me a resume of what especially was going on in the Air Force. I cannot remember at this moment of dictation exactly what it was, but I know it was something important which will be before us very soon."

Lovett believes that bombing can be used to break civilian morale. He is, in his own way, a moralist: he believes in giving the Germans a dose of their own medicine. He works closely with the army air forces commander, Gen. Henry "Hap" Arnold, who has observed that Lovett possesses a "hidden power." Indeed, when Arnold suffered his fourth heart attack in three years in January 1945, Lovett, though a civilian, increasingly assumed Arnold's air force duties. There is no record of Lovett's views on the bombing of Dresden. But it is doubtful he shares much with Stimson, which may help explain why the secretary of war is still learning about the extent of the firebombing of Dresden from *The New York Times* three weeks after the fact.

The use of a far more overwhelming, destructive force is much on Stimson's mind during the first two weeks of March 1945. He is distracted, and the weather matches his mood, dank and gray, "abominable," he records. On March 5, after agitating about Dresden in the Operations and Intelligence staff meeting in Marshall's office, he needs to take a nap. In the afternoon, he records later that day, "I called in Harvey Bundy, who has been anxious to see me as to S-1."

Bundy is one of Stimson's valued assistants, a reserved, brainy lawyer by way of Yale College and Harvard Law School. "S-1" is the code name for the atomic bomb project. (The Americans call it "the Manhattan Engineering Project," and the British, "Tube Alloys.") The scientists at work on the bomb call it "the gadget." In his periodic diary entries about S-1, Stimson refers to the weapon as "the dire," "the dreadful," "the terrible," "the awful," and "the diabolical."

The secretary of war first learned of S-1 in November 1941, just before Pearl Harbor. For some time, largely unnoticed by the larger world, scientists in various countries had been working on the secret of splitting the atom to release energy—in an instantaneous, massive, primal spasm—creating, potentially, a bomb big enough to destroy a city. Fleeing Hitler's Germany, Jewish scientists had brought their atomic expertise to England and America in the 1930s. (It might be said that Hitler lost World War II on April 7, 1933, when Germany banned

Jews from government.) At first tentatively, President Roosevelt's government took up the project (already started by the less well-resourced British) in extreme secrecy, but with gathering determination and ever more resources to create a workable bomb.

The fear back in 1941 had been that Germany would be the first to build an atomic bomb. Not until late 1944 did the tight circle of Americans charged with developing the bomb understand that the Germans were too far behind to catch up. In early 1945 Nazi scientists were getting close to building a missile powerful enough to reach New York, but thanks to Hitler's disdain for "Jewish science," the Führer had no atomic bomb to put atop the missile. But by then, Germany was no longer the primary target. In May 1943 a top-secret "Target Committee," composed of scientists and military officers, had provisionally decided to aim the first atomic bomb at Japan— probably at a Japanese fleet in a harbor. The scientists feared that if a dud were to land on Germany, the Nazis might be able to reverse-engineer their own "gadget." No one seems to have worried much about the ingenuity of Japanese scientists.

Secretary of War Stimson has been overseeing S-1 as a kind of chairman of the board. His chief role, through 1943 and 1944, was to keep the money flowing from Congress without divulging too much about the work. Now, at the beginning of March 1945, he realizes that the bomb is nearing readiness, and that the hour to act is drawing near. After "a most thorough and searching talk" with the straitlaced Bundy, Stimson records in his diary that night of March 5:

> We are up against some very big decisions. The time is approaching when we can no longer avoid them and when events may force us into the public on the subject. Our thoughts went right down to the bottom facts of human nature, morals, and government, and it is by

far the most searching and important thing that I have
had to do since I have been here in the office of the
Secretary of War because it touches matters that are
deeper than even the principles of present government.

Stimson does not say in his diary just what he and Bundy
discussed, but Bundy's notes do: the need for an international
arms control agency to hold on to the atomic bomb after the
war. Surprisingly, perhaps, the two men do not talk about
whether to drop the bomb in this war. The focus is on how
to avoid the use of more and bigger bombs in the next one.

In his conversation with Bundy, Stimson suggests a curious
choice for the kind of man who should run the postwar international arms control agency: Phillips Brooks, a late-nineteenth-
century Episcopal priest and Bishop of Massachusetts. By later
generations, Bishop Brooks will be remembered, if at all, for
writing the lyrics to the Christmas hymn "O Little Town of
Bethlehem." In the bishop's time, the Gilded Age, a period
when the sermons of moral crusaders were sometimes front-
page news, Brooks was an apostle of a movement called Muscular Christianity.

What the country—and the whole world—needs now,
Stimson tells Bundy, according to Bundy's notes, is a spiritual
revival based in Christian principles. Only through faith will
mankind find the self-discipline to control its powerful deadly
weapons.

Stimson's existential worry, of long duration, is that man's
technical capacity to do evil will outrun man's human capacity to do good. He hopes that man can be made more moral—
indeed, can one day achieve moral perfection—but he fears
that science, and its temptations, will overcome morality first.
Specifically, he worries that the emotions stirred up by this
war will lead to a more terrible next war.

Stimson doesn't doubt that Americans are willing to use

the atomic bomb in *this* war. There was no public outcry protesting the firebombing of Dresden; indeed, apart from some newspaper columns and a sermon or two, the public did not react at all to the burning of large numbers of civilians by the Allies in the once-lovely historic city. Americans want to punish Germany, which has overrun continental Europe, and even more, they want vengeance against Japan for attacking Pearl Harbor. Atrocity stories have been appearing in the newspapers about the Japanese starving or abusing American POWs and Asian citizens alike, sometimes horribly, with rapes and beheadings.

Mostly Americans want the war to end, so that their husbands and sons can come home. By March 1945, war weariness is settling in, certainly among congressmen under pressure from business leaders and their lobbyists chafing at war rationing and regulatory red tape. Stimson's immediate concern is that Americans will not be willing to make the added sacrifices necessary to finish the fight.

In the winter of 1945, the U.S. armed services appear to face a manpower shortfall. The war is far from over: Germany is reeling but is still threatening the Allies with secret weapons like missiles, jet planes, and a rumored "death ray." Japan's home islands have been barely pricked by American weaponry, much less conquered. The Joint Chiefs of Staff predict the Allies will need another six months to defeat Germany and another year to grind down Japan. Draft allotments are barely enough to fill the ranks. Nonetheless, in March, with the war dragging on, Congress is still balking at a compulsory service act. Stimson has been frustrated by lawmakers, reflecting their constituents, who want to declare victory and be done with it. Soon veterans of combat in Europe with enough "points" will be discharged, and few of the American soldiers and sailors rotating home from the battlefields of Europe will be eager to fight in an even uglier war in the Pacific.

Stimson knows that America probably will have to use the atomic bomb to end the war. President Roosevelt and Prime Minister Winston Churchill have already signed an agreement that the bomb "might" be used "against Japan . . . after mature consideration."

Much is at stake for the men creating S-1. The bomb will be successfully tested in July, after which Stimson will tell Bundy and McCloy, "Well, I have been responsible for spending two billion dollars on this atomic venture. Now that it is successful, I shall not be sent to prison in Fort Leavenworth." (He is joking, but not lightly.) There is no discussion at the higher levels of government about *not* using the bomb. It is simply understood that the American public would want to use a weapon that could save the lives of thousands of American soldiers, regardless of the humanitarian cost. The inevitable use of "the gadget" is taken for granted, even though it will almost surely kill large numbers of Japanese civilians.

Stimson does not question this informal consensus, not in any formal way, not in any written record he will leave behind, including his diary. But that does not mean he does not think about what he has referred to as "the terrible," "the awful," "the dreadful," especially in the hours before dawn. Jack McCloy will later be asked how his boss thought about the bomb. "On his knees," McCloy will answer.

At dinner on the night of March 8, in his elegant but spare dining room, lined with the heads of stags that he has shot, Stimson is feeling a little revived. He and Mabel always sit down at a precise hour, no cocktails beforehand. But then "just as we finished dinner Mabel suddenly toppled over unconscious at her end of the table and gave me the fright of my life," a shaken Stimson will write the next day. The seventy-seven-year-old Stimson leaps up and carries Mabel to the sofa, and a doctor is summoned. Mabel quickly comes to, "but it was a desperate time for about five or ten minutes," Stimson will record.

As it turns out, nothing is really wrong with Mabel. She may have been dehydrated from her cold. Physically, she is soon up and reading aloud with her husband at dinner. But it is not uncommon for one spouse to carry the stress of another—indeed, through a bit of mysterious alchemy clinically known as "projective identification," a person can sometimes mentally transfer his or her cares and woes to another. It is one of the human psyche's myriad ways of defending oneself from deep inner conflict. (In 1967, as Secretary of Defense Robert McNamara struggles over the quagmire of the Vietnam War, his wife, Margie, and his son Craig will develop painful stomach ulcers. McNamara will later ruefully remark, "They had my ulcers.")

On March 9, just as Stimson speaks into his recording device about his "desperate time" with Mabel, an armada of B-29 bombers is taking off from airfields on Guam and Tinian, two of the Mariana Islands in the far Pacific, bound for Tokyo. In the summer of 1944, in hard fighting, American soldiers and Marines liberated the Marianas from the Japanese, and Seabees set to work building the largest airfields in the world—launching pads, finally, for bombing the Japanese homeland, a twelve-hour round trip, fifteen hundred miles away.

For many months, the army air forces tried daytime "precision" bombing against Japanese aircraft factories, but the bombs almost always missed. Japan was, it seemed, even cloudier than Germany. The B-29s, magnificent new flying machines that could climb to thirty thousand feet, barely in range of Japanese fighters, were being blown about by a never-before-observed meteorological condition later dubbed "the jet stream." The 130-to-230-mph winds either stopped the west-bound planes cold or blew east-bound planes right past their targets.

Desperate for results, the head of the XXI Bomber Command, Maj. Gen. Curtis LeMay, tried a new strategy. He sent the bombers in low, at night, when they had a better chance to evade flak and the dwindling number of Japanese fighters. Since the newfangled but finicky Norden bombsight was next to useless at night, precision bombing was out. So using a new, improved incendiary bomb filled with a jellied gasoline called napalm, LeMay set out to light a fire on the ground that would spread. He knew that Japanese cities, made largely of wood, would burn. On the night of March 9–10, by setting off a ferocious firestorm, the B-29s burn out sixteen square miles of the Japanese capital. The crews in the planes can smell the burning flesh. It will eventually be determined that roughly 85,000 residents of Tokyo, or probably more, die in the conflagration. According to the U.S. Strategic Bombing Survey, the fires started by the B-29s and their napalm bombs killed more people in a six-hour period than at any time in the history of war.

On March 10, the scope of the damage in Tokyo, though not the death toll, is widely reported with banner headlines in the American papers. "B-29s Pour Over 1,000 Tons of Incendiaries on Japanese Capital; Tremendous Fires Leap Up Quickly in Thickly Populated Center of Big Enemy City" reads *The New York Times*.

On March 13, three days after the Tokyo firestorm, Stimson, feeling the stress of the job, reports in his diary, "After lunch which I took at home with Mabel, I had a nice talk in the afternoon with Bob Lovett who had just returned from the South, and I also had a nice little game of deck tennis— gentle and quiet, which did me a lot of good."

Assistant Secretary of War for Air Lovett had been in Florida meeting with Hap Arnold, the army air forces commander, who was recuperating from his fourth heart attack in three years. The firebombing of Tokyo seemed to signal a momentous strategy shift by U.S. Army Air Forces. After Dresden, Stimson had publicly stated that the United States did not engage in terror bombing of cities. Now it appeared that they were doing so, or something close to it.

The scowling LeMay has been portrayed, unfairly, as a merciless killer. Especially in later years as strategic air commander, he was prone to making cold-blooded statements. (He wanted to threaten to bomb North Vietnam "back into the Stone Age.") He did not smile (in fact, he couldn't; his face was frozen by a condition called Bell's palsy), and he was easy to caricature. But he was not reckless with the lives of his pilots.

Though he did not get direct orders to firebomb Tokyo from Arnold or anyone in Washington, he was not acting entirely on his own. The taciturn, cigar-chomping general had been told that he might, like his predecessor, Gen. Haywood Hansell, be replaced as the head of the XXI Bomber Command if he failed to get results, measured by aerial photos of targets destroyed. Precision bombing was failing, so he needed to find something that worked, and incendiary bombs had promise; indeed, at the Dugway Proving Grounds in Utah, the air force had erected a Japanese-style village to practice burning it down. The air force later explained that LeMay wasn't targeting civilians—that the bombers were aiming at small industries widely dispersed in residential neighborhoods—but this seemed to be a rationalization for the sort of area bombing of cities that, in Europe, had long been the province of the British RAF, not the USAAF.

If Lovett and Stimson discuss the Tokyo firebombing in their talk on March 13, Stimson does not say so. Nor, for the next two months, will he mention in his diary anything about bombing civilians.

✳ ✳

Stimson badly needs a prolonged rest. Every weekend throughout the war, he has flown with Mabel in his Army DC-3 to Highhold, his estate on the North Shore of Long Island. Highhold is large and comfortable, though Stimson notes in his privately printed memoir that it has none of the faux-château grandeur of the robber baron estates dotting the so-called Gold Coast nearby. (Stimson's estate is "a gallop apart" from Theodore Roosevelt's house, Sagamore Hill, in nearby Oyster Bay.) On clear days, gazing out at the thin strips of blue to the south (the Atlantic Ocean) and the north (Long Island Sound), Stimson has been able to regain his bearings, at least on most weekends. With its bridle paths and tree-shaded lawns, Highhold, he tells Mabel, soothes him as soon as he sets foot there.

But he needs to get farther away and for longer than a weekend. The army has requisitioned the Biltmore Hotel in Miami for R&R, and it has rooms available to the secretary of war. On March 18 Stimson records in his diary, "This morning after a rather tortured night, a good deal of doubt and uncertainty, Mabel helped me out by deciding that she thought we ought to go to Miami after all and give up going to Highhold because I could not possibly get the freedom from the care that is weighing me down there and get the absolute rest that I apparently need. So we have decided to go to Miami tomorrow, and once we decided it has been a great relief."

Ten days later he picks up his diary again to report that "we had delightful weather and a very complete rest, but we were both so tired that it seemed like a long time before we could get over the fits of depression that were natural to such a situation." He swam, twice a day, in the surf. He went deep-sea fishing and caught a bonito. And he visited an army air forces "redistribution center," where men who fought in Europe are being reassigned to units to fight in the Pacific.

Recounting the trip in his diary on March 28, Stimson praises the "sympathetic work" of the officers preparing the airmen to go back into battle. "All the men whom I met were . . . very grateful for it," he records.

He is speaking two days after the Americans have finally won the Battle of Iwo Jima, a five-week struggle, costing the lives of almost seven thousand U.S. Marines and virtually all twenty thousand Japanese soldiers, to capture an island that is about one-sixth the size of Nantucket. (The Americans want the island to serve as an air base to support bombing raids on Japan.) The men at the Miami redistribution center are being sent off to fight much greater numbers of equally fanatical Japanese on their far larger home islands.

Two years after the war, Stimson will sit with Harvey Bundy's son, McGeorge Bundy, to write his memoir, titled *On Active Service in Peace and War*. The writing, which is mostly by McGeorge Bundy, is arch and self-consciously literary and refers to Stimson in the third person. But it probably captures Stimson's true feelings as he lay awake—at Woodley, at Highhold, and in his hotel room in Miami—thinking about the atomic bomb and remembering that visit to the men at the Miami redistribution center in the spring of 1945:

> In March, he [Stimson] visited an Air Forces redistribution center in Florida. There he met and talked with men on their way to the Pacific after completing a term of duty in Europe. The impression he received was profound. These men were weary in a way no one reading reports could readily understand. They would go to the

Pacific, and they would fight well again, but after this meeting Stimson realized more clearly than ever that the primary obligation of any man responsible for and to these Americans was to end the war as quickly as possible. To discard or fail to use effectively any weapon which might spare them further sacrifice would be ir-responsibility so flagrant as to deserve condign punish-ment. Paraphrasing Shakespeare (but with life and not death as his end), Stimson could have said, as he felt, that "He hates them who would upon the rack of this war stretch them out longer."

And yet to use the atomic bomb against cities popu-lated mainly by civilians was to assume another and scarcely less terrible responsibility.

2.

Target Practice

"May [be] *Frankenstein* or means for World Peace"

Nuclear physicist J. Robert Oppenheimer was the genius behind the atomic bomb; Gen. Leslie Groves, his boss, drove the Manhattan Project relentlessly.

Washington, D.C.
April–June 1945

ROOSEVELT IS DEAD. IT IS A WARM SPRING DAY, APRIL 15, 1945, and Stimson is standing in the garden of FDR's house at Hyde Park, New York, looking at the late president's caisson. The secretary of war is moved by the hymns ("Faith of Our Fathers," "Eternal Father, Strong to Save") and by the phalanx of West Point cadets, in their dress gray uniforms, marching solemnly by. Stimson had dreaded the wearying trip from Washington to the Hudson River Valley for Roosevelt's burial. The weather was hot and muggy when he left Washington, and he feared that he would not be able to sleep, but more than duty has brought him north. Stimson may have regarded FDR as "foxy," but he misses the president's great heart as well as his vast experience.

Stimson is unsure about the new president, who is also at the ceremony, head bowed, hat in hand. Harry Truman "seemed willing and anxious to learn and do his best," Stimson recorded in his diary after Truman's first war council two days earlier, Truman's first full day in office, April 13.

Stimson had been summoned to the White House along with General Marshall and other top brass to brief the new president. Afterward the secretary of war had stayed behind to have a private word with Truman. He told the president that he needed to talk to him about a "new explosive of unbelievable power." Stimson did not elaborate. Truman was obviously overwhelmed by an overload of new responsibility and, as Stimson noted, by "the terrific handicap of coming into such an office where the threads of information are so multitudinous." Truman does not pretend otherwise. "Boys," he had told reporters on taking the presidential oath on April 12, the day FDR died, "if you ever pray, pray for me now."

Stimson waits patiently, letting Truman settle into his new role. On April 24 he dictates a note to the president.

Dear Mr. President,

I think it is very important that I should have a talk with you as soon as possible on a highly secret matter. I mentioned it to you shortly after you took office but I have not mentioned it since on account of the pressure you have been under.

On April 25 at noon, Stimson enters the Oval Office through a side door (to avoid reporters hanging around the anteroom) and formally greets the new man he calls "Mr. President."

Truman and Stimson are correct with each other but also wary. Truman is a populist Democrat and an ardent New Dealer. Stimson is an upper-crust Republican and anti–New Dealer. Truman is mindful that Stimson, with his patrician accent, was a Wall Street lawyer. Stimson knows that Truman, with his snappy suits and two-tone shoes, was called "the senator from Pendergast," meaning the corrupt Pendergast machine in Kansas City. Both men will overcome their doubts, but not right away. A year earlier, when Truman's Senate committee investigating government procurement was beginning to poke around the top-secret Manhattan Project, Stimson put a stop to it. In his diary afterward, Stimson described Truman as a "nuisance and a pretty untrustworthy man. He talks smoothly but acts meanly."

Now, standing stiffly erect as always, Stimson reaches into his briefcase and pulls out a memorandum, just finished that morning, and hands it to Truman. The words are meant to shock:

> Within four months we shall in all probability have completed the most terrible weapon ever known in human history, one bomb of which could destroy a whole city.

The memo goes on to sound out the theme that has preoccupied Stimson for weeks, that if the new, dark science of the atomic bomb is not somehow controlled, civilization itself will be at risk. The United States has a monopoly now, but that won't last, and a less scrupulous nation—he specifically mentions Russia—will build its own weapon. "The world in its present state of moral advancement compared with its technical development would be eventually at the mercy of such a weapon," the memo warns.

Truman is a good politician. In a genial tone, he recalls how the secretary of war stopped his Senate committee from looking into the top-secret project. Now, he says, he understands why. "He was very nice about it," Stimson will record that night.

In the Oval Office that noontime, after he lectures the president on the broader philosophical issues, Stimson hands Truman a second document, detailing the work of the Manhattan Project. Just then another man, portly in the uniform of a U.S. Army general, enters the room. It is Leslie Groves, who has been running the Manhattan Project for the past three years.

Smuggled into the White House through an underground passage, Groves has been kept waiting for an hour in a separate anteroom. Truman starts to read the second document, which is long and technical, then hesitates. He says he doesn't want to tackle so much at once. Stimson and Groves prod him to keep reading. "This is a big project," says Groves.

After about forty-five more minutes, Truman says he entirely agrees with the necessity of the project. Stimson asks if he can form a committee of senior government officials to look into the weighty questions about the future of the bomb, and Truman agrees.

Leslie Groves is not used to waiting and cooling his heels, even for the president. General Groves of the U.S. Army is an entirely self-confident man. At the outset of the war, he ran the building of the Pentagon. He is accustomed to giving orders and does so with self-assurance bordering on arrogance. His only known weakness is an addiction to chocolate, which makes his uniform fit too snugly. While Stimson agonizes all night, Groves falls asleep the moment his head hits the pillow. Groves pretends to disdain "long-hair" scientists and "woolly" academics, but he has chosen a brilliant physics

professor, J. Robert Oppenheimer, to run the Los Alamos
lab, even though he suspects Oppenheimer is, at heart, a
Communist. (He is not, but he has consorted with Communist Party members and "fellow travelers," including his mis-
tress, who has been followed by Groves's security men.)
Subtly shrewd about human relations, despite his outward
bombast, Groves knows that Oppenheimer's ego is fully in-
vested in creating a bomb that will shock the world.

General Groves reports to Stimson, but the secretary of
war largely leaves him alone. Groves admires Stimson as a
gentleman of integrity, if a bit ancient, and Stimson, in turn,
is thoroughly impressed by Groves's energy and efficiency.*
From a small office in the War Department building off
Constitution Avenue in Washington, the Manhattan Project
chief runs a secret labyrinth of labs and factories planted
around the country. Groves is perfectly content to let Stimson have a committee to ponder the future of nuclear weapons. Groves has his own committee, the Target Committee,
to propose and, if Groves has his way, decide on which city
or cities to drop the bomb. Two bombs at least—one to
show the Japanese that the Americans have an A-bomb, the
other to let them know that the Americans have more than
one.

Groves's Target Committee, run by his deputy, Brig. Gen.
Thomas Farrell, and populated by junior army air force offi-

---

* Groves undertook to explain atomic energy to Stimson with a simple
one-page drawing of the atom. Stimson was cross at first: "Don't try to tell
me that. I can't understand a word that you're saying." Groves gingerly
tried to go on. "Just look at this for a minute. This is helium." Stimson
brightened. "Oh helium," he said. "That comes from Helios the Sun,
doesn't it?" "Yes, sir," said Groves. "Oh," said Stimson, "I know all about
helium." Groves later recalled, "From then on, he would listen, but before
that he just closed his mind completely. As soon as I could get a Greek
analogy to it, he was all set."

cers and scientists working at Los Alamos, has its first meeting on April 27, two days after Stimson and Groves meet with Truman. ("I don't mind committees," says Groves, "if I pick the people on them.")

An earlier idea—to build an A-bomb that would detonate underwater to sink the Japanese fleet (in effect, a giant depth charge)—has been discarded as unworkable. An air-burst bomb is chosen, but it will have to be dropped from a great height—thirty thousand feet—or the B-29 delivering it will not be able to get safely away from the blast. According to the ordnance experts, the bomb will not be particularly effective against concrete reinforced structures like bunkers and factories, but it will be devastating against ordinary buildings, especially if they are built of wood. Thus the best target is not a military base or an industrial site but a large Japanese city.

Some of the scientists at Los Alamos are queasy about devastating a city full of civilians. "Some tender souls are appalled at the idea of the horrible destruction which this bomb might wreak," Capt. William "Deak" Parsons, the chief of ordnance at Los Alamos, wrote Groves back in September 1944. These "tender souls" were pushing for a "demonstration"—setting off a bomb in a desert or an island somewhere in the Pacific, and inviting the enemy to watch. Such a demonstration would be a "fizzle," Parsons wrote Groves. "Even the crater would be disappointing." It would make a big flash but would not leave a huge hole in the ground.

Groves and his Target Committee agree. On April 27, 1945, they decide that the target should be a "large urban area of not less than three miles in diameter existing in large populated areas." There is another wrinkle. Dropping a bomb from thirty thousand feet is not a precise science, as the air force has discovered with its B-29 raids tossed about by the jet stream's hurricane-force winds. So at a second set of meetings, held in Oppenheimer's office at Los Alamos on May 10–11, the Target Committee rejects aiming at a purely military or industrial target. It concludes that "any small or strictly military objective should be located in a much larger area subject to blast damage in order to avoid undue risks of the weapon being lost due to bad placing of the bomb." In other words, the bomb should be aimed at the center of the city.

The scientists are aware that the atomic bomb will be radioactive over a large area, maybe two-thirds of a mile, and that radiation can be fatal. Indeed, when a pair of German émigré scientists, Rudolf Peirels and Otto Frisch, first pondered the explosion that could be achieved by splitting the atom, they wrote, "Owing to the spread of radioactive substances with the wind, the bomb could probably not be used without killing large numbers of civilians." Since using such a weapon against a city would be "unsuitable," these scientists suggested that an atomic explosive might be used as a "depth charge at a naval base"—the idea first proposed, then discarded by the bomb makers at Los Alamos. But at the meetings of the Target Committee, there is little discussion of radiation. The long-term impact of radioactive fallout is not well understood; the targeters are focused on the blast, not on its aftereffects. (A purely radiological bomb—a conventional explosive bomb scattering radioactive material, to be known as a "dirty bomb"—was earlier ruled out.)

Henry Stimson knows none of this. He is not kept abreast of the minutes of the Target Committee. No one briefs him about radiation.

There is no active conspiracy to keep him in the dark. True, Leslie Groves is a bureaucratic genius at the art of compartmentation—to preserve security but also to ensure that only he controls the information. Still, James Conant, the president of Harvard and an important scientific adviser

to the president in Washington, regularly visits Los Alamos*
and understands at least the basic principles of radiation, as
does the lab's director, J. Robert Oppenheimer. Either man
might have told the higher-ups in Washington that the bomb
would produce radiation. But Conant and Oppenheimer
want to show the world what the weapon can do, and they do
not want to raise comparisons with poison gas, generally
avoided by both sides in World War II after its hideous effects
in World War I. Some things, it seems to them, are better left
unsaid.

On Tuesday, May 8, 1945, the remnants of the Third Reich
formally surrender to the Allies in Germany. Stimson goes to
a service of thanksgiving in church. "The spirit was somber
but very united and strong," he recounts to his diary. "It was
just the kind of meeting which I think was appropriate to the
occasion for which it was held."

The next day, May 9, Stimson meets in his roomy Pentagon office with three senators who have just been to Germany to see for themselves the liberated concentration camps
Buchenwald, Dachau, and Nordhausen. All three men, Stimson records, think "the so-called atrocities represented a de-
liberate and concerted attempt by the government of Germany
to eliminate by murder, starvation and other methods of death
large numbers of Russians, Poles, Jews, and other classes of
people whom they did not wish to have survive." Stimson's

---

* Conant, a distinguished chemist, ran interference for Groves with scientists at Los Alamos, who were skeptical of a military man. It also helped
that Conant was the president of Harvard. "Yes," Groves later said in an
oral history, "they were all interested in the possibility of being invited to
be professors at Harvard after the war."

language is detached ("so-called atrocities"), but the stark evidence of mass murder is deeply unsettling.*

Stimson is feeling particularly low, which he blames on exhaustion. He is undergoing medical tests, which the surgeon general has ordered, but little is understood about heart disease in 1945. The doctors tell him he must have a sustained rest. Stimson and Mabel decide to retreat to Highhold for a week or two.

First, though, Stimson goes to see President Truman to talk about the ongoing war against Japan. Afterward, on May 17, he sends the president a memo:

> For the reasons I mentioned to you, I am anxious to hold our Air Force, so far as possible, to the "precision" bombing which it has done so well in Europe. I am told that it is possible and adequate. The reputation of the United States for fair play and humanitarianism is the world's biggest asset for peace in the coming decades. I believe the same rule of sparing civilian populations should be applied as far as possible to the use of any new weapons.

Stimson's intentions are worthy, but these are the words of a man who is uninformed, if not misinformed—or possibly willfully incurious. He is writing the memo six days after General Groves's Target Committee has decided to aim the atomic bomb at the center of a city. Also, Curtis LeMay's XXI Bomber Command of the Twentieth Air Force has al-

---

* The War Department knew of the concentration camps and made a conscious decision in 1944 not to bomb them. It was felt that bombing the camps would be largely symbolic and divert resources from other important targets. The lead actor on this decision was Assistant Secretary Jack McCloy, but as historian Michael Beschloss has shown, President Roosevelt quietly supported McCloy, and Stimson likely did as well.

ready been firebombing Japanese cities for weeks, precisely because precision bombing, which LeMay initially tried, was a failure. Stimson knows about the firebombing just by reading the newspapers. But he is under the misapprehension that the indiscriminate bombing will soon stop. Sometime that spring—it is not clear exactly when—Stimson extracted a promise from Assistant Secretary Lovett that the army air forces would use "only precision bombing in Japan." But this is a promise that Lovett cannot deliver on—if indeed he means to.

Lovett has already read LeMay's full "Record of Operations" of the Twentieth Air Force, detailing the firebombing of Tokyo and four other cities, which he got on April 27. "It's a superb record and I am delighted to have it," Lovett wrote the command's chief of staff, Brig. Gen. Lauris Norstad. (LeMay had stopped firebombing for a time in March, but only because he ran out of incendiaries.) On April 25, LeMay wrote Norstad that he is beginning to think that Japan can be defeated by bombing alone—no need for the army or navy to mount a costly invasion. This is what Lovett, as assistant secretary of war for air and a true believer in airpower, wants to hear.

Lovett wants the air force, after the war, to be a separate service branch, equal with the army and the navy. He and the top brass at the air force chafe at the idea that they play a supporting role for the army. Working with *Time/Life* publisher Henry Luce, Lovett has started an in-house air force magazine called *Impact*. It features images from *Time* and *Life* magazine photographers showing how air force bombers destroyed buildings in Rome and other European cities without hitting churches and other cultural shrines. Lovett and the air force brass are particularly eager to impress their chief customer, Secretary of War Stimson. Shown photos of precision bombing in 1942 and 1943, Stimson exclaimed in his diary, "mar-

velous" and "miraculous!" On February 5, 1945, Gen. Carl
"Tooey" Spaatz sent Stimson "a pictorial report showing the
results of some of our strategic bomber operations carried out
during the past year." On February 13, Stimson wrote back to
say that he was "very much impressed with the accuracy and
the effect of the bombing." That was one day before bombers
from Spaatz's command dropped bombs into the firestorm of
Dresden, trying to hit railroad marshaling yards but unable to
know if they had.

Stimson rests at Highhold, preparing himself. "I did little for
the first few days except sleep and stroll about the place, not
even riding horseback. Later I rode two or three times without apparently damaging my leg," Stimson writes on May 27,
as his ten-day sojourn at Highhold is drawing to an end. The
next day he writes:

> On Monday we flew back to Washington, reaching
> there at eleven A.M. For some reason or other I felt
> used up that day and confined myself to conferences
> with Bundy, Harrison, and Marshall over matters relat-
> ing to S-1. I have made up my mind to make that sub-
> ject my primary occupation for these next few months,
> relieving myself so far as possible from all routine mat-
> ters in the Department.

   While trying to recover at Highhold, Stimson had been on
the phone with Jack McCloy, telling his assistant to get to
work on the draft of a presidential statement to be released
after the first use of the atomic bomb. "The moral position of
the U.S. weighs greatly upon him," McCloy noted in his own
diary. McCloy and Stimson's Long Island neighbor, Arthur

Page, the head of public relations for the giant phone con-glomerate AT&T, tried to reflect Stimson's moral concerns in an outline of the presidential statement prepared on May 25. It stressed that the United States would "choose a military target like a naval base" to avoid the "wholesale killing of ci-vilians."

The killing of civilians is much on Stimson's mind when he comes to his office on the morning of May 29. He has slept well, for once, and feels "refreshed," but his reading of the morning newspapers has alarmed him—and made him won-der what happened to Assistant Secretary Lovett's promise that the air force would engage "only" in precision bombing in Japan. According to news accounts bannered on the front pages, General LeMay's napalm-laden B-29s have returned to Tokyo, scorching another nineteen square miles. The press does not report, because it does not know, that the loss of life in Tokyo is much less this time—several thousand, as opposed to the 85,000 or so who perished in March—because many of Tokyo's residents have fled. The flames from the incendiary bombs have spread through the Imperial Palace grounds, leaving many buildings charred and uninhabitable. "The Sec-retary," McCloy writes in his diary that night, "referred to the burning of Tokyo and the possible ways and means of em-ploying the larger bombs"—that is, the atomic bombs.

Joining Stimson from his office next door, General Mar-shall offers a suggestion. McCloy takes notes:

> General Marshall said he thought these weapons might
> first be used against straight military objectives such as a
> large naval installation and then if no complete result
> was derived from the effect of that, he thought we
> ought to designate a large number of manufacturing
> areas from which the people would be warned to
> leave—telling the Japanese that we intend to destroy

such centers. . . . Every effort should be made to keep our record of warning clear. We must offset by such warning methods the opprobrium which might follow from an ill-considered employment of such force.

Marshall does not know that he is out of step with General Groves's Target Committee, which is looking at targeting a city center. Like Stimson, Army Chief of Staff Marshall is thinking in terms of striking a naval base—a truly military target. If it's necessary to destroy a broader manufacturing area with the atomic bomb, the army chief wants to spare civilians with a warning. Marshall shares Stimson's worry about America's moral standing.

The next morning, May 30, the *Times* runs a second story. LeMay has met with the reporters and shown them photos of swaths of smoking rubble in Tokyo. The *Times*'s front-page, top-of-the-fold headline reads: TOKYO ERASED, SAYS LEMAY. The chief of the XXI Bomber Command seems cavalier about the civilian deaths and the fate of the emperor (reported by the Japanese press to be safe). "General LeMay made it clear tonight that while the bombing of the palace area, so far as he was concerned, was inadvertent, he was not going to worry about it," the newspaper account noted.

Stimson feels blindsided and means to speak to General Arnold, the army air forces commander, about why the air force violated Secretary Lovett's promise of "only" precision bombing. But first, he is going to make sure the Target Committee has not similarly sidestepped his wish, as he put it in his May 17 memo to President Truman, to apply "the same rule of sparing civilian populations" to the list of A-bomb targets.

As it happens, just the day before, the Target Committee, meeting in Groves's office, has finalized its target list. The committee's main concern has been to showcase the power of the new bomb. There is some urgency to its task. LeMay's bombers have been so methodical at burning Japanese cities that the members of the Target Committee are concerned that by the time S-1 is ready, there will be none left. Tokyo is already too burned out to be a good target. Indeed, Groves has asked the air force to preserve a number of cities from firebombing, to, in effect, save them for the atomic bomb.

Three undamaged cities are "reserved": Kyoto, Hiroshima, and Niigata. All have military bases or industries or both. The committee makes no effort to choose "aiming points" for the bombs; that is to be left to later determination, "when weather conditions are known." But the guidelines laid out by the Target Committee clearly show that, while the members of the committee have not dispensed with destroying military or industrial targets, necessity dictates taking no chance on a misplaced bomb. The bombs should *not* be aimed at industrial areas as "pinpoint" targets, since in all three cities, "such areas are small, spread on fringes of cities, and quite dispersed." Rather, the "first gadget" should be placed "in center of selected city." Kyoto, Hiroshima, and Niigata are all densely populated urban areas, largely built of wood.

At 9:20 A.M. on the morning of May 30, General Groves receives a message to report to the office of the secretary of war "at once." Stimson is waiting for him. He wants to know: has Groves selected the targets yet?

Groves stalls. Yes, he has prepared a report, and he expects to take it over—the next day—to show General Marshall.

"Well, your report is all finished, isn't it?" Stimson demands. This morning, judging from the dialogue later recalled by General Groves, Stimson is not a sleepy old man, but more like the prosecutor he once was.

Momentarily taken aback, Groves stalls some more. "I

haven't gone over it yet, Mr. Stimson. I want to be sure that I've got it just right."

Stimson: "Well, I would like to see it."

Groves: "Well, it's across the river and it would take a long time to get it."

Stimson: "I have all day and I know how fast your office operates. Here's a phone on the desk. You pick it up and you call your office and you have them bring the report over."

Groves makes the call, and the two men sit in silence, waiting. Groves tries a new diversion: Isn't the report something that General Marshall should pass on first?

Stimson's scratchy patrician voice takes on a hard edge. "This is one time I'm going to be the final deciding authority. Nobody's going to tell me what to do on this. On this matter I am the kingpin, and you might just as well get that report over here."

General Groves, with his round, full face and tiny mustache, stares impassively. The two men continue to wait. Stimson directly asks Groves which cities he is planning to bomb. Groves answers that Kyoto is the preferred target. It was chosen because its size—a million people—"will leave no question about the effects of the bomb."

Immediately, Stimson says, "I don't want Kyoto bombed."

Kyoto was the ancient capital of Japan. The secretary of war went to Kyoto with Mabel in the late 1920s, during his tour as governor general of the Philippines. He knows it to be a beautiful city, full of sacred temples and shrines, still the cultural center of the nation.

Stimson explains the timeless glories of Kyoto to Groves in some detail. By the time the Target Committee report is handed to him, the secretary's mind is already made up. What's more, Groves stands no chance of winning an appeal to General Marshall.

Or so Groves will tell the story in a later interview:

He read it [the report] over and he walked to the door separating his office from General Marshall's, opened it and said, "General Marshall, if you're not busy, I wish you'd come in." And then the Secretary really double-crossed me because without any explanation he said to General Marshall: "Marshall, Groves has just brought me his report on the proposed targets." He said: "I don't like it. I don't like the use of Kyoto."

Indeed, Stimson does not approve of any of three targets proposed by Groves. Back in his office, a disappointed Groves writes General Norstad, chief of staff of the Twentieth Air Force (who also wears the hat of assistant chief of plans for the army air forces), "Will you please inform General Arnold that this AM the Secretary of War and the Chief of Staff did *not* approve of the *three targets* we had selected, particularly Kyoto." Norstad in turn informs his boss, General Arnold, army air forces commander, that the "targets suggested by General Groves for 509th Composite Group [the special unit created to drop the atomic bomb] have been disapproved, supposedly by the Secretary of War."

Stimson is feeling invigorated. "It was a beautiful clear day, cool, very unusual for Washington in May," he records in his diary. He allows himself a small moment of triumph.

"I celebrated what was a pretty successful day by having a pretty barbaric night so far as sleeping was concerned," Stimson records in his diary the next day, May 31. He gets to the Pentagon early, apprehensive about the momentous event on his calendar. He is meeting with the Interim Committee, a secret high-level group he has appointed to advise the president on the use and future of the atomic bomb. (Stimson wisely chose the unpretentious name for the committee to signal his awareness that any final decisions about ongoing nuclear policy would rest with Congress.) In addition to high-ranking representatives of the State, Navy, and War departments, Stimson has invited leading scientists, including, he notes, "three winners of the Nobel Prize."

Stimson's notes for his presentation to this august group are unusually dramatic for so buttoned-up a man. Under the heading "S-1," he writes, by hand:

> Its *size* and *character*
> We don't think it *mere* new *weapon*
> *Revolutionary Discovery* of Relation of man to universe
> Great History Landmark like
> > *Gravitation*
> > *Copernican* Theory
> But,
> Bids fair [to be] *infinitely greater,* in respect to its *Effect*
> > —on the ordinary affairs of man's life
> May *destroy* or *perfect* International *Civilization*
> May [be] *Frankenstein or* means for World Peace

Stimson wants to impress the scientists that "we were looking at this like statesmen," he records in his diary that night, "and not merely soldiers anxious to win the war at any cost."

He succeeds with at least one important scientist. As Robert Oppenheimer listens to Stimson make his introductory remarks, he sees that Stimson understands that atomic science "meant a very great change in human life," as Oppenheimer will later recall. Chain-smoking cigarettes, his body rail thin after months of riding herd on disputatious physicists on a remote mesa in New Mexico, Oppenheimer is a striking, almost haunting figure. Speaking in a hushed voice, he is a magnetic presence amid a score of sober-looking, middle-aged men discussing the future—or the end—of the world. The intense, visionary Oppenheimer is relieved to hear that Stimson believes the bomb must be internationally controlled by a group of enlightened wise men. On the other hand, he wonders if a committee is capable of producing statesmen.

At the meeting of the Interim Committee, held in a dark-paneled conference room near Stimson's office, it is up to Oppenheimer to describe what the atomic future might look like. The two atomic bombs now being built (named Fat Man and Little Boy) may explode with blasts the equivalent of 2,000 to 20,000 tons of TNT. But those are just the early models. Future so-called thermonuclear bombs, hydrogen bombs that magnify atomic fission with fusion, might range in explosive power from 10 million to 100 million tons of TNT.

In the room is James "Jimmy" Byrnes. The compact, wily Irishman from South Carolina has been designated as President Truman's personal representative on the Interim Committee. A former senator and former Supreme Court justice, he will soon be named secretary of state. Byrnes is "thoroughly frightened," he will later recall. Like the others, he wants to know: how long before the competition—Russia—catches up? About six years is the answer.

If international control of the weapon is desirable, General Marshall suggests, maybe this is the time to begin sharing information with the Russians. Marshall asks whether it would be a good idea to invite two Russian scientists to witness the test of the bomb, scheduled for early or mid-July.

Absolutely not, says Byrnes. Stalin, he says, would surely demand to be brought into the atomic partnership, which would be unacceptable. The Kremlin cannot be trusted; after all, Russia is making a puppet state out of Poland, breaking a gauzy promise made at Yalta to permit democracy in the country, newly liberated from Nazi rule. The others in the room are aware that Byrnes presumably speaks for the president. The official notetaker at the meeting records:

> *Mr. Byrnes* expressed the view, *which was generally agreed to by all present*, that the most desirable program would be to push ahead as fast as possible in production and research and make every effort to better our political relations with Russia.

Byrnes does not say, and no one asks, how it will be possible to better political relations with Russia while refusing to share the secret of the atomic bomb. Actually, the Russians are already stealing atomic secrets with spies planted among the scientists at Los Alamos. No one quite knows it, but the arms race has already begun.

At lunch, as the group splits into two tables, the conversation devolves into cross talk. Oppenheimer is again struck by Stimson's anxieties over the growing tide of civilian casualties, as well as his yearning to lift up a fallen world. Some years later, in remarks describing Stimson's lunchtime musings at the Interim Committee, Oppenheimer will say that Stimson emphasized

> the appalling lack of conscience and compassion that the war had brought about . . . the complacency, the indifference, and the silence with which we greeted the mass bombings of Europe and, above all, Japan. He was not exultant about the bombing of Hamburg, of Dresden, of Tokyo. . . . Colonel Stimson felt that, as far as

degradation went, we had had it; that it would take a
new life and a new breath to beat the harm.

At lunch, someone brings up the idea of demonstrating the
bomb on a deserted island or wasteland before dropping it on
a city. The idea is quickly dismissed. What if the bomber is
ambushed? What if the bomb is a dud? What if the Japanese
bring American POWs into the test area? What if the Japanese simply are not impressed?

Oppenheimer is queried on what the Japanese might see.
"An enormous nuclear firecracker detonated at great height
doing little damage," he says.

Oppenheimer can be curiously dismissive of his own creation. On the day before the Interim Committee meeting,
Oppenheimer ran into Leo Szilard, a Hungarian-born physicist who was one of the first scientists to see the explosive
potential of splitting the atom. Szilard had fled Germany with
his secret in 1932 and joined the Allied effort to beat the
Nazis to the atomic punch. Plagued by second thoughts about
the bomb, he has come to Washington to beseech President
Truman not to use it. Szilard will later recall:

> I told Oppenheimer that I thought it would be a very
> serious mistake to use the bomb against the cities of
> Japan. Oppenheimer didn't share my view. He sur-
> prised me by starting the conversation by saying, "The
> atomic bomb is shit." "What do you mean by that?" I
> asked him. "Well, this is a weapon which has no mili-
> tary significance. It will make a big bang—a very big
> bang—but it is not a weapon which is useful in war."

It's not clear what Oppenheimer means by this, perhaps
even to Oppenheimer himself. He has trouble grasping the
implications of his own invention. After lunch the discussion

among the members of the Interim Committee turns to the question of how to use the weapon against Japan. Someone asks Oppenheimer how many people would be killed by an atomic bomb detonating over a city. About twenty thousand, says Oppenheimer. He is guessing, but he is regarded as the expert in the room. (In truth, no one really knows what the bomb will do: estimates range from fizzle out as a dud to ignite the entire universe.)

Stimson brings up Kyoto as "a city that must *not* be bombed." He insists that "the objective is military damage, not civilian lives." The discussion rattles around the room. Someone else notes that the atomic bomb would not do any more damage or take any more lives than one night of LeMay's B-29 firebombing attacks. There is some confusion over just what a "military" target is. Does that include industry? Industry dispersed through residential neighborhoods? The note-taker sums up:

> After much discussion concerning various types of targets and the effects to be produced, *the Secretary expressed the conclusion, on which there was general agreement, that we could not give the Japanese any warning, that we could not concentrate on a civilian area; but that we should seek to make a profound impression on as many inhabitants as possible. At the suggestion of Dr. Conant* [scientific adviser to the president, deeply involved in the Manhattan Project], *the Secretary agreed that the most desirable target would be a vital war plant employing a large number of workers and closely surrounded by workers' houses.*

Historians will later pick apart the doubletalk, the muddled product of men straining for consensus when faced with the impossible moral dilemma of total war: how to save lives by killing people.

✳ ✳

During most of the debate over choosing a target, Oppenheimer is unusually circumspect. He does say that "the neu-
tron effect of the explosion would be dangerous to life for a
radius of at least two-thirds of a mile." But there is no discussion of radioactive fallout or the fatal long-term effects of
radiation. Oppenheimer himself favors using the bomb. He
has convinced himself that its military use in this war might
mean an end to all wars. It will make war so horrific that hu-
mankind will ban it.

General Groves has been invited to the meeting as a "guest."
He stays quiet. He does not point out that it is highly unlikely
that a bomber flying at thirty thousand feet can hit a "vital
war plant" with anything like assurance. Groves, the skilled
military bureaucrat, is biding his time. He already has a place
in mind—Hiroshima—that will fit any broad definition of a
military target, at least as Groves understands the term. True,
Stimson has apparently ruled out Hiroshima—along with the
other two cities on the target list, Niigata and "especially"
Kyoto, largely for sentimental reasons, in Groves's opinion.
But given time, decisions can be revisited. Hiroshima is
known as a "military city"—*gunto*—by the Japanese themselves. It houses the army headquarters for the forces defending Kyushu, the southernmost Japanese island and the landing
point for the anticipated Allied invasion of Japan. Hiroshima
has a port and industry as well, though they are located on the
periphery of the city, miles from the center. Factories are hard
to hit and built of reinforced concrete. A surer aiming point—
one that has a far larger margin for error—is a bridge in the
middle of Hiroshima, easy to spot from bombing range, in
the midst of acres of wooden homes.

Hiroshima would work to show off the bomb—surrounding
hills would create a "focusing effect" of the blast, containing

and bouncing back the shock waves. At the same time, Groves hasn't given up hope of getting his number one choice, Kyoto, back on the target list. The old capital is huge—with a population of a million people. Groves wants to destroy Kyoto for the same reason Stimson wants to protect it—to cut out the cultural heart of Japan.

The next day, June 1, Stimson makes good on his intention to confront General Arnold on the subject of civilian bombing. That night the secretary will record in his diary:

> I had in General Arnold and discussed with him the bombing of the B-29s in Japan. I told him of my promise from Lovett that there would be only precision bombing in Japan and that the press yesterday [actually, the day before, May 30] had indicated a bombing of Tokyo which was very far from that. I wanted to know what the facts were. He told me that the Air Force was up against the difficult situation arising out of the fact that Japan, unlike Germany, had not concentrated her industries and that on the contrary they were scattered out and were small and closely connected in site with the houses of their employees; and thus it was practically impossible to destroy the war output of Japan without doing more damage to civilians connected with the output than in Europe. He told me, however, that they were trying to keep it down as far as possible. I told him there was one city that they must not bomb without my permission and that was Kyoto.

Arnold is fudging with Stimson. It is true that some of Japan's industry is dispersed in private homes. Months later, after the Japanese surrender, LeMay will recount that, making his way across the charred landscape of Japan, he observed the metal frames of drills and lathes sticking up amid the ashes of residential neighborhoods. But by 1945 Japan has largely given up on home industry, and in any case, Arnold's strategic justification for the firebombing is an effort to paper over the real reason: the precision bombing of factories and industrial targets was not working. Back in March, LeMay chose to firebomb cities for the same reason. Claiming that it is necessary to use firebombs to destroy dispersed industry is a "pretty thin veneer," the blunt LeMay will later admit in an incautious moment.* Though the air force, equipped with improved radar, hopes to return to precision bombing, by the end of the war LeMay will burn out more than sixty cities.

Stimson does not know the true ins and outs of the plan for the bombing campaign because Arnold—and Stimson's trusted aide, Robert Lovett—do not tell him. Perhaps Stimson is too old and weary to pursue "the facts" with the sort of zeal he showed as a young prosecutor or even at the beginning of the war. The unremitting grind of running the War Department, the constant need to make life-and-death decisions based on imperfect information while navigating the shoals of power, the lifelong weight of duty "to God and country," have worn Stimson down.

It may also be that, in some part of his mind, he does not really wish to know.

---

* LeMay has been accused by historians of using bombing to kill civilians in order to break Japanese morale. More recent scholarship suggests that LeMay was focused on trying to destroy Japan's economy, not on killing or terrorizing civilians—but that he had to burn acres of workers' homes as kindling in order to generate fires that were big enough and hot enough to consume any factories, power stations, warehouses, etc., located in the targeted city. To put it in raw terms, he wasn't aiming at citizens; they merely got in the way.

✳ ✳

Five days later, on June 6—the first anniversary of D-Day, the 1944 Allied invasion of Normandy—Stimson calls on President Truman at the White House to discuss S-1. Truman says Byrnes has already briefed him on the work of the Interim Committee, and that Byrnes is "highly pleased." The implication is that Truman is, too. Stimson turns to the subject that has been gnawing at him. That evening Stimson will record their exchange:

> I told him that I was busy considering our conduct of the war against Japan and I told him how I was trying to hold down the Air Force to precision bombing, but that with the Japanese method of scattering its manufacture it was rather difficult to prevent area bombing. I told him I was anxious about this feature of the war for two reasons: first, because I did not want to have the United States get the reputation of outdoing Hitler in atrocities; and second, I was a little fearful that before we could get ready the Air Force might have Japan so thoroughly bombed out that the new weapon would not have a fair background to show its strength. He laughed and said he understood.

Truman's laugh must have been thin and dry. In his diary, Stimson does not say if he laughed along with Truman during their meeting on S-1, but the secretary of war too can see the grim irony in saving the village now in order to destroy it later.

Both men are realists experienced in the exercise of power. Truman spent most of his early political career as an important cog in the Kansas City machine of Boss Tom Pendergast, dispensing patronage as a county "judge" (administrator).

Though personally honest—with a meager bank account to show for it—Judge Truman occasionally needed to look the other way when others in the machine were lining their own pockets.

Stimson is rigidly scrupulous in matters of personal probity, but his idealism is balanced by a relentless streak and even a touch of ruthlessness. He is a believer in the direct approach, of seizing the initiative and getting to a quicker and more certain result by the overwhelming use of force. As a hunter, he seeks not to wound the animal but to kill it. In his earlier iteration as secretary of war, during the Taft administration, Stimson once commented, "I preferred to use a big gun rather than a small gun. When I had to deal a blow, I believed in striking hard." As an amateur historian of the Civil War, he faults Gen. George Meade, the victorious Union Army commander at Gettysburg, for letting Robert E. Lee's defeated Confederate Army slip away. Stimson is glad that his friend Gen. George Patton, commander of the Third Army that chased the German Wehrmacht out of France, did not make the same mistake. (Patton once rented Woodley from Stimson, keeping his polo ponies in the stable.)

Stimson and Truman want to end the war. The only alternatives are invading Japan, at the cost of many American lives; continuing to bombard Japan while starving its people with a naval blockade; or dropping the atomic bomb.

Unless, that is, Japan can be persuaded to surrender before she is destroyed.

"Our demand has been, and it remains—Unconditional Surrender!" President Truman had fairly shouted, banging the rostrum, as he delivered his first address to Congress on April 16, four days after FDR died. The lawmakers roared their approval.

In June, polls show that most America[ns]
like the Germans before them, to surrende[r]
(while, at the same time, wishing for their sons a[nd]
to be brought safely home from the war withou[t]
About a third of Americans wish to hang the Japanese [em]-
peror, and most of the rest want Hirohito imprisoned, preferably for life.

The public anger is understandable to Joseph Grew, the
acting secretary of state, a dapper Boston Brahmin and career
foreign service officer who is temporarily running the State
Department before Jimmy Byrnes takes over in July. But
Grew worries that the average American doesn't understand
just how difficult it will be to make the Japanese give up.
Grew spent nine years as the American ambassador to Japan.
He knows that Japanese officials are not allowed to use the
word *surrender;* indeed, Japan claims to have *never* surrendered
in its 2,600-year history.* Japanese soldiers are sworn to fight
to the death in the name of the emperor, who is regarded as
a god; they are very rarely taken prisoner.

Grew fears that Japanese soldiers will simply refuse to
surrender—unless they are commanded to do so by the emperor himself. Grew has read the stories appearing in the
newspapers at the end of May, describing how fires set by
B-29 incendiaries have burned down many of the buildings at
the Imperial Palace in Tokyo. He feels a sense of urgency to
extract a surrender from Japan before Hirohito is killed, intentionally or not, by the U.S. Army Air Forces. Without
orders from the emperor, the Japanese diehards may never
give up.

---

* "Never surrender" was a modern propaganda invention. In earlier eras,
surrender was widely practiced during periods when Japanese states were
warring with each other. Japan, as such, did not exist prior to about
A.D. 700.

The best way, Grew believes, is to abandon the demand for unconditional surrender and instead offer the Japanese terms: principally, in return for surrender, Japan can maintain its emperor.

Grew takes the idea to Henry Stimson, who listens attentively. Indeed, the acting secretary of state believes he has found an ally in the secretary of war. They have much in common. Grew, of Groton and Harvard, and Stimson, of Andover and Yale, are fellow members of a gentlemen's hunting club, the Boone and Crockett Club; as young men, both heard the call to public service from Theodore Roosevelt. Stimson, too, has spent time around Japanese diplomats, negotiating at peace conferences in the late 1920s and early '30s, and he believes that what he calls "a submerged class" of liberals and moderates exists in the Japanese aristocracy. If they can be saved from the militarists, these statesmen can rebuild Japan after the war. On the need to offer the Japanese moderates a good reason to surrender—preserving their emperor—Stimson and Grew see eye to eye.

But there is a catch. Grew, the diplomat, is congenitally eager to placate—too eager, according to some of his State Department colleagues, who call him "the prince of appeasers." Stimson has a colder eye. At meetings at the end of May and early June, Stimson tells Grew that the United States should not make any offer, not yet. U.S. forces are sure to win the Battle of Okinawa, but the Japanese are taking heart from their fierce resistance, and Stimson thinks it would be a mistake to show weakness.

In World War I, Harry Truman, like Henry Stimson, volunteered to go to France as a soldier. Captain Truman experienced more fighting than Colonel Stimson; he was with his artillery unit at the front lines on several occasions when the German shells began to fall. Truman saw panic as well as courage, and he witnessed the bloodied corpses on the ground.

More than twenty-five years later, in July 1945, as he enters his third month as president, Truman is appalled by the American casualties (dead and wounded) on the embattled island of Okinawa—fifty thousand and counting. Now the Pentagon is proposing Operation Downfall, the invasion of Japan. The plan is that on November 1, the first massive sea-borne landing—bigger than D-Day—will envelop the southern island of Kyushu, and on March 1 a second, even greater force will land on Honshu, where most of the Japanese population lives, spread across the Kanto plain around Tokyo. Truman knows that the Japanese homeland will be defended by fight-to-the-end soldiers holed up in caves, *kamikaze* suicide planes, and, reportedly, women and children armed with pitchforks. The Battle of Japan will be, as he puts it, "Okinawa from one end of Japan to the other."

In early June, Truman receives a letter from Herbert Hoover, the former president, who says he has been talking to informed sources at the Pentagon. The unnamed colonels chatting with Hoover predict that an invasion of Japan will take the lives of upward of half a million American men. Truman is rattled by this butcher's bill.

On June 18 he summons the top brass to a meeting at the White House to learn the facts. The navy and air force favor a siege to strangle Japan. They would like to avoid an invasion—the navy has faced two thousand *kamikaze* planes during the battle for Okinawa—though the generals and admirals concede that it may be necessary to seize Kyushu, the southern island, to make it into a giant aircraft carrier. General Marshall of the army believes that a strategy of blockade and bombardment will take too long. Marshall is worried that America is becoming increasingly war weary and will give up before the job is done. Just as the sailors favor ships and the airmen tout airpower, Marshall has the army bias for boots on the ground. American troops, he insists, will have to land in massive numbers to conquer Japan.

Marshall is not unmindful of the cost, measured both in human lives and in lost moral standing as the rules of war are rewritten or just cast aside. But the normally rule-bound Marshall is beginning to push the limits. In a fit of exasperation in May, the army chief of staff declared that it might be necessary to "drench" the Japanese soldiers in mustard gas to flush them out of their hiding holes. Marshall himself is showing signs of war fatigue, if not spiritual exhaustion. Two days earlier LeMay flew all the way to Washington from his headquarters on the Pacific island of Guam to make the case for defeating Japan by conventional air bombardment. Marshall fell asleep at the briefing.

Knowing that Truman is worried about high American casualties, Marshall has lowballed the estimates. Though the chief of staff is revered for his honesty and rectitude, he has colluded with the designated commander of the invasion force, Gen. Douglas MacArthur (an egotist Marshall thoroughly dislikes), to suggest that about 31,000 American soldiers will perish or be wounded in the initial assault. At the White House meetings, Truman's senior military adviser, Adm. William Leahy, a crusty old salt, scoffs at the Marshall/ MacArthur number as too low by at least half. A confusing argument breaks out among the generals and admirals; President Truman cannot get a straight answer about casualty estimates.

Stimson says little. During his May retreat from Washington, over lunch at Highhold with former president Hoover, Stimson heard his old boss predict that an invasion of Japan would cost between a half million and one million men.

Stimson knows that Hoover has good sources in the military. Indeed, around the Pentagon, Stimson himself has been using the battle casualty number of 500,000. But he is too worn out to engage in tendentious debate over necessarily squishy numbers, and he doesn't want to cross his old comrade-in-arms General Marshall. Stimson has been suffering from such bad migraine headaches that he considered staying in bed that day.

Finally, as the conversation goes in circles, Stimson speaks up, though a little obliquely. According to the meeting's note taker, the secretary tries to make his case that there is "a large submerged class in Japan who do not favor the present war." He says, "I feel something should be done to arouse them." Shouldn't the United States be exploring some diplomatic alternative to a costly invasion?

Anxious that he might flag during the late afternoon meeting, Stimson has invited his energetic and resourceful aide, Jack McCloy, to join him. Prodded by President Truman, who knows Stimson's ubiquitous assistant (everyone important in the war effort knows him), McCloy jumps into the debate with more vim than his boss. "Really, we should have our heads examined," says McCloy, "if we don't seek some other method by which we can terminate this war successfully."

No one at the meeting has mentioned the atomic bomb, still a closely held secret, even though everyone in the room knows about it. Now McCloy does bring up S-1. Why not "send a strong message to the emperor" describing the atomic bomb and saying the United States will use it unless Japan surrenders? McCloy suggests that Japan can keep "the Mikado," calling the emperor by the traditional Japanese title, to serve as a constitutional monarch.

The image of McCloy invoking the bomb as a goad to "the Mikado" will enter the history books, partly because McCloy, in later years, will describe the scene with gusto to historians. As McCloy will tell the story, at the mention of the atomic bomb, "there was a gasp in the room." He uses an arcane comparison: "It was like mentioning Skull and Bones in good Yale society." Members of Stimson's secret society were supposed to leave the room at the mere mention of its name. McCloy may have been wondering how Stimson had managed to fly to New Haven ten days earlier for a secret gathering in the Skull and Bones "tomb," in the midst of his headaches and all his duties as secretary of war.*

McCloy likely exaggerated for posterity. In his later retelling of the story, he will certainly overstate Truman's response. According to McCloy, Truman instructed him to "get the political processes moving" to craft a diplomatic opening to Japan. Truman may have given some bland approbation to McCloy's remarks, but the president has a way of seeming to agree with people when he is really minding his own counsel. As June passes into July, Truman is far from sold on the idea of abandoning "unconditional surrender."

Still, over the next two weeks, McCloy and Stimson work closely with Acting Secretary Grew and James Forrestal, the secretary of the navy, to fashion a diplomatic overture to Japan. It boils down to modifying unconditional surrender, perhaps without quite saying so, with the incentive that Japan can keep her emperor. Stimson is not quite sure of the timing. He wants a final show of force, a heavy ordinary bombing attack, or—if the Japanese balk at the surrender demand—perhaps even "an attack of S-1."

"Japan is susceptible to reason," he writes. "Japan is not a nation composed entirely of mad fanatics of an entirely differ-

---

* "At 8'clock I went down to Bones," Stimson recorded on June 8. "I never felt more dull in my life, but I was received very warmly, in fact tumultuously, and managed to get off a few words."

ent mentality than ours." In the ruling elite, he believes, there must be a liberal voice, there must be *someone* who is in a position to make a difference, who is ready to surface and push aside the militarists.

In fact, there is one.

3.

The Stomach Art

"THERE ARE NO CIVILIANS IN JAPAN"

Foreign Minister
Shigenori Togo was
the only member of
Japan's Supreme War
Council to seek peace.

Tokyo
April–July 1945

I T IS EARLY APRIL IN JAPAN, THE TIME WHEN THE
cherry blossoms fall. As Shigenori Togo enters Tokyo, all he
can see outside his train window is rubble and ash. Almost a
month after the firebombing of the capital, burial parties have
just interred the last of the melted bodies of humans, stacked
two or three meters high in piles of charred flesh and pow-
dery bones that resemble "rice-plant mounds," or so they are
called by the dazed survivors.

Togo is about to become one of the most powerful men in Japan. As foreign minister, he will be one of the "Big Six," a member of the Supreme Council for the Direction of the War, along with the prime minister, the navy and war ministers, and the army and navy chiefs of staff. These men run the war effort, which means they run Japan, for no part or person of Japan is beyond the sacred duty of waging war to protect the *kokutai,* the imperial system.*

Togo is an unlikely leader in Japan. He is not in the military, although in Japan the military effectively rules. He is also not, strictly speaking, Japanese. His father's family was originally Korean; his surname was Park. The Parks came to Japan in the sixteenth century. Although they were admired for their artistry at pottery, as Korean-born they were considered racially inferior. The prejudice persisted three hundred years later, so when Shigenori was a little boy, his father bought the Japanese surname Togo from an ancient samurai family, the hereditary warrior caste.

At university, Shigenori Togo studied German philosophy. He liked discussing Goethe and Schiller and high European culture; he avoided geishas and the group drinking bouts with the other students. He thinks Nazis, including Hitler, are thugs and has never been afraid to say so. He is married to a German woman, the widow of a distinguished architect whom he met while serving at the Japanese embassy in Berlin. Togo spent most of his foreign service career as a diplomat in the West, where, a bit of a dandy, he developed a taste for starched white shirts and white pocket handkerchiefs,

---

* The meaning of the word *kokutai,* resonant with the Japanese, can have different shadings—most narrowly, the emperor and his dynastic rule through the Shinto religion; but, more broadly, and practically speaking, it refers to the governance system all around the emperor, dominated by the military.

French cuffs, and imposing neckties. As first secretary at the Japanese embassy in Washington in the early 1920s, he envied Americans their sense of freedom as well as their industrial capacity.

Most atypically for a Japanese, particularly a Japanese diplomat, Togo is blunt. Japanese can be masters at the art of indirection. In a society where walls are paper thin, they are careful not to say anything offensive. The Japanese language is often spoken in the passive voice, and sentences do not require subjects. Togo can be direct, at times abrasively so. His face seems fixed in a grimace, challenging subordinates as if to ask, "So, what do *you* want?" One of his colleagues at the Foreign Ministry, Shigeru Yoshida—later to become prime minister in postwar Japan—describes him thus: "taciturn, expressionless, and singularly bereft of anything that could be described as personal charm." He is, however, warm with his family; he is a family man, which in mid-twentieth-century Japan also sets him apart.

And yet he has been a highly successful diplomat. Possibly because he plays against Japanese type—saying what is on his mind, declaring what he really wants—he has been able to reach agreements with Japan's traditional enemy, Russia. In 1939 it was Togo who arranged a truce between Russia and Japan following a pitched battle in the Mongolian desert (on the border between Russia and Japanese-controlled Manchuria) at the cost of seventeen thousand Japanese casualties. A year later, after Togo negotiated a mutual nonaggression pact between Russia and Japan, Stalin gave him a banquet, where the Soviets' hard-eyed foreign minister, Vyacheslav Molotov, toasted him for his stubborn persistence—"not just as a statesman, but as a man."

Promoted to foreign minister in 1941, Togo strenuously opposed going to war with the United States. A true patriot, he was briefly heartened by the wave of Japanese victories following Pearl Harbor, but he knew that the surprise attack had, as the Japanese fleet admiral Isoroku Yamamoto put it, "awakened a sleeping giant." His wife, Editha, caught a dose of the "victory disease" and in April 1942 told a fellow diplomat's wife that, really, there was no need to worry about moving one's furs and jewels from Tokyo because the capital was perfectly safe from American air raids. The next day Gen. Jimmy Doolittle's raiders attacked Tokyo and four other cities. Chastened, Togo remained an outspoken realist about the long odds facing Japan, and less than a year into the war, he fell out with Japan's bullheaded prime minister, Gen. Hideki Tojo. Sidelined, he retreated to his home in Nagano, in the mountains away from Tokyo, where he undertook a study of fallen nations—reading deeply into all the ways Russia and Germany were fractured by internal unrest after defeat in World War I.

In the spring of 1945, Togo can see that Japan is thoroughly beaten, and he is eager to find a way out before revolution comes from a long suppressed and starved people. He is not the only one. Some of the men now running the Japanese government want to bring the war to an end, but in a society where even the word *surrender* is forbidden, they cannot admit it. One of those men who wants peace is Emperor Hirohito, although he has trouble acknowledging it even to himself.

At ten-thirty P.M. on the night of April 7, Togo reports to the art-deco-styled official residence of the prime minister, known as the Kantei, where he is formally greeted by a bent-over septuagenarian wearing a stiff wing collar and a morning coat. The Japanese prime minister, Adm. Baron Kantaro Suzuki, seventy-seven years old, has been watching the cherry blossoms fall like delicate snowflakes (the prime minister's garden was spared from the firebombing) and thinking, off and on during the last few days, about the fall of the Roman Empire. Suzuki was once a navy hero, commanding torpedo boats and destroyers in sea battles against the Russians and Chinese at the turn of the century. He has served in high navy posts, including navy minister. Now he is old and deaf. His hands shake, and he can seem slightly muddled. He spends most of his days reading Taoist philosophy and appears to believe what his religion preaches: that "obscurity is virtue" and "passivity is more potent than action." Suzuki is Japan's third prime minister in less than a year. He has been chosen by a murky process rife with hidden agendas and unstated assumptions. "I'm just a sailor," he protested when offered the premiership. Nonetheless, he was the nominee of the *jushin,* the group of ex-premiers who advise the emperor, chosen in part because every other candidate had too many enemies.

Late in the April evening, as he sits down in Suzuki's office at the Kantei, Togo gets right to the point, as is his way. How long, he asks, does the prime minister expect the war to go on?

"I think we can carry on for two or three years," answers the elderly gentleman.

Togo has to struggle to maintain his wooden expression. He knows that Japan cannot possibly hold out so long. With Suzuki, he tries to be realistic, practical. "Modern war," he lectures the old admiral, "depends mainly on material and production. Because of this, Japan cannot continue even one more year." Togo knows that factories, starved of resources, are going idle, and that the island nation of Japan, strangled by the enemy, is running out of food and fuel.

Togo has assumed he is being invited back as foreign minister to seek an immediate end to the war. Now he thinks he is being drawn into a quagmire. It is getting late; the prime minister is tired. Regretfully, Togo declines the position. He plans to head back to Nagano to return to his morbid studies of postwar disintegrations by nations too proud and foolish to seek peace.

But over the next two days, in private conversations with some colleagues who know—or think they know—what the prime minister is thinking, Togo intuits that Suzuki was intentionally opaque during their initial audience. The prime minister was engaging in the ancient practice known as *haragei*, literally, "the stomach art" (*hara*, "stomach"; *gei*, "art," or "stage performance," sometimes "game"). In Japanese culture, it can be perfectly acceptable to say one thing while meaning another and somehow expect the other person to know it. A man gifted at *haragei*, the stomach "art" or "game," can disguise his gut feeling with words, while signaling, by inference or with the barest winks and nods, sometimes *invisibly*, his true intentions. *Haragei* can be an extremely subtle and deft way to work around awkward situations, to communicate truth without mentioning the unmentionable. It can also serve as a convenient excuse when things go wrong. Too often, *haragei* breeds confusion and mistrust. How can one know if the other person really meant what he or she said?

Togo is impatient with the custom of *haragei*. But he understands its place in polite Japanese culture, as well as its usefulness in politics. The next day he goes back to see Suzuki. The ancient Taoist admiral is blandly supportive of whatever Togo wants to do in the role of foreign minister. Togo accepts the job, even though he knows he is putting himself at serious risk, and not just from American bombs. He is an obvious target for assassination by pro-war fanatics.

The Japanese of Togo's time, by custom and history, feel a heavy sense of obligation, called *giri*. It is a debt that must be repaid—to the emperor, always and above all others; to one's superiors, to one's friends and family, and even, ultimately, to oneself. Naturally, obligations can conflict and can lead to a sense of moral paralysis or a strange lassitude. Or to lashing out—against others, or against oneself, through suicide.

Taking one's life can be seen as honorable. In the Japan of 1945, every schoolchild knows the *Tale of the 47 Ronin*. The story is based on actual events that took place in what is now the prefecture of Hyogo in the year 1702, at a time when Japan was ruled by a supreme warlord, called the *shogun,* and power belonged to the *daimyos,* great feudal landowners. The knights of these realms were called *samurai.* They were known for their privilege—they could, with impunity, strike down lesser beings with the long and short swords tied at their waists; and for their duty to *bushido,* a warrior code of un-yielding stoicism and loyalty. In the story, a high official in the court of the *shogun* insulted a *daimyo* and, in response, the *daimyo* struck the court official with a dagger. The *daimyo* was required to commit *seppuku,* to stab and disembowel himself, for violating his *chu,* his duty to his superior lord. The *daimyo's* followers, some forty-seven samurai, became *ronin,* samurai who are leaderless, wandering, lost—but, in this case, not morally lost. They vowed to seek revenge for their fallen master. For a year, these medieval knights plotted; finally, on a snowy night, they cut down the high court official. All through the land, the *ronin* were hailed as heroes for their fidelity, for fulfilling their *giri* to their lord. Still, they too had violated their *chu.* So they took the only honorable way out: they killed themselves.

With its convoluted plot and twisted strands of duty and obligation, *The 47 Ronin* is a national epic, at the core of popular mythology. It sets a tone and expresses a deep feeling. In Japan during World War II, popular patriotic movies typically end in tragedy and death, often with spectacular suicides.

In the 1930s and '40s, Japan is caught in an agony of conflicting obligations. Young army and navy officers are repeatedly, openly insubordinate to their superiors. This may seem odd in a deeply hierarchal society, but *gekokujo*—the overpowering of seniors by their juniors—is widely accepted and even condoned. The young emulators of *The 47 Ronin* can be excused or expect only mild punishment if they are deemed to be sincere. Sincerity has a deep purchase on the Japanese imagination. *Sincere* does not mean candid. It means true to one's inner spirit.

Typically, the mutinous officers claim they are acting in the name of the emperor. They are fulfilling their highest obligation to the figure who is divine, a direct descendant of the sun goddess. They are ever loyal to the throne that has, in Japanese mythology, ruled the ancient Yamato race, as the Japanese call themselves, for 2,600 years. They wish to restore a quasi-mythic Japan ruled by a warrior caste—before the politicians, bureaucrats, and greedy businessmen came along. Gangs of midlevel officers, typically captains and colonels, form secret societies with names like the Blood Brotherhood Association and plot to remove anyone who stands in the way of their noble quest to restore Japan to its feudal glory.

In the 1920s, Japan briefly flirted with democracy, but economic hard times fueled a populist movement that took hold especially in the army, whose ranks are filled with the sons of impoverished farmers. Army and navy salaries are low—but officers are made to feel that they are noble samurai, adhering to a code of *bushido* that makes them as fierce and righteous (if ultimately doomed) as *The 47 Ronin*.

They believe they are engaged in what they call "the Showa Restoration." Emperor Hirohito's reign is called *showa,* translated as "enlightened peace" or "radiant Japan." The junior and midlevel officers secretly conspire to take away power from politicians and business interests and restore it to the emperor—by violence, if necessary.

The period will, in later years, be remembered as "government by assassination." Between 1921 and 1936, there were sixty-four major acts of political violence, including five attempted coups. An egregious example was the so-called League of Blood Incident in 1932, when eleven young naval officers shot and killed Japan's prime minister, Tsuyoshi Inukai, in his residence. (Inukai's last words were, "If I could speak, you would understand." The killers replied, "Dialogue is useless.") The naval officers attacked other government officials and tossed grenades into the Tokyo office of Mitsubishi Bank. The plotters also tried to kill the American comic actor Charlie Chaplin, who was visiting Tokyo, in hopes of sparking a war with America. The coup failed, but the soldiers were only lightly punished, inviting more insubordinate *gekokujo*.

In the 1920s and '30s, three sitting prime ministers, numerous high officials, admirals, and generals were murdered.* In 1923 a madman even took a shot at Hirohito, though the emperor is generally regarded as sacrosanct, since revolts are always in his name.

Throughout the country, the assassins are regarded as heroes, popular avengers, ridding the world of politicians and corrupt businessmen. In 1931 the hotheads in the army gained stature when some young officers in the so-called Kwantung Army, based in Manchuria, in northern China, staged a prov-

---

* The following were casualties of right-wing violence: Prime Minister Hara Kei (Takashi), assassinated in office, 1921. Prime Minister Osachi Hamaguchi, shot in November 1930, died of complications in August 1931. Prime Minister Tsuyoshi Inukai, shot dead on May 15, 1932. Former prime minister Makoto Saito, shot dead on February 26, 1936, while serving as privy seal. Future prime minister Kantaro Suzuki shot and left for dead February 26, 1936. Prime Minister Keisuke Okada, escaped assassination on February 26, 1936, when his brother-in-law Denzo Matsuo sacrificed himself in Okada's place, convincing the assassins he was Okada.

ocation to seize the region for Japan.* The officers were acting on their own; their superiors, right up to the emperor,
embraced their actions after the fact. Like Hitler's *Lebensraum*
(literally, "living space," the conquest of territory for an ex-
panding population), the annexation of Manchuria offered
the densely populated Japanese home islands room to grow.
The Japanese Empire was swept up by an aggressive nationalism and plunged into an ill-considered war to take over the
rest of China. In 1941, when America sanctioned Japan for its
aggression with a crippling oil embargo, Japanese armies
launched offensives into Southeast Asia and the Southwest
Pacific.

As always, racial enmity and pride are inflammatory. The
first Asian nation ever to defeat a European power in its war
against Russia in 1905, modern Japan wanted and expected to
be treated as an equal by the Western nations after World
War I. Embittered to encounter continued racism and condescension by white nations, the Japanese became—or postured
as—racial avengers against white supremacy. They declared
that their aim was to unite Asia for Asians by expelling the
white man. Instead, imbued with their own sense of the su-
periority of the Yamato race above all others, the Japanese
conquerors proved to be crueler than the European colonial-
ists. Atrocities abounded—villages burned, women violated—
excused as zeal. In the fifth year of its existence, the so-called
Greater East Asia Co-Prosperity Sphere can better be described as a charnel house. The military fanatics who control
Japan cannot stop, not even when, three and a half years after

* In 1932 Henry Stimson, acting as President Hoover's secretary of state,
presciently foresaw what lay ahead, announcing that the United States
would never accede to any nation's violation of another nation's sovereignty (the Stimson Doctrine). But to Stimson's disappointment, Hoover
lacked the will to do anything about it. "A tragedy of timidity," wrote
Stimson.

Pearl Harbor, they are reaping a whirlwind of napalm fire-storms set by an awakened—and vengeful—America.

Although in 1945 they are the most powerful men in Japan, the four military members of the so-called Big Six—the war and navy ministers and the army and navy chiefs of staff—are wary, perhaps even frightened, of their own subordinates. At meetings of the Supreme Council for the Direction of the War, they try to outdo each other with displays of fight-to-the-death defiance. Togo suspects they are putting on a good show to impress their hotheaded young staff officers, who draw up the official papers and plans.

The prime minister, Admiral Suzuki, seems haunted by his own experience with *gekokujo*. During the most audacious coup attempt, known as the February 26th Incident in 1936, Suzuki was serving as the emperor's grand chamberlain, running the palace. He was shot four times and still carries a bullet in his back. He will remember, nine years later in 1945, the feeling of a gun muzzle pressed against his temple.

Togo finds the other members of the War Council as hard to read as he found Suzuki. Gen. Yoshijiro Umezu, the army chief of staff, is known as "the Ivory Mask" because his expression reveals nothing. Adm. Mitsumasa Yonai, the navy minister, is thought to be pro-peace, but he can seem slippery. Adm. Soemu Toyoda, the navy chief of staff (who comes on board in June), is also supposed to be pro-peace, but, as time goes on, he will make the most bellicose statements of anyone.

The great question mark is the war minister, Gen. Korechika Anami, arguably the most powerful member of the Big Six. Anami plays the part of a true samurai: unblinking in his fealty to ancient martial virtue. He is a champion archer with the long seven-foot bow and keeps fit at *kendo*—fencing with bamboo swords. Anami believes in spirit over intelligence (he twice flunked the military academy exam) and is prone to statements like "morality is fighting strength." *Morality* is a relative term in the Japanese army. Unlike modern Western armies, Japanese forces do not bother to set up long lines of supply. They live off the land and harvest the spoils of war, raping and pillaging, which explains why, as the Japanese advance, millions of Chinese refugees clog the roads fleeing before them.

Anami has been an aggressive combat commander, though not a notably successful one. In China earlier in the war, his overextended forces were outflanked and forced to retreat. But he is a successful politician with ties to the emperor, for whom he served as a military aide-de-camp before the war. With a bluff, genial manner, he is popular with junior officers, who approve of his determination to fight one last "decisive battle" to humble America.

Anami is also, to all appearances, a hard-liner against peace. One of his first acts as minister of war was to order the special higher police, sometimes called the thought police (charged with controlling political groups and enforcing ideological purity), to arrest four hundred people suspected of "end the war" sentiments. Those arrested include friends of Togo, among them Shigeru Yoshida, who had been Japan's ambassador to Great Britain before the war.

Togo will have to be careful with Anami. Already, the military police, the *kempeitai,* have started coming around Togo's own house, questioning his wife and daughter. Still, Togo has hope for Anami, who is personally loyal to the emperor. Togo suspects that the war minister, for all his sincerity, is performing *kabuki,* a stylized dance—as if wearing a ferocious mask—to keep his own troops in line.

Togo wants to begin a discussion on the forbidden subject—

ending the war. But how, without winding up in jail or assassinated? His first move, a clever one, is to persuade the other members of the Big Six to meet secretly—just the six of them together in a room without staff or aides. Togo is encouraged that his fellow members of the Supreme Council for the Direction of the War are willing to get together without any second-guessing colonels lurking about. It suggests that the other members of the Big Six, even the hard-line Anami, wish to speak words they don't want their subordinates to hear.

Still, Togo proceeds cautiously. The first secret meeting of the Big Six comes just after the collapse of Germany in early May. Japan will now have to go it alone against the Allies. The propaganda machine cranks out the message that the Germans surrendered because they lack the "spirit" of the Japanese. The Japanese population, while suffering from privation and fearful of the B-29s, which they call "*B-san,*" are sullen but largely docile. They have been conditioned to believe in the empire's invincibility. The Big Six know better. They have seen a comprehensive recent report, ordered by Togo, that shows that Japan is running out of oil, steel, and even food. As a condition of taking the job as foreign minister, Togo insisted on an honest accounting of Japan's economic condition. It is dire. Japan may have no more airplane fuel by September, and the rice crop is the worst in a half century. People are trying to coax fuel out of pine cones and cook dinner from acorns.

At a series of meetings on May 11, 12, and 14, Togo hopes to convince his colleagues that necessity dictates sending out some peace feelers. Taking the straightforward approach, he proposes talking directly to the United States about a cease-fire. He is summarily rebuffed. America, the others say, will demand unconditional surrender, which is unthinkable. Togo suggests various go-betweens, including the Vatican, Sweden, and China. Again, the answer from the others is a flat no.

Togo's colleagues are willing to reach out to only one country: the Soviet Union. Russia may seem an unlikely partner for peace. Japan fought a major war against Russia in 1904–5 and the two countries battled in 1939 on the Manchurian border. Already there are ominous signs that Russia is preparing for war against Japan. With Germany defeated, trainloads of Russian soldiers and tanks are moving east, preparing, it would appear, to seize Manchuria and retake Russian ports lost to Japan in 1904–5.

But perhaps Russia can be persuaded to take a friendlier view. General Anami points out that Russia and the United States, now allies, will become adversaries as soon as the war is over. Already the two nations are butting heads as Russia seeks to dominate eastern Europe in the wake of Nazi Germany's collapse. Might not the U.S. versus U.S.S.R. rivalry extend to the other side of the Eurasian continent as Japan's empire folds up? In that case, he suggests, maybe Russia can be convinced to use Japan as a buffer to America. Admiral Yonai goes a step further. Japan should propose to obtain oil from the Russians in exchange for giving Russia some naval cruisers.

Togo makes little effort to disguise his scorn for Yonai, telling him that he couldn't possibly know anything about Russia if he thinks Moscow will become Japan's trading partner. With characteristic bluntness, Togo says it is "hopeless to try and get Russia on our side now." He notes that Stalin met with Churchill and Roosevelt at Yalta during the winter, and Russia has said it will not renew the neutrality pact with Japan that was signed in 1941. Togo suspects, correctly as it turns out (and with some intelligence to support his view), that Russia may have agreed to enter the war in the Pacific on the side of the Allies.

Anami is unmoved. Japan is not losing the war, he insists. The empire still controls vast amounts of territory throughout Asia. The time is coming, he says, for a decisive battle that will humble the Americans. In the meantime, Togo agrees to contact the Russians—not to try to end the war but simply to establish friendlier relations. Disappointed but resigned, he starts looking for a back channel to Moscow.

✳ ✳

In early June, the ultranationalist zealots who serve on the staff of the Supreme War Council strike back. Excluded from meetings by the Big Six, these junior and midlevel officers spend their time preparing a fire-breathing document entitled *The Fundamental Policy to Be Followed Henceforth in the Conduct of the War.* It declares, simply, that Japan will "fight to the bitter end."

To Togo's surprise and regret, the report has the full backing of Suzuki, the prime minister. At a meeting of the Supreme War Council on June 6, Togo is caught flat-footed when Suzuki introduces a resolution approving of the *Fundamental Policy*. The document calls for the enlistment of a national volunteer army, including women and children. Physically ill—he is suffering from pernicious anemia, whose chief symptoms are fatigue and weakness—Togo labors to stand up from his chair. Still, he rallies to ridicule the notion that the nearer the battlefield is to Japan, the more advantageous to the Japanese. Not to the women and children fighting, he dryly points out.

At this, Admiral Toyoda explodes: "Even if the Japanese people are weary of the war, we must fight to the last man!"

General Anami joins in, sounding like the lord who killed himself in *The Tale of the 47 Ronin*: "If we cannot fulfill our responsibilities as advisers to the throne, we should offer our sincere apologies by committing hara-kiri!"

Togo is rolled. The Supreme War Council adopts the *Fundamental Policy* of no surrender. On his way out, Togo confronts Admiral Yonai. "I expected support from you today," he says coldly. "But I got none." Togo is particularly disappointed in Suzuki. "I cannot understand what Prime Minister Suzuki is thinking," he will write in his diary that night. "I understand and expected the army's stance, but where in the world does the prime minister think he's taking the country?" He worries that Suzuki has "a split personality."

On June 8 the *Fundamental Policy* is presented to the emperor. The Big Six and various other officials make their way to the Imperial Household Ministry for an audience with Hirohito. They cannot visit him in the palace because it was burned down in the firebombings.

Sitting on his throne, Emperor Hirohito says nothing as usual. He is not expected to speak; it is considered unseemly to trouble "the August Mind." The emperor is presented with the consensus views of his government and silently assents. But several of his faithful servants note that his expression is particularly dour.

Hirohito, the 124th emperor in a line of succession "unbroken for ages eternal," has been raised to revere the army and navy, who are themselves jealous rivals for his divine sanction. At the age of eleven, he was made a second lieutenant in the army and an ensign in the navy. In his infrequent public appearances, he usually sits astride a white horse, wearing the bemedaled uniform of a field marshal. As a boy, in war games with his playmates, he was always the commander in chief and always victorious.

After the war, it will be said that he was an innocent figurehead. This is not true. Hirohito was only reluctantly persuaded to approve the surprise attack on Pearl Harbor, and he at first questioned the suicidal *tokko* tactics of the military. But he has publicly bowed in a show of respect for *kamikaze* pilots who crashed their planes into American ships,* and, behind closed doors, he has sanctioned the use of poison gas against the Chinese. He is not merciless: he did tell the army not to execute a group of American airmen captured after the daring Doolittle raid on Tokyo in 1942; in the end, the army executed three of eight. On an almost daily basis, military leaders keep the emperor briefed on the progress of the war, but they shade and dissemble, exaggerating American losses. Hirohito can be understandably peevish and critical with the military as his empire disintegrates. He pleads, "Isn't there some way, some place, where we can win a real decisive battle with the Americans?"

Hirohito is not a commanding presence. His voice is reedy, and he is seen slouching about the palace in slippers, talking to himself. He is happiest observing fireflies in the garden and pursuing his passion for sea anemones as a marine biologist. His courtiers try to cheer him up with humorous Walt Disney cartoons of Mickey Mouse and Donald Duck, seized when the Japanese captured Wake Island. More querulous than confident, Hirohito slumps under the weight of duty.

Still, he has shown flashes of character. He is faithful to the empress. When she seemed capable of producing only daughters instead of a male heir, Hirohito was strongly pressured by his ever-present courtiers to take a concubine, in the custom of his ancestors. Hirohito refused—and in time, Empress Nagako gave birth to a boy, Crown Prince Akihito.

He has not always been cowed by the military. Learning

---

* In October 1944 the Japanese navy adopted the tactic of diving their planes directly into American ships. The pilots called themselves *kamikazes* after the "winds of the gods" that destroyed invading Mongol armadas twice in the late thirteenth century. The notion that Japan was divinely protected had great currency among the Japanese people and their leaders.

that his grand chamberlain had been shot and the lord keeper of the privy seal had been murdered by fanatical army officers during the February 26, 1936, coup attempt, he was at first fatalistic. "So they have finally done it," he sighed. But then he braced himself, put on his uniform, and ordered the army high command to get control of their subordinates, ending the uprising.

The army, the navy—the whole nation—are sworn to protect the emperor. There are outlandish stories, like the one about a high school principal who committed hara-kiri after failing to rescue the emperor's portrait from a burning schoolhouse, or the motorcycle policeman who committed hara-kiri after making the wrong turn in the emperor's motorcade. When the palace was bombed in May 1945, Minister of War Anami offered to resign.

Since the autumn of 1944, when the first B-29s appeared over Tokyo, the emperor and empress have been living in the *obunko,* the imperial family library, a columned one-story structure set away from the main palace buildings in the formal gardens. Beneath the *obunko* is a bomb shelter. When air raid sirens sound, as they did with growing frequency in the winter of 1945, Hirohito and his wife began spending nights in the shelter. It was damp and cold, and they had trouble sleeping.

The firebombing in March only grazed the palace complex, a 240-acre green island set amid stone walls, surrounded by a moat, in the heart of the capital. Some trees and hedges caught fire from embers blown in the wind; the emperor and empress, sheltering in the *obunko,* could smell the acrid smoke. The May firebombing was devastating. It swept away most of the palace structures, built of cypress wood, and only frantic efforts saved priceless portraits and artifacts, as well as the crown prince's toys. Thirty-three firemen died. Hirohito was shaken. Now he wonders if he is being deliberately targeted by the Americans.

On June 13 he is informed that the military wishes to move him away from the palace to a fortress of underground tunnels the army has built deep in the mountains of Nagano province. An armored train has been readied to carry him to safety.

But the emperor refuses. He says simply, "I'm not going."

Hirohito is not regarded as self-reflective, but he is not unaware of his peculiar position, at once semigod and dependent. He has described himself as "a bird in a cage." It has begun to dawn on him, however slowly and reluctantly, that the army is using him to commit madness—national self-immolation—in his name. Despite the divine mythology surrounding his name (and the irony that the *showa* emperor was leading his nation in an era of anything but "radiant peace"), Hirohito knows that his throne has always been held at the sufferance of men with swords. Until the Meiji restoration of Hirohito's grandfather in the 1860s, emperors were kept isolated, and sometimes impoverished, while the nation was ruled by an all-powerful warlord, the *shogun*. Now, Hirohito knows, if he disappears into the mountains under the protection of the army, he will, in effect, become its captive. Hirohito prays to his ancestors for strength. He will swallow his fear and stay in Tokyo.

But the decision is gut-wrenching. His own mother, the empress dowager, a hard-line hawk, has berated him for not taking a more bellicose stand as a war leader. At the same time, she is demanding a better bomb shelter for herself. Hirohito, who is normally healthy, begins suffering from diarrhea and vomiting.

The Marquis Koichi Kido is lord keeper of the privy seal. His formal duties are keeping track of the seals affixed to various imperial pronouncements, known as rescripts. His real job is to be the emperor's eyes and ears in the world beyond the palace. In the era of *gekokujo,* the job is demanding and dangerous. Fanatics killed Kido's predecessor in the February 26 Incident, and the prior privy seal had to quit after a mental breakdown.

Small and compact, with a tidy mustache, Kido is a man of regular habits. His golf swing is so regular that he is known as "the Clock." As cynical as he is reverent, Kido has tried to ride the tiger, hoping to keep the military under control by forming alliances with military leaders and supporting the war effort.

But he knows that Japan has lost the war. On the afternoon of June 8—the same day the emperor sullenly assented to the *Fundamental Policy* to fight to the last man—Kido picked up his brush and began writing:

> The progress of the war in Okinawa, to my regret, makes me believe that it is destined inevitably to result in a miserable fiasco. Moreover, it is almost certain that this result will come about in the very near future.
> [Japan will formally surrender Okinawa on June 22.]

Kido is as worried about the anger of his own people as he is about B-29 firebombings. He knows the level of privation, that women are exchanging their kimonos for sweet potatoes; that popular magazines are running recipes for acorn stew; and that because soap is scarce, the Japanese, who love their bath, have begun to stink.

He continues to write:

> The extreme shortage of provisions and foodstuffs that will sweep the country in the latter part of this year and thereafter—in light of the approaching chilly season—

will cause serious unrest among the people at large.

And in consequence, the situation will be beyond salvation.

He fears, more than anything, a revolution that will sweep away the imperial system, the *kokutai*. Kido knows that the time has come to act, to do something, to try to save "the situation." But what?

Kido would like to approach the United States and Great Britain directly to sue for peace. But he knows the military would never hear of it. So he thinks instead of the Soviet Union as the go-between. Russia may be Japan's natural enemy, but the two countries have a neutrality pact for the time being. Working into the night, Kido writes a "Draft Plan for Controlling the Crisis Situation," proposing that Russia mediate a peace agreement, though one stuffed with conditions favorable to Japan, especially the preservation of the *kokutai,* rule by the emperor (which, in practice, means rule by the military).

Kido, supposedly the emperor's emissary to the political world, is unaware that the Big Six have already launched a diplomatic feeler to Russia. Prime Minister Suzuki has not told him.

With some trepidation, Kido sets out to enlist the Big Six in his plan, which would go further than theirs—not just looking to improve relations with the Kremlin, but seeking Russia's active mediation to end the war.

Kido starts with Admiral Yonai, hopeful that he will not betray him. Yonai approves, in a guarded sort of way. "Of course, very good idea, but I wonder how the prime minister really feels about the war?"

Kido approaches the prime minister. Suzuki has been giving fiery fight-to-the-end speeches to the Diet, Japan's rubber stamp legislature. He is also wary. "I wonder what Admiral Yonai thinks about all this?" Suzuki inquires of Kido.

The privy seal answers, "Yonai said the same thing about you." Suzuki found this to be amusing; he is entertained by the *haragei,* the undisguised playing of the artful stomach game. But Kido is not. He worries that neither man knows what is in the other's "stomach."

Foreign Minister Togo is encouraged to learn of Kido's idea and greatly relieved. He can see that Kido shares his idea of reaching out to Russia as a way of getting the military on board for some sort of peace initiative, however tentative. But first he asks, what of the fight-to-the-end vow of the *Fundamental Policy* endorsed by the emperor on June 8?

"Oh!" Kido replies. "That! It is all right."

The privy seal seems a little breezy about an imperial vow to commit national suicide, but Togo is eager to seize the moment nonetheless. On June 20 he is granted an audience with the emperor.

It has been cloudy and rainy in Tokyo, and Togo can see that Hirohito's mood reflects the weather. As it happens, the emperor has just been briefed on the war situation, and for once, the generals have not tried to cover up the military's perilous want of resources. Hirohito has learned that the *tokko* suicide forces are scrounging for old automobile engines to power their planes and boats, and that the army troops building redoubts are making shovels out of the iron fragments of American bombs. The emperor glumly recounts these details to Togo.

Gingerly, Togo walks the emperor through the steps his government is taking to reach out to the Russians and expresses his hopes that Russia can broker an end to the war. Hirohito "approves of the steps taken as entirely satisfactory," Togo records. Then the emperor says the words his foreign minister has been longing to hear: "Please terminate the war as quickly as possible."

✳ ✳

The emperor has spoken. But nothing in the ruling circle is simple or straightforward. On June 22 Hirohito summons the Big Six to an audience and—disregarding custom—speaks first. He backs into his agenda. The *Fundamental Policy* had been set on June 8, he says: the war should be fought to the end. Nonetheless, he says, it is necessary to consider other methods to cope with the crisis. Do the others have any ideas?

Togo weighs in, but he too steps carefully. He says an emissary is meeting with the Russian ambassador, but he notes that Japan will have to be prepared to pay a substantial price—giving up chunks of the empire to Russia—to gain Moscow's help, which is no sure thing in any case.

General Anami, the samurai warrior of old, faithful to the code of *bushido,* the "way of the warrior" who yearns to die for his emperor, sternly insists that Japan must not show weakness. Speaking in aphorisms about moral purity, he might as well be fencing with bamboo *kendo* sticks, not debating subtle geopolitics. General Umezu, his face as impassive as ever, warns against rushing into negotiations. The emperor interjects that it would be too bad to miss the right moment. This counts as a rebuke to both Anami and Umezu, and Umezu agrees that yes, they need a concrete plan to end the war. The emperor abruptly stands to leave. The meeting has lasted thirty-five minutes.

Togo's hopes are raised, but they are soon frustrated. He attempts to reach out to Russia's ambassador, Jacob Malik, but Malik ducks; he is sick, or he is busy, or he fails to respond. Feeling some urgency, the emperor himself steps in. Hirohito suggests to Prime Minister Suzuki that it would be wise to send Prince Konoe, a former prime minister, to Moscow immediately to plead Japan's case: that Japan and Russia—despite their history of bloodshed and rivalry—can be allies against the Anglo-Americans.

On July 12 Togo sends a "very urgent" telegram to Naotake Sato, Japan's ambassador to Russia:

> His Majesty the Emperor, mindful of the fact that the
> present war daily brings greater evil and sacrifice upon
> the peoples of all belligerent powers, desires from his
> heart that it may be quickly terminated. . . .

Momentous news, it might seem, but there quickly comes
the hedge:

> But so long as England and the United States insist
> upon unconditional surrender the Japanese Empire has
> no alternative but to fight on with all its strength for
> the honor and the existence of the Motherland.

In Moscow, Japanese ambassador Sato scoffs. He has already been coldly rebuffed by Molotov, Stalin's steely foreign
minister, and he can see that the Kremlin, fresh from defeating Germany, is in the mood to grab, not to give. He answers
Togo that Japan is completely unrealistic to hope that anything *but* unconditional surrender will end the war. There is
"no hope," he writes Togo, that Russia will do anything to
help Japan surrender under any terms other than unconditional surrender, with the possible exception of preserving
the imperial structure of government. With bracing frank-
ness, Ambassador Sato chides Togo for using "academic fine
phrases." Still, Sato is mildly apologetic: "I have expressed my
views frankly, and I fear that I must apologize for the uncer-
emoniousness of my words. I am filled with thoughts of fear
and heartbreak."

Togo remains unyielding. When Sato presses the Japanese
government to accept unconditional surrender with the one
exception of preserving the emperor, Togo wires back:

> We are unable to consent to it under any circumstances
> whatever. Even if the war drags on and it becomes clear

that it will take much more than bloodshed, the whole country as one man will pit itself against the enemy in accordance with the Imperial Will so long as the enemy demands unconditional surrender.

Read today, Togo's telegrams have an odd rigidity. Normally, Togo is the blunt one, cutting through the verbiage to get to the underlying point. And Togo all along has been a sober realist in a country where newspaper headlines are proclaiming JAPAN'S 100 MILLION WILL DIE FOR THE EMPEROR! But in the exchange of telegrams between Sato and Togo, which runs on throughout July, it is Sato who comes across as the truth-teller. Togo sounds like a mouthpiece for the military, because by circumstance and necessity, he is. He is not answering Sato for himself or even for the emperor. He is channeling the Supreme Council for the Direction of the War, and Togo's colleagues are nowhere near surrender. At meetings of the Supreme War Council, war minister Anami insists that Japan has not lost the war, that it is merely readying itself for the final Decisive Battle; indeed, the army has been preparing for months.

The plan is called Ketsugo Sakusen, an operation to achieve the final, decisive battle (*hondo kessen*). The Japanese have guessed exactly where the American landing force plans to land, on the beaches of Kyushu, the southern island of the homeland. The armed forces are ready to greet the invaders with some seven thousand *kamikaze* planes, aimed to fly into the landing ships, in waves of three or four hundred. They are patchwork planes, manned by pilots who know only how to take off, but the plan, by no means unrealistic, is to sink up to half of the American invasion fleet before the boats can reach the beaches. The *kamikazes* in the air will be supported by a thousand suicide bombers in small speedboats, midget submarines, and swimmers sticking ten-kilo TNT charges to the bottoms of landing craft.

In Washington on June 18, when President Truman met with his generals and admirals to discuss the human cost of the invasion of Japan, the top brass estimated that Kyushu would have about 350,000 Japanese defenders, against about 700,000 American invaders. Meanwhile, in fact, the Japanese army has almost tripled the force for Kyushu, to about 900,000 men. That number counts just regular soldiers. All men from ages fifteen to sixty and all women from ages seventeen to forty—nationwide, some 28 million civilians—have been required to join the National Volunteer Corps. Their weapons include muzzle-loading muskets, longbows, sharpened bamboo spears, and pitchforks. Published by the government earlier in the year, the *People's Handbook of Resistance Combat* instructs:

> When engaging tall Yankees, do not swing swords or spears sideways or straight down; thrust must be straight into their guts.

It is perhaps understandable that an intelligence officer with the U.S. Army Air Forces writes on July 21, "The entire population of Japan is a proper military target. THERE ARE NO CIVILIANS IN JAPAN" (all caps in original).

There is little Togo can do to head off this Armageddon. The military controls the government. Under the Japanese constitution—"given" to the people by Hirohito's grandfather, Emperor Meiji—only the army and the navy have direct access to the emperor. The war minister, chosen by the army—in this case, Anami—can bring down the government anytime simply by resigning. Then there is the ever-present threat of assassination of any government leader deemed to be "traitorous." As a practical matter, government ministers are beholden to their staffs, fanatical young army officers with swords and guns.

Japan, in the summer of 1945, can be seen through a glass

darkly. *Hondo kessen* at Kyushu may seem like suicidal madness, but in a way, it makes perfect sense. The Japanese do not have to "win" the Decisive Battle. They just have to make the cost of victory unbearable to the Americans. It is called *shukkettsu,* "the bleeding strategy." Facing waves of suicide planes and the task of burning Japanese soldiers out of caves while battling women and children armed with pitchforks, America—already showing signs of war weariness—could be reasonably expected to back off from unconditional surrender and offer good terms: no longer demanding the end of the imperial system, the *kokutai,* or disarming the army, or occupying Japan, or even stripping it of all the conquered territory from Indonesia to Manchuria. The strategy is plausible, and it might have worked in part, but for two bombs that are shortly to arrive on the island of Tinian, 1,500 miles from the Japanese coast, within the range of a *B-san.*

4.

The Patient Progresses

"You judge it; I can't"

President Harry
Truman and
Stimson in the
Oval Office; the
two men were
wary but
respectful of
each other.

Washington, D.C.
Potsdam, Germany
July 1945

THE SECRETARY OF WAR IS WRAPPING UP A MEETING
with President Truman in the Oval Office. Stimson is aware
that people are "fretting at the door," but before he leaves, he
needs to raise an awkward subject. Truman is going to meet
with Stalin and Churchill in Potsdam in two weeks to discuss
the end of the Pacific War and the reconstruction of Europe,
and Stimson has not been invited. Stimson wishes to know

why. "I asked him to tell me frankly," he records in his diary, whether the reason was concern over Stimson's health. Truman laughs. "Yes," says the president. "That's just it."

Stimson is aware that Truman prefers the company—and the advice—of his new secretary of state, Jimmy Byrnes. The president is more comfortable with Byrnes, his former Senate colleague and organizer of "bullbat" time—whiskey, poker, and political talk.* Truman is respectful of Stimson, and vice versa, but the two men are still guarded. Truman cannot help but feel, in Stimson's patrician manner, a slight edge of condescension.

Still, Stimson is determined to go to the meeting in Germany. Nothing is more important to him than the use of S-1 to end the war and the rebuilding of the world in its wake. The next day he asks the president if he can travel separately to the meeting, scheduled to begin in mid-July in the Berlin suburb of Potsdam, in the Russian zone of occupation, and bring his aide, Jack McCloy. "All right," Truman says, curtly.

Truman, Byrnes, and some of the president's poker-playing pals sail on the *Augusta,* a U.S. Navy cruiser, escorted by two destroyers. Stimson makes his way on a slow steamer, the *Brazil,* via Marseille, arriving two days late.

The Americans are quartered in an abandoned film colony on a lake in a once-posh suburb now overrun by the Red Army. Truman is installed by the Russians in a showy villa that once belonged to a German film producer. When the Russians had commandeered the villa as they marched into Berlin, they killed the owner and raped his daughters. After

---

* A bullbat is a night hawk that sings after dark. Byrnes was also director of the Office of War Mobilization from 1943 to 1945, during which time he functioned as a kind of "assistant president." The cocksure Byrnes felt slighted when FDR passed over him for the vice-presidential nomination in 1944 in favor of Truman.

the house was looted of its art and furnishings, the Soviet secret police, the NKVD, wired it with electronic listening devices. Stimson is accommodated in a smaller house, which is hot and mosquito-y and surrounded by Russian guards. Stalin stays in a fifteen-room villa once owned by a German World War I general, Erich Ludendorff.

"I received important paper in re Japanese maneuver for peace," Stimson writes in his diary on July 16, his first full day in Potsdam. Stimson has been reading Togo's mail. More precisely, he has been reading a summary of the United States' MAGIC intercepts of Japanese diplomatic messages, compiled and analyzed by army intelligence and the State Department. U.S. code breakers have picked up Foreign Minister Togo's telegram to Ambassador Sato on July 12, the message stating that the emperor "desires . . . that the war may be quickly terminated."

This could be very dramatic news indeed—the first real breakthrough toward surrender. But the analyst writing the report, Brig. Gen. John Weckerling, deputy assistant chief of staff, G-2 (army intelligence), warns of a ploy: the Japanese are hoping to appeal to "the war weariness" of America to "stave off defeat," using a diplomatic smokescreen while they build up their defenses. The "Japanese government clique" is not making a serious offer for peace, or so concludes the report that Stimson reads.

Although General Weckerling cannot know all the machinations of the Supreme Council for the Direction of the War, his suspicions about the Japanese military are not far off. Stimson is instinctively a realist; still, he wants to seize an opportunity to head off a looming bloodbath.

Shortly before dawn on that same morning of July 16, scientists and military men are rubbing suntan lotion onto their faces in the pitch black of the New Mexico desert. At 5:29 and forty-five seconds, a giant column of fire ascends heavenward, mushrooming into a fantastic fireball. Kenneth Bainbridge, one of the scientists in charge of arming "the gadget," whacks Robert Oppenheimer on the back and exclaims, "Now we are all sons of bitches!" The Manhattan Project has succeeded in building the world's first nuclear weapon. Oppenheimer thinks of a line from Hindu scripture:

Now I am become Death, the destroyer of worlds.

General Groves, the head of the Manhattan Project, is standing nearby. His deputy, General Farrell, says, "The war is over." Groves replies, "Yes, after we drop two bombs on Japan."

✳ ✳

In Potsdam on the afternoon of July 16, eight hours ahead of New Mexico, an "eyes only" telegram arrives for Stimson from his aide handling S-1, George Harrison. It is written in an easily decipherable code:

Operated on this morning. Diagnosis not yet complete but results seem satisfactory and already exceed expectations. . . . Dr. Groves pleased.

"The Secretary cut a gay caper," Jack McCloy writes in his diary that night, "and rushed off to tell the president and Jimmy Byrnes about it." McCloy himself is less buoyant. He writes, "I hope it does not augur the commencement of the destruction of modern civilization."

Stimson wants to take advantage of the moment. Early on the morning of July 17, heading over to "the Little White

House," he wishes to impress upon the president that the time has come to warn Japan with a stick—that America has the A-bomb—and a carrot—that if Japan agrees to surrender, she can keep her emperor.

Truman cannot meet with the secretary of war. He is busy. Instead, Stimson gets Byrnes. The secretary of state gives the secretary of war a flat no: no early warning, no deal on keeping the emperor.

On the voyage across the Atlantic on the *Augusta,* in between poker games, Byrnes had already convinced Truman to reject Stimson's and Joseph Grew's proposal that Japan be allowed to retain its emperor in return for surrendering. Byrnes has told Truman that he will be labeled "an appeaser" and politically crushed if he allows the Japanese to keep "the Mikado," who most Americans wish to see banished, if not strung up. Byrnes and Truman are also influenced by hard-line New Dealers in the State Department, who believe that Japan's feudal hierarchy needs to be torn out by the roots and replaced by a system that honors the people's choice.

Truman listens to Byrnes, whom he admires for his "keen" intelligence and his "conniving" skills as a politician. But the president has his own worldview, shaped by his ascent in the populist politics of Kansas City, Missouri. It is fundamentally different from that of patricians like Stimson and Grew. When Ambassador Grew was in Japan, he compared the moderate gentlemen of high lineage that he encountered—men like the Marquis Kido—to the families he grew up with in Brahmin Boston, the Saltonstalls, the Peabodys, and the Sedgwicks. Stimson as well was impressed by the Japanese statesmen he met at international peace conferences in the late 1920s and early '30s, by their impeccable manners and moderate views, even by their sense of fiscal responsibility—to Stimson, no different from the better sort on Wall Street.

To Harry Truman, Imperial Japan looks more like the Pendergast machine. Truman is on record comparing Stalin to Tom Pendergast, "the Boss." Truman has never met Hirohito, who is nothing like either Stalin or Pendergast, but he certainly understands the top-down nature of power closely held by a strongman. Truman leaves no record of thinking deeply about the Japanese imperial system, or *kokutai,* a word that may have no meaning to him. But he is clear, in at least one private conversation with a former congressional colleague, that he does not like "the Jap Emperor," as he calls him, and wants him gone.

More code breaking hardens Truman's unwillingness to cut a deal with the Japanese. MAGIC intercepts of Japanese diplomatic cable traffic show the futility of Foreign Minister Togo's exchange with Ambassador Sato; the militarists are not serious about finding acceptable terms for surrender. At the same time, the American code breakers' ULTRA intercepts of Japanese military communications show that the Japanese are rapidly reinforcing Kyushu to repel the expected American landings there. Military analysts believe they have seen this trap before: in the late autumn of 1941, Japanese diplomats kept negotiating with their American counterparts in Washington while the carrier strike force of the Imperial Japanese Navy, the Kido Butai, steamed under cover of clouds and storms toward the American naval base at Pearl Harbor.

Put off by Byrnes, Stimson decides to take a tour of Berlin. In his diary that night, he describes the city as "dead." It is skeletal. Bombing—the "dehousing" campaign by the British Royal Air Force—has reduced entire square miles to mazes of chimneys and hollowed-out shells of buildings. Eerily, there are no young men on the streets—they are apparently dead or gone. Stimson sees only "despondent looking groups of homeless people going from place to place with all their worldly goods pushed by them in little carts, baby carriages, bicycles, etc." To his wife, Stimson writes that the scene is "depressing beyond words."

Back at the secretary's villa, another "eyes only" cable arrives from Harrison in Washington:

> Doctor has just returned most enthusiastic and confident that the little boy is as husky as his big brother. The light in his eyes discernible from here to Highhold and I could have heard his screams from here to my farm.

The "Doctor" is Groves, back in Washington from Los Alamos. The "little boy" is the plutonium bomb exploded at the Trinity test site in New Mexico; the "big brother" is the gun-type uranium bomb also being built.* Highhold, Stimson's estate on Long Island, is 250 miles from the Pentagon, while Harrison's farm in the Virginia countryside is fifty miles away.

Back in May, as Stimson talked to McCloy, he had regarded the A-bomb as a "mastercard" in dealing with the Russians. "I called it a royal straight flush and we mustn't be a fool about the way we play it," he wrote in his diary on May 14. Stimson hoped that by sharing the secret of the atomic bomb with the Russians, the Soviets might be persuaded to open up their closed system of government and join the rebuilding of

---

* The official code name for the plutonium bomb described by Harrison as "little boy" is actually Fat Man. Somewhat confusingly, the code name for the gun-type uranium bomb Harrison refers to as "the big brother" is Little Boy.

Europe. In May he had allowed himself to mix his idealistic hope that Russia could be made trustworthy with his more realpolitik instinct-for-power: perhaps a show of overwhelming force can induce the Russians to behave.

But as Stimson sees Russian repression all around him in Berlin, right up to the Russian secret policemen outside his gate at Potsdam, he realizes that he has been wishful, if not uncharacteristically naïve. He is particularly "troubled," he records, when Ambassador Averell Harriman explains why, after twenty months in Moscow, he sees no hope that Russia will open up to the West. The Kremlin is not about to stop repressing its own people or scheming to tighten its grip on eastern Europe. Like his fellow Yale man Stimson, Harriman may have learned the bonds of brotherly trust in the "tomb" of Skull and Bones, but spending time at the Kremlin with Stalin has acculturated him to a different, darker reality in international relations.

McCloy is similarly pessimistic about America's erstwhile ally. "Personally," Stimson's aide McCloy writes in his diary, "I think they have their political religion and we have ours."

Sitting in the sun outside their villa (and outside the range of Soviet eavesdropping devices), Stimson, McCloy, and Harriman have plenty of free time on their hands to talk about Russia while Truman, Churchill, and Stalin meet in the Cecilienhof Palace, an ornate Tudor-style villa that had been adapted (and thoroughly bugged) by the Russians as they prepared to host the conference in their occupied zone. Stimson and his retinue have been effectively shut out by Jimmy Byrnes. "He gives the impression that he is hugging matters in the conference pretty close to his bosom," Stimson writes in his diary. Years later Harriman will recall of Byrnes, "He threw me out," and McCloy will sigh to an interviewer about the secretary's snub, "It was pretty pathetic."

"I got up and found myself rather stalled with not much to do," Stimson writes on July 21. He cheers himself up by writing Mabel:

Dearest little Misty,

This [letter] is a little token of the fifty-seven years of happiness we have spent together. No other man has ever received such happiness as I have with you.

"Patient progressing rapidly," Harrison cables Stimson that morning, "and will be ready for final operation first good break [in the weather] in August." The president's group has just received General Groves's eyewitness description of the Trinity test of the atomic bomb, along with the effusions of his deputy, General Farrell, about the visual effects: "unprecedented, magnificent, beautiful, stupendous, and terrifying." President Truman is "tremendously pepped up," Stimson writes in his diary. "It gave him an entirely new feeling of confidence."

Stimson cables Groves for the latest target list, "always excluding the particular place against which I have decided. My decision has been confirmed by highest authority." The "particular place" is Kyoto, the old Japanese capital; the "highest authority" is the president. Stimson has been informed that tireless General Groves has been at it again: agitating to put Stimson's "pet city," as Groves calls it, back on the target list. Groves is relentless: he knows the Japanese revere the ancient capital, and he will try at least two more times to make Kyoto the target, without success.

Hiroshima and Niigata are on the list—cities Stimson also rejected, if less forcefully, back in May, when he threw out the entire selection from the Target Committee during his confrontation with Groves in his office. Groves has basically just waited out Stimson, who has no targets of his own to offer. At the insistence of General Marshall, Groves has added Kokura, a plausibly military target because of its enormous arsenal at the center of town. As a secondary target in case the others are socked in by weather, General LeMay has proposed Nagasaki, a port town with munitions factories. Nagasaki is one of the few major cities left in Japan that LeMay has not burned out.

The "eyes only" cables about S-1 create a sense of momentum. The conference at the Cecilienhof Palace is going badly. The Russians are obdurate, seizing control of states in eastern Europe, especially Poland, and eyeing contested territories in other parts of the world, including the territories conquered during the war by Japan. The progress of the atomic bomb—from testing to targeting—is the only "good" news that Truman and his coterie get.

Stimson is carried along. Still, he is starting to stir again about civilian casualties. Driving through the shell of Berlin, looking at the blank-eyed survivors, he is wondering about the effects of the atomic bomb on a Japanese city. As it happens, General Arnold is in Potsdam for the conference, and on July 21 Stimson spends an hour grilling the air force chief on atomic targets—on the "where, why, and what effects," as Arnold puts it in his diary. The next day Stimson badgers Arnold some more. Arnold writes in his diary that Stimson is worried about "the killing of women and children." And then a third day, once again. This time Arnold tells Stimson that he will just have to wait for a report he has ordered from Washington.

But the time for waiting, or second-guessing, or doing anything to stop the inevitable is running out. Truman came to Potsdam with the hope of persuading Stalin to make good on his promise at Yalta that Russia would declare war on Japan. But the Americans are starting to think that with the A-bomb, they won't need the Russians. Indeed, Truman and Marshall wish to force Japan to surrender before Russia can gobble up too much territory—Manchuria, Korea, possibly even Hokkaido, Japan's northernmost home island.

Truman has been putting off telling the Russians about the atomic bomb, but on July 24 he finally does, in a cryptic and roundabout way. Strolling over to Stalin at the end of the day's session, the American president says that his country has developed "a new weapon of unusual destructive force," without mentioning the word *atom*. Stalin is impassive. "All he said," Truman later writes, "was that he was glad to hear it and hoped we would make good use of it against the Japanese." In fact, Stalin knows about S-1 from his spies planted at Los Alamos. The Kremlin leader is not as nonchalant as he appears: he immediately sends a telegram to Moscow to speed up efforts to build Russia's own A-bomb.

On that same day, July 24, Stimson goes to Truman and tells him that S-1 will be ready for use as early as August 1—only a week away. That night Stimson records in his diary:

> He said that was just what he wanted, that he was highly delighted, and that it gave him his cue for his warning.

The "warning" is the diplomatic approach that Stimson has been pushing, off and on, for the past month, the carrot-and-stick offer to Japan that surrender will be rewarded by magnanimity—specifically, that Japan will be able to keep her emperor. Only now the carrot has been removed, replaced in the Potsdam Declaration with the stipulation that "subject to suitable guarantees against further aggression, the Japanese people will be free to choose their own form of government."* In Japan, where power has come from heaven and the point of a gun, such democratic enticements are almost sure to fall flat.

Stimson has not entirely given up on trying to entice the Japanese to surrender by diplomacy. He records in his diary:

> I spoke of the importance which I attributed to the re-assurance of the Japanese on the continuance of their dynasty, and I felt that the insertion of that in the formal warning was important and might be just the thing that would make or mar their acceptance.

But, he concedes, "I had heard from Byrnes that they preferred not to put it in [the Declaration]." Stimson makes a last plea:

> I hoped that the President would watch carefully so that the Japanese might be reassured verbally through

---

* It has become conventional wisdom among many historians that Jimmy Byrnes was to blame for "removing the carrot." Byrnes, it is said, wanted to guarantee Japanese rejection of the Potsdam Declaration in order to pave the way for the use of atomic bombs—perhaps with the ultimate intention not of ending the war but of intimidating the Soviets. Byrnes was a hard-liner, there can be no doubt, and he had considerable influence over Truman. But the story is more complicated than a nefarious plot. Historian Rich Frank points out that the actual change in language in the Potsdam Declaration came not from Byrnes but from a subcommittee of the Joint Chiefs of Staff. These officers, brainy generals who operated as a kind of "think tank" to the joint chiefs, objected to a dangerous ambiguity in the language originally proposed by Stimson, which seemed to suggest that the Allies might depose or execute the existing emperor, while at the same time continuing the institution of emperor worship. The language ultimately chosen—and agreed to by Stimson—was consistent with the principles of the Atlantic Charter, the pro-democracy war aims laid out by Britain and America in 1941.

diplomatic channels if it was found they were hanging fire on that one point.

Truman tells Stimson that he has the secretary's suggestion "in mind" and that he "will take care of it." By now Stimson can read the signals. What Truman means is: *Don't hold your breath.*

The talk turns to S-1. Once again Groves has put Kyoto on the target list, and once again Stimson has removed it. The secretary of war gives Truman his reasons, and the president agrees—"with the utmost emphasis," Stimson records. Truman reflects that "such a wanton act" would leave "bitterness" among the Japanese people, who regard Kyoto as a sacred place, and make it much harder to "reconcile" the Japanese people to the Americans than to the Russians. Already, in the last days of July 1945, the coming competition between the United States and the Soviet Union is driving policy.

But geopolitics are not the only consideration. Harry Truman, too, is thinking about the lives of women and children. The next day, July 25, Truman writes about them in his diary:

> We have discovered the most terrible bomb in the history of the world. It may be the fire destruction prophesied in the Euphrates Valley, after Noah and his fabulous Ark.
>
> Anyway, we "think" we have found a way to cause a disintegration of the atom. An experiment in the New Mexico desert was startling—to put it mildly. . . .
>
> This weapon is to be used against the Japanese between now and August 10th. I have told the Sec. of War, Mr. Stimson, to use it so that military objectives and soldiers and sailors are the target and not women

and children. Even if the Japs are savages, ruthless, merciless, and fanatic, we as the leader of the world for the common welfare cannot drop this terrible bomb on the old Capital or the new.

He & I are in accord. The target will be a purely military one and we will issue a warning statement asking the Japanese to surrender and save lives. I'm sure they will not do that, but we will have given them the chance. It is certainly a good thing for the world that Hitler's crowd or Stalin's did not discover this atomic bomb. It seems to be the most terrible thing ever discovered, but it can be made the most useful.

It will be later said that, by making this fantastical entry in his diary, Truman was deceiving either himself or history or both. It is possible that he did not really know what he was doing, that he had simply not been informed that the atomic bomb was sure to kill tens of thousands of women and children. Alex Wellerstein, a close student of the archival record of the dropping of the atomic bomb, has argued that Truman was misled—innocently, not intentionally—by Stimson. The secretary of war was so adamant that Kyoto was a civilian target, Wellerstein contends, that Truman may have gotten the mistaken impression that, by contrast, Hiroshima was a "purely military" target. Truman probably has no idea where Hiroshima is on a map until, on July 26—the day after his diary entry—he is handed a page torn out of *National Geographic,* with Hiroshima circled in pen. The president is given two hours to look at a report evaluating Hiroshima as a strategic target. (It is the report requested by General Arnold, who has been trying to answer, and fend off, Stimson's "where, why, and what effects" questions earlier in the week.) The report states that "Hiroshima (population 350,000) is an

'Army' city; a major POE [point of embarkation]; has a large QM [quartermaster] and supply depots; has considerable industry and several small shipyards." Truman is not told that the bomb will be placed in the middle of the city, and he has no way of knowing that of the seventy thousand or so people who will be instantly killed, only about 10 percent will be soldiers.

Perhaps Truman is largely ignorant. He continues to refer to Hiroshima as a "purely military" target right up to the moment, more than two weeks later, when he is shown aerial photographs of the erased landscape where Hiroshima once stood. But Truman, a much subtler and slyer figure than the "Give 'Em Hell Harry" of popular myth, is no stranger to moral ambiguity. As a cog in the Pendergast machine, Jefferson County judge Truman once wrote in his diary that he had allowed a crooked contractor to steal $10,000 to forestall the man from stealing ten times more. "You judge it; I can't," Truman wrote at the time. Of course, political graft can't be compared to nuclear destruction. Still, Truman is having to weigh impossible choices in late July 1945. The casualty estimates for the invasion of Japan are murky and disputed, but—at a minimum—they predict the deaths of tens of thousands of American soldiers.

On July 27, before he leaves Potsdam, Stimson has dinner with Gen. Dwight Eisenhower, the Supreme Commander of Allied Forces in Europe. They talk about the atomic bomb, and Stimson reveals that the air force is about to use it against Japan, with the hope of saving the lives of hundreds of thousands of American soldiers. Years later Eisenhower will recall, "I listened, and I didn't volunteer anything because, after all, my war was over in Europe, and it wasn't up to me. But I was getting more and more depressed just thinking about it. Then he asked my opinion, so I told him I was against it on two accounts. First, the Japanese were ready to surrender and it wasn't necessary to hit them with this awful thing. Second, I hated to see our country be the first to use such a weapon. Well . . . the old gentleman got furious. And I can see how he would. After all, it had been his responsibility to push for all the huge expenditure to develop the bomb, which of course he had a right to do and *was* right to do. Still, it was an awful problem."

Some scholars have questioned Eisenhower's account, which became more vivid in the retelling as the years wore on. Eisenhower had his facts wrong; the Japanese were far from being "ready to surrender." Moreover, if Eisenhower's opposition to using the bomb ran deep, he could have protested to President Truman, but he did not.*

Still, Ike's recollection of Stimson's angry outburst at Ike is credible; the secretary, for all his self-control, can be tempestuous, and he is feeling the strain as he leaves Potsdam. Eisenhower's reluctance for America to be the first to use the A-bomb may have struck a chord in Stimson, who once opposed submarines as too underhanded. Ike's son John, who in July 1945 is a young army officer traveling as an aide to his famous father, will later describe the depth of his father's de-

---

* Eisenhower inherited the bedeviling problem of a nuclear world when he became president in 1953. He considered using "tactical" nuclear weapons on the battlefield to end the Korean War, and he also made a sincere, if ineffective, attempt to turn over nuclear energy for civilian use ("Atoms for Peace") while allowing the existing nuclear powers to aerially monitor each other's weapons development ("Open Skies"). As I discuss in my book *Ike's Bluff* (2012), President Eisenhower ended up spending massively on nuclear arms development and then codifying nuclear deterrence. The doctrine, now known as MAD—Mutual Assured Destruction—prevails to the present day.

pression on learning from Stimson about the coming deployment of the atomic bomb. "Dad was sitting on the edge of his bed, just shaking his head back and forth," he will recall. If Stimson's fury at General Eisenhower is understandable, so is Ike's depression.

5.

Prompt and Utter

"Shall the worst occur"

Tokyo
July 27–August 4, 1945

O N JULY 26 THE ALLIES BROADCAST THE POTSDAM
Declaration. Article 13, the last article in the declaration, reads:

> We call upon the government of Japan to proclaim now
> the unconditional surrender of all Japanese forces, and
> to provide proper and adequate assurances of their good
> faith in such action. The alternative for Japan is prompt
> and utter destruction.

In Japan during the Age of Showa, it is considered unseemly,
and even a little ridiculous, to blurt out one's feelings. "Behold the frog who when he opens his mouth displays his
whole inside" goes a derisive saying. Rather than risk giving
offense, it is better to speak indirectly, or conceal one's feelings altogether, or perhaps play the artful stomach game—
haragei.

Togo takes the unusual—and risky—step of expressing his
honne, his innermost voice, when he is confident that he can

persuade others. He is a stubbornly proud man, and he often believes that if he can just argue the logic and reason of his case, his cause will prevail. His stubborn faith in himself and his single-minded powers of persuasion have carried him far—to a place among the Big Six in the climactic days of August 1945. But on at least one critical occasion in the past, at the outset of the war, his pride came before a fall.

In the late fall of 1941, Togo was able to convince himself that he could head off war between Japan and the United States. As foreign minister, he gave strict instructions to his emissaries in Washington to seek a modus vivendi, to find a way to avoid an open confrontation between Japan and the United States while the two nations searched for a solution to Japan's desire to remove America's oil embargo—and America's desire to remove Japanese troops from China and Southeast Asia.

So on November 27, when Japan received a message from the American secretary of state, Cordell Hull, that Togo read as a rebuff, Togo "was struck by despair," he later recalled in his memoir.* His daughter, Ise, saw a physical change come over her father. Togo's normal verve vanished. He became despondent and seemed to drag about. Friends and colleagues tried to counsel him to resign, to make one last effort to slow down the march to war by disrupting the government. But Togo would not. Overcome with a mixture of resignation and reflexive patriotism, he went along with the navy's planned surprise attack on Pearl Harbor ten days later. During the climactic negotiations, he had been naïve about American defiance and indeed the defiance of his own mili-

---

* Hull's note was not, in fact, the inflexible ultimatum that Togo (and some later historians) saw it to be. Hull indicated a willingness to keep negotiating. But Togo believed that he had run out of time because he was up against a deadline for attack set by Japan's military.

tary, who were not to be stopped at this late stage. As true world war broke out, the prideful Togo felt dispirited—"the Hero wronged," as one historian put it—and sank into lassitude. He resigned from the cabinet eight months later.

Early on the morning of July 27, 1945, Togo is given a translation of the Potsdam Declaration, taken from a shortwave radio broadcast out of San Francisco (sixteen hours behind Tokyo time). The foreign minister reads the words:

> Following are our terms: We will not deviate from them. There are no alternatives. We shall brook no delay.

That might seem like an "or else" ultimatum, but not to Togo. He focuses on the word *terms*. The declaration demands "unconditional surrender" but goes on to add "of all Japanese armed forces." To Togo, that is a signal that the Americans will settle for something less than unconditional surrender, that there is time to work out a deal that will preserve the emperor and mitigate the harshness of an enemy occupation.

What's more, Togo believes that his voice is being heard. He sees that the Russians have not signed the declaration promulgated by the rest of the Allies—the United States, the United Kingdom, and China—which tells him that Moscow is paying attention to Togo's attempts to appeal to Russia as a mediator between Japan and the Allies. Even though he warned the Supreme War Council back in May that Russia would make a poor partner for peace, having renounced its neutrality pact with Japan the month before, he has convinced himself that his diplomacy is paying off.

He is unaware that he is being overheard—that the American code breakers are listening to the intercepted signals of his conversations with Japan's Ambassador Sato in Moscow. Rather, he wants to believe that Moscow has stepped in on Japan's behalf, to tell the Allies that Japan is looking for acceptable terms of surrender.

Excited by the possibilities, Togo immediately seeks an audience with the emperor. Before noon, he is shown into Hirohito's chambers in the *obunko*. After bowing low, Togo gets on with it: he emphasizes that it is important not to reject the Potsdam Declaration, but rather to treat it with "the utmost circumspection"—to play for time while continuing to seek an audience between the emperor's personal emissary, Prince Konoe, and Molotov, the Russian foreign minister.

Hirohito, saying little, goes along. The emperor's mind is in another world. Twice in the last week of July, he prods Marquis Kido, his keeper of the privy seal, to make sure that the Three Sacred Treasures are being protected. These ancient symbols—a sword, a jewel, and a mirror—are kept inside wooden boxes, housed in shrines in southern Honshu. They are so sacred that even the emperor is not allowed to look upon them.

The emperor fears an American airborne assault to capture the relics. "Shall the worst occur, I shall guard them myself and share their fate," he says melodramatically (or is recorded as saying by court scriveners). The Three Treasures are legacies from earlier emperors back through "ages eternal." Hirohito is fixated on securing them. He believes he owes his dynastic ancestors his true *on,* the ultimate form of *giri,* his greatest obligation. Because he can have little impact on day-to-day matters, he believes he serves his people best as the high priest of the Shinto religion, which worships the imperial dynasty above all else.

Equipped with his somewhat vague remit from the palace,

Togo goes to meet with the Big Six at the premier's office. Again, Togo argues strenuously against rejecting the Potsdam Declaration; for once, Prime Minister Suzuki sides with him, or appears to. Better just to say nothing while continuing to work the Russian angle, urges Togo. But the military men hotly protest. The Potsdam Declaration is not a secret they can keep. The American *B-sans* have become so brazen that they are dropping leaflets warning residents a day or two before burning their cities. What if the Americans drop leaflets laying out the Potsdam Declaration? Along with threats of imminent destruction, the Potsdam Declaration promises that Japanese soldiers will be allowed to peacefully return to their homes if they surrender, and that Japan will not be enslaved. Such temptation could sap the will to resist. The generals and admirals say they are concerned about "a serious impairment of morale." The military men do not say so, but they are also worried that if they appear to be going soft, their own fanatical officers will kill them.

An awkward compromise is reached. Rather than make a statement, the government will give an expurgated version of the declaration (minus the talk of soldiers going peacefully home) to the state-controlled press, with instructions to print a small article without commentary.

The plan goes awry. Rather than blandly play down the declaration as instructed, the popular newspapers scoff at the surrender conditions—one calls them "laughable"—while omitting any reference to the provision that would allow Japanese soldiers to return home to a peaceful life. The papers continue to promise that Japan will fight to the end. Some journals say the government will just ignore the declaration. They use the somewhat obscure word *mokusatsu* to describe the government's response.

Togo is furious. The newspapers are cowed by their censors and the thought police; they never act on their own authority. The foreign minister suspects backdoor meddling by his Big Six military colleagues. (He is correct; the military men who control the Supreme War Council, determined to deep-six the Potsdam Declaration, barely hide their true intentions.)

The damage is compounded at a press conference on July 28. While Togo is attending to other matters, five of the Big Six get together at an "informational meeting" at Imperial Staff Headquarters, where they lean on Suzuki to add his official voice to the *mokusatsu* chorus. Meeting reporters that afternoon in the grand drawing room of his official residence, Prime Minister Suzuki uses the word *mokusatsu* to describe Japan's official reaction to the Potsdam Declaration. The foreign press reports that the Japanese government has rejected the Potsdam Declaration—even though, literally speaking, it has not. The word *mokusatsu* (*moku,* "silence," *satsu,* "killing") has several meanings, ranging from "take no notice" to "treat with silent contempt." The last definition gets the most play in the Western press.

"If this was a form of national *haragei* [the stomach game], it was completely lost on America and Britain," the scholar Robert Butow will later write, and in fact, the evidence strongly suggests that the Big Six—minus Togo—are utterly defiant. In Washington, President Truman assumes that Japan is doing just what he expected.

Togo gamely, stubbornly, tries to press ahead on the diplomatic track. He wants to build on the Potsdam Declaration to agree on terms favorable to Japan, using the emperor's emissary, Prince Konoe, to show the Russians that Japan seriously desires peace with the Allies. He orders Ambassador Sato to seek a date for Prince Konoe to meet with Foreign Minister Molotov in Moscow.

Sato is informed by the Russian Foreign Ministry that Molotov will not be available until eleven P.M. on August 8. The suspiciously precise delay might have raised an alarm with the Japanese, who should know from experience that what goes around can come around: on December 7, 1941, Japan's ambassadors in Washington, D.C., delivered Japan's declaration of war to the State Department about an hour after the bombs started falling on Pearl Harbor. At the Kremlin, Stalin orders the invasion of Japanese-occupied Manchuria to begin on August 8, at about the same moment Molotov is scheduled to meet Ambassador Sato to discuss Prince Konoe's peace mission.

6.

A Bucket of Tar

"What the hell, let's take a chance"

Col. Paul Tibbets named the *Enola Gay*, the B-29 that dropped the atomic bomb on Hiroshima, after his mother.

Washington, D.C.
Guam and Tinian Islands
July 28–August 6, 1945

To Gen. Carl Spaatz, CG, USASTAF [commanding general, United States Army Strategic Air Forces]

1. The 509th Composite Group, 20th Air Force will deliver its first special bomb as soon as weather will permit visual bombing after about August 3, 1945 on one of the targets: Hiroshima, Kokura, Niigata and Nagasaki. . . .

2. Additional bombs will be delivered on the above targets as soon as made ready by the project staff.

THE ORDER HAS BEEN DRAFTED BY GEN. LESLIE GROVES. He wants to allow the local commanders as much control as possible, given the tricky weather over Japan. The order does not name other cities because the United States has no way of knowing for sure how many A-bombs it will take to end the war. Groves guesses it will take two, but he wants to be ready for a more drawn-out bombardment. He expects to have three bombs in August, three more in September, and seven more by December. The order for the bombs is sent to Potsdam and approved by Secretary of War Stimson on July 25. There is no record that President Truman ever saw the actual order.

The order might not have been written at all, if not for the insistence of the man who received it.

Gen. Carl "Tooey" Spaatz has been summoned back to Washington from Europe, where he was the commander of strategic bombing, to be the chief of strategic air forces in the war against Japan. His writ includes the 509th Composite Group, a special unit created by General Groves and the air force to drop the atomic bomb.

On this hot day in late July, as the sun shimmers off the hoods of thousands of cars parked in the Pentagon parking lot, Spaatz is standing in the office of Gen. Thomas "Tom" Handy, General Marshall's number two as deputy chief of staff of the army. A freckled redhead as a boy, Spaatz is an unremarkable-looking fifty-four-year-old man with a trim, bristly mustache and an unreadable gaze. He can be round-about in conversation. But he is firm with Handy, who is standing in for Marshall while the chief of staff is in Potsdam.

Marshall has already verbally given the order to drop the bomb, but Spaatz wants it in writing. "Listen, Tom," he says to General Handy, "if I am going to kill 100,000 people, I'm not going to do it on verbal orders. I want a piece of paper."

✳ ✳

Tooey Spaatz has learned to live with death. Low key and unemotional, he can appear indifferent. As chief of staff of the newly created independent air force after the war, he will attend the funeral of some airmen from a downed C-47. Spaatz remains impassive as he walks back to his office from Arlington Cemetery with air force secretary Stuart Symington. Finally Symington says to Spaatz, "You know something, Tooey, you are a cold bastard, aren't you?"

Spaatz explodes. "God damn it! My life has been nothing but one long attendance at the burial of my friends!"

Spaatz has always been taciturn. Ill at ease in formal situations, he dislikes speaking to groups and is not good at it. On several occasions, his superior at supreme headquarters, General Eisenhower, has felt the need to step in and finish briefings given by his tongue-tied air commander.

But Eisenhower values Spaatz for the same reason others do. Like Henry Stimson, Spaatz is known for his integrity. Unlike some wartime generals, most notably Douglas MacArthur, Spaatz never seems to be self-seeking, to be acting to advance his own glory. Spaatz is his "own man," as a future historian will note, but without the arrogance sometimes shown by self-made men.

His military career began modestly. At West Point he was a "clean sleeve" cadet, no stripes on his uniform, never bestowed any rank in the corps. More devoted to playing risqué songs on his guitar than to cadet "bull"—spit and polish—he walked off his last demerits only twenty minutes before graduation. (The customary punishment was—and is—to "walk the area" back and forth in uniform, shouldering a rifle, for hours at a time.)

In 1914, standing at attention in formation on the Plain, he watched a small, rickety biplane fly down the Hudson River

Valley and knew right away that flying was his calling. This was only eleven years after the Wright Brothers' historic flight at Kitty Hawk in 1903. In World War I, Spaatz shot down two German Fokkers before running out of gas and crash-landing just beyond enemy lines. He watched his friends, daredevils in the fledgling army air corps, die in peacetime crack-ups and was lucky to survive flying the thoroughly unsafe planes of early aviation.

A group of Spaatz's fellow pilots became visionaries for the possibilities of airpower. A few well-placed bombs—taking out a bridge here, an electricity-generating plant there—could reduce a city as large as New York, without the sort of ghastly trench warfare that had made World War I horrific. Or so the airmen ardently argued to political and military leaders like Secretary of War Stimson (himself a fan of the new heavy bomber, the B-17 "Flying Fortress"), who were eager to avoid the carnage of another Great War. These airpower pioneers became known as the Bomber Mafia.

Most of the Bomber Mafia were friends or close colleagues of Spaatz, but he was not a zealot like them. He understood, more realistically than the others, that precision bombing was, as he put it, "a relative term." Spaatz's clear eye and steady hand attracted the attention of General Arnold, the army air forces commander. Spaatz was quiet, modest, and even-keeled, while Arnold was loud, boastful, and ambitious yet smart enough to see that he needed Spaatz, so much so that he made Spaatz his chief of staff. In 1942 Arnold sent Spaatz to run the strategic bombing of Germany. "Don't worry," Spaatz told his wife, "Hap will fire me in six months." Six months stretched to nearly three years.

The air war in Europe tested Spaatz's equanimity. In the cloudy skies over Germany, the Luftwaffe was waiting. The radar didn't work. American planes bombed Switzerland by mistake—twice. The British badgered the Americans to give up hit-or-miss daylight bombing of military and industrial targets and join them in "area bombing"—"dehousing"—to break German morale by night.

Spaatz did not want to. He wrote General Arnold that he did not wish the American air force to be "tarred" with the opprobrium surely awaiting the British, once the war was over, for bombing civilians. Eisenhower noted that he too preferred "precision bombing" of military targets—but, significantly, added, "I am always prepared to take part in anything that gives real promise to ending the war quickly."

Spaatz wanted to concentrate on the German oil industry— and he did with good effect. The Nazis had plenty of steel, but American bombing had severely depleted their meager supplies of oil and synthetic fuels. To conserve fuel, the Luftwaffe had resorted to using oxen to drag fighter planes onto the runway.

For the D-Day invasion, Spaatz's instructions were to bomb transportation targets in France—marshaling yards in the middle of towns and cities and railways. Anxious to keep civilian casualties to a minimum, Spaatz insisted on visual bombing (no relying on hit-or-miss radar) and dropping leaflets in advance to warn away civilians.

Spaatz is no military martinet. He prefers to deliver orders—or to generally make his will known—in a relaxed, sometimes indirect manner. "Come on over and see me," he might say to a subordinate, or "Better drop in tomorrow." At the gloomy Victorian pile outside London that served as his quarters in 1944, Spaatz was to be found, sometimes in pajamas, playing poker, with the head of a kitten peeking out of his uniform blouse for good luck. He likes highballs, but pale ones. He has no restraint at poker, bluffing outrageously. "That's where the flying pay goes. It's an old Air Force custom," his wife "philosophically" tells *Time* magazine. "They all have that feeling: 'What the hell, let's take a chance.'"

His wife, Ruth, a former actress, understands that he needs to relieve the pressure from making enormous bets on an almost daily basis with the lives of men. Between the summer of 1942 and the spring of 1945, in the Eighth Air Force's thousand-day air war over Germany, 26,000 airmen died or went missing, more than all the U.S. Marines who perished in World War II. In 1943 three out of four airmen did not complete their twenty-five combat missions—they were killed, wounded, or developed severe shakes (what they called "the clanks") and could not fly anymore. The airmen began referring to Germany as "the Land of Doom": their most common prayer, constantly repeated, was "Dear God, I don't want to die," and after a mission, the bar at the officers' club was more often eerily quiet than boisterous. In 1944, when the odds improved somewhat, Spaatz upped the number of missions to thirty-five before a man could go home. It was a practical decision: pilots were more likely to survive—and to drop their bombs—on their last five missions than on their first five.

Spaatz does his best to wall off sentiment or remorse, no matter what the cost. In January 1944, after a raid on Germany lost sixty bombers, General Eisenhower, the supreme allied commander, asked Spaatz "whether we could take the losses." Spaatz replied, "What's that got to do with it? Are we getting control of the German Air Force? If we have to take the losses to control them, then we have to take it, that's all." (Indeed, wresting control of the skies made the Normandy landings possible a few months later.)

Spaatz tries not to get dragged into political squabbles between the Allies, he seeks to avoid tests of will and ego, and he expects his subordinates to do the same. The transcript of a phone conversation in April 1944 with Gen. Jimmy Doolittle, commander of the Eighth Air Force, shows the Spaatz way. Doolittle tells Spaatz that the British bombing commander, Gen. Arthur Harris, has summoned him to a top-level meeting with Eisenhower and British officials, including Prime Minister Churchill:

> DOOLITTLE: Any suggestions you have?
> SPAATZ: No, except to be a little cagey, that's all.
> DOOLITTLE: I can't hear you.
> SPAATZ: Be a little cagey.
> DOOLITTLE: Yes, I figure that he [General Harris] will try to put me in the middle on [the debate over whether to bomb] Transportation v. Oil, and I also figure that he's very apt to ask what my opinion is regarding our fighters supporting the RAF.
> SPAATZ: Yes.
> DOOLITTLE: And I think I know your desires . . . and I'll avoid getting myself into a spot where I'm on the spot.
> SPAATZ: Yes.
> DOOLITTLE: Anything else?
> SPAATZ: Not a thing, Jimmy.

He seems almost nonchalant. Still, the responsibility, day after day, night after night, weighs on Spaatz. After the fire-bombing of Dresden in February 1945, newspaper headlines declared that America had joined Britain in "terror bombing" German cities. Spaatz received a cable from General Arnold that seemed to question his judgment—were the headlines true? Had Spaatz's planes targeted civilians? For a moment, Spaatz lost his confidence; if Arnold had lost faith in him, he felt he should resign or be relieved. After a flurry of cables, misunderstandings were smoothed out, and Spaatz remained on the job. Spaatz wrote his wife that he could handle the day-to-day stress of running an air force. But in the small hours of the morning, he confessed, he lay awake, wondering about all the people he had caused, one way or another, to die. His aide-de-camp, Maj. Sarah "Sally" Bagby, wrote to Ruth to convey Spaatz's apologies for blowing $1,700, about two months' pay, in five nights of poker after the Dresden bombing.

Drained, he wanted to go home, after the German surrender in early May 1945, and rejoin his wife, whom he had seen only twice in three years, and his three daughters. "My one hope was to get this job over with, return home, retire, and starve to death with my harem," he wrote Ruth. It was a futile hope. Arnold had told Spaatz in late April that his next assignment was to run the strategic air war (long-range bombing) in the Pacific against Japan.

Sometime in early July, during a home leave in Washington, Spaatz was briefed about the still-secret atomic bomb. He told Arnold that he was, and had always been, against bombing cities, causing mass civilian casualties. But Arnold knew that Spaatz would, in the end, obey orders. He was told that the A-bomb would save the lives of thousands of American men slated to invade Japan.

Spaatz remained deeply disturbed. At their home in Alexandria, Virginia, his daughter Katharine overheard him talking one night with Ruth. Katharine heard her mother say that "as a West Point man, you have to carry out your orders." Late into the night, her father was pacing back and forth. In the morning, she asked him why he couldn't sleep. "Dresden," he answered. He could not tell his daughter—or his wife—about the atomic bomb; he had been sworn to secrecy.

Spaatz arrives on the island of Guam on July 29, the day after Prime Minister Suzuki said *mokusatsu* ("to treat with silent contempt") to the Potsdam Declaration. He has flown across the Pacific aboard his personal B-17, the *Boops,* which is the nickname of his youngest daughter, Carla. In addition to his orders to drop the bomb "after about August 3" on one of four Japanese cities, he has in his briefcase a whole set of new directives for the strategic bombing of Japan.

LeMay's B-29 bombers have scorched more than sixty cities. The cigar-chomping general says he is running out of cities to burn. Back in Washington, his superiors have decided to switch away from "burn jobs" to hitting transportation targets and ammunition dumps. "Precision bombing" is back; new and improved radar promises that the B-29s will hit their targets with better accuracy. This does not quite mean that the civilian population will be spared, however. Some planners have argued that the Twentieth Air Force should drop chemicals to kill the rice crop. This idea was rejected because "indigenous food supplies may be very important to the commander charged with occupation." Nonetheless, cutting the rail lines could starve millions of Japanese who depend on the transport of rice, especially those on the vast Kanto Plain around Tokyo, where most Japanese live. Already, air-dropping mines in the Inland Sea—Operation Starvation—has badly disrupted the supply lines that Japan counts on to feed the general population. Japanese soldiers are less likely to go hungry than civilians; the army has hoarded food supplies in caves.

In any case, Spaatz does not rush to stop LeMay's relentless firebombing. He knows he cannot: the pilots have been trained to fly low-level nighttime missions, and the bomb stockpiles are stacked with incendiaries. Spaatz is not one for giving formal orders in any case. He sets himself up in quarters overlooking the bay on Guam and resumes his nightly poker games. Years later LeMay will describe the Spaatz method to an air force symposium on leadership:

I never got any direct orders from General Spaatz on anything. We had three or four poker games in that two weeks. I knew somehow what he wanted at the end of that time.

Spaatz keeps his own orders—to drop the atomic bomb—in his billfold, folded up three times. One day while he is taking a shower, an orderly comes in, takes his pants, and sends them to the laundry. A frantic search recovers the billfold, the orders still tucked inside.

On August 1, Spaatz flies to Manila aboard the *Boops* to brief General MacArthur, who is to lead the invasion of Japan, on the atomic bomb and the coming attack on Hiroshima. Weather permitting, the mission is as early as two days away. Spaatz records: "He looked at me and he said, 'This changes warfare.'"

The air war that Spaatz began on August 17, 1942, standing on the runway of an airfield in Britain as the first American daylight "precision bombing" raid over Europe took off, has reached its climax. On that day back in 1942, at the controls of the lead plane, *Butcher Shop,* was a twenty-seven-year-old major named Paul Tibbets.

The American's first-ever raid, on the railroad marshaling yards in Rouen, France, caught the Germans by surprise, although not for long. A few weeks later Tibbets was piloting another mission over France when a yellow-nosed Me-109 attacked his B-17 head on, blowing a cannon hole in the plexiglass windshield and ripping off part of the left hand of Tibbets's co-pilot. Blood spewed over what was left of the control panel. Standing behind Tibbets, an RAF officer along for the ride panicked and lunged for the controls. Tibbets, who was slightly wounded by the flying glass, had to knock the man out with a sharp jerk of his elbow.

At the U.S. Army Air Forces airfield in Britain, Spaatz presented Purple Hearts to Tibbets and the co-pilot. The photograph of the three of them took up a whole page of *Life* magazine. In an interview with the Associated Press, Tibbets spoke at length about how proud he was that on their bombing raids, the Americans (unlike the British) took every precaution not to kill the civilians below. "My anxiety is for the women and kids," he said. "You see, I have a three-year-old boy of my own at home." The headline in Tibbets's hometown *Miami Herald* read: MIAMI HERO FORGETS OWN DANGER TO SPARE CIVILIANS IN EUROPE RAIDS.

Tibbets flew forty-three combat missions in Europe and, in time, decided that he could not afford to be anxious. He realized, as he later put it, "If I get to thinking about innocent persons getting hit on the ground, I won't be worth anything." He was tapped to pilot planes for Generals Patton and Eisenhower, then was made the lead test pilot of the air force's new "Superfortress" bomber, the B-29, being rushed into production. In 1944 Tibbets's combat record, plus his skill at flying the B-29, won him an assignment to command the eighteen-hundred-man 509th Composite Group that would drop the atomic bomb. Colonel Tibbets handpicked the pilots, who referred to him as "Old Bull." (He was just turning thirty years old.)

The group trained in Utah and Cuba, practicing dropping Fat Man–look–alike bombs called "Pumpkins." In July 1945, while Spaatz was preparing to fly to his new army air forces headquarters on Guam, more than a dozen B-29s of the 509th and a vast support chain arrived on nearby Tinian Island in the Marianas.

The Twentieth Air Force base on Tinian is a marvel of modern military engineering. In the summer of 1944, the

Seabees had begun scraping runways out of the coral as soon as the Marines had driven the last Japanese into the hills. Now, on bombing days, every fifteen seconds or so, a B-29 rumbles down the runway to get on "the Hirohito Highway." The B-29 is a "buggy" plane; its engines have a tendency to catch on fire. At the end of the runways are the carcasses of planes that, heavy with fuel for the twelve-hour flight to Japan and back, failed to gain altitude and instead blew up, setting off spectacular fireballs with the loads of napalm in their bomb bays.

The 509th Composite Group is quartered in one corner of the island. The food and facilities are superior to those of other air groups. Even the group's Silverplate B-29 planes are state of the art, causing some grumbling, especially since what the 509th does remains shrouded in mystery. Someone writes a poem:

> Into the air the secret rose,
> Where they're going, nobody knows
> Tomorrow, they'll return again,
> But we'll never know where they've been.
> Don't ask us about results and such
> Unless you want to get in Dutch.
> But take it from one who is sure of the score
> The 509th is winning the war.

Tibbets's planes keep training by dropping Pumpkins filled with high explosives on targets on a dozen Japanese cities. One of his more rambunctious pilots has the inspiration to drop a Pumpkin on the grounds of the Imperial Palace. (It misses.) He is severely dressed down by Tibbets.

It is the beginning of August, a month known in Japan for viewing the moon, when Spaatz delivers the A-bomb order to Tibbets. The countdown—"weather permitting"—has begun. A typhoon brushes Japan. On August 4 the forecasters predict that the weather over the home islands will improve. On the morning of August 5, as soon as the rain stops, Tibbets's plane, which he has named the *Enola Gay* after his mother, is towed over a large pit, where the atomic bomb, nicknamed Little Boy and weighing almost five tons, is winched into its belly. Tibbets briefs his crew that in the morning they will be dropping a bomb of almost indescribable destructive power on Japan. He does not use the word *atomic*. The men are handed welders' glasses to protect their eyes from the bomb's flash—"brighter than the sun"—and Tibbets pockets a box of twelve cyanide pills, one for each man, in case they are forced to land in enemy territory.

In the middle of the night of August 5–6, Tibbets, pretending to be perfectly calm, climbs with his crew into the *Enola Gay*. From his open cockpit window, he waves to the crowd, a gaggle of officers with stars and bars on their collars, surrounded by enlisted men in khaki cutoffs, as a movie camera whirs. Shortly before three A.M., the *Enola Gay* starts down the runway. Tibbets causes some consternation in the control tower by waiting to the last possible moment to pull back the stick and loft the superheavy bomber out over the dark sea.

The night is lovely. The faint glow of a crescent moon lights up the cloud banks below. Colonel Tibbets smokes "like a chimney," he recalls: a pipe, cigars, and cigarettes.

The day dawns clear. In bright sunshine, the *Enola Gay* passes over the coast of Japan. A shining city lies ahead. "Are we agreed this is Hiroshima?" Tibbets asks his crew. The bombardier searches for his aiming point, a T-shaped bridge in the middle of the city. At eight-fifteen and fifteen seconds, the bomb bay doors swing open, and Little Boy falls away. Tibbets puts the plane into a violent, diving right-hand turn. After forty-three seconds, the cockpit fills with blinding light. A shock wave slaps the plane, and Tibbets cries out, "Flak!," though there is none. He looks back and sees a cloud boiling up toward the *Enola Gay* "like something terribly alive," he will later recall. Down below, what was once Hiroshima looks like a seething bucket of black tar.

There is silence in the plane, then everyone starts talking at once. Tibbets explains, as best he can, the history of the weapon just loosed on mankind.

In Hiroshima, about 70,000 people die quickly. About 70,000 more die slowly, over time. Historians still debate the numbers.

General Spaatz, who saw Tibbets off a thousand days earlier on the first daylight bombing mission over Europe, is standing on the runway on Tinian when Tibbets pulls the plane up to its hardstand. (The day before, Spaatz went fishing for seven hours; he caught no fish.) Tibbets climbs out of the plane and is taken aback when Spaatz walks up to him and pins a Distinguished Service Cross on the lapel of his dirty coveralls.

There is a lot of chatter about the end of the war. But Spaatz puts his arm around one of the crew members, Lt. Jacob Beser, the radar countermeasures operator, and asks, "How did it go, son?" Beser is having trouble grasping the reality of what he saw. It was as if the earth emitted some dark passion, he thinks to himself, and the *Enola Gay* just seemed to be passing by. Spaatz quizzes Beser for ten minutes. The general, unlike the others in the welcoming party, which seems to include all the air force top brass in the western Pacific, seems to be skeptical about the damage estimates.

The crew is debriefed for two hours. When they are finished, they are free to go to the victory celebration at the mess hall. By then, all the hot dogs have been eaten, and the beer is gone.

A message is sent to "War"—Secretary of War Stimson in Washington:

> [Hiroshima] attacked visually one-tenth cloud cover. . . . No fighters and no flak. . . . Results clear cut, successful in all respects. Visible effects greater than Trinity.

Part Two

7.

Terrible Responsibility

"I had a rather sharp little attack"

General Spaatz at the time of the bombing of Hiroshima and Nagasaki. He wrote in his diary that he initially opposed using the atomic bomb but came to accept the necessity.

Gen. Carl "Tooey" Spaatz (lighting cigarette) with Gen. Curtis LeMay (center left), commander of the B-29 bomber force, and other officers on Guam. Spaatz wanted to replace LeMay's firebombing of Japan with "precision" bombing

Washington, D.C.
Highhold, Long Island
Tinian and Guam Islands
August 5–9, 1945

GEN. LESLIE GROVES, WHO LIKES TO BE IN CONTROL, is not. He is sitting in his office on the fifth floor of the New War Building in Washington, a minimalist art deco–style building on Virginia Avenue, not far from the White House, waiting for word on the atomic bomb attack on Hiroshima. He expected to get a report at about dinnertime (it is still August 5; Washington is fourteen hours behind Tinian), but none came. He returned to his office, and now he sits there while his aides anxiously hover. He unbuttons his collar, takes off his tie, and rolls up his sleeves. "While this was completely out of character for me, I did it for the specific purpose of creating a more informal, relaxed atmosphere," he will later write. Not fooled, his aides and his faithful secretary, Mrs. O'Leary, start playing poker. A little pile of one-dollar bills grows by her elbow; Mrs. O'Leary is winning.

Finally, at eleven-thirty P.M., a messenger bursts through the door with a telegram bearing the news. (Incredibly, the top-secret cable from Tinian is about four hours late because the army signal corps has misdirected it through Manila.) Groves calls General Marshall, who politely thanks him, but it is not until morning that Groves, Marshall, General Arnold, and George Harrison, Stimson's aide handling S-1, call the secretary of war on a secure phone. Stimson is at Highhold, recovering from his trip back from Potsdam.

"A very rainy day but in the morning I got the news that the S-1 operation was successful," Stimson records in his diary that evening, Tuesday, August 6. No other reaction; no expression of feeling of any kind. Back at the Pentagon, General Marshall tells the others they should guard against showing too much gratification, since undoubtedly masses of Japanese civilians were killed. Groves responds that he is thinking not so much about those casualties as about all the American soldiers killed in the Bataan Death March. On the way out, General Arnold slaps Groves on the back and says, "I'm glad you said that—It's just the way I feel."

Back at Highhold, Stimson, once more the lawyer, wants to see the evidence. Patched into a "scramble" phone call between the Pentagon and the 509th Composite Group's base on Tinian, the secretary of war asks General Farrell, Groves's deputy who is at the air base, "Have you any more information from interrogation of the F-13 crews?" The F-13 crews are from the three B-29s that flew over Hiroshima—the *Enola Gay* and two others carrying cameras and measuring instruments.

Early photos show the city still wreathed in smoke. But the next day—after the enormous dust cloud settles, and the fires cease to rage—another photoreconnaissance plane flies over Hiroshima. The photos show that the city has been 60 percent destroyed. About four square miles show no rubble, "as if swept clean by a terrific wind," says one report.

At Tooey Spaatz's flag officer's quarters overlooking Tumon Bay on Guam, the poker game breaks up early on the night of August 6. One of the players is a newsman, Charles Murphy of *Time-Life*; the Luce publishing empire has been granted inside access to the top brass of the army air forces, thanks in part to publisher Henry Luce's connection to Stimson's man, Bob Lovett. Among the "young wing commanders" playing at Spaatz's table, "there was more talk about the peculiar properties of the new bomb than the run of the cards," writes Murphy in a draft of a story for *Time-Life*. The airmen wonder: what lies beneath the pall of brown smoke shrouding Hiroshima?

"Next morning, Generals Spaatz and LeMay finally had on their desks the photographs that answered the question," Murphy types in the draft, which he will give to Spaatz for his inspection and approval. The newsman continues: "General LeMay let me see them." LeMay has been showing Murphy photos of burned-out cities ever since the *Time* correspondent arrived at Guam on a reporting trip at the beginning of July. "I could tell at once that there was a city quite completely destroyed. It was a flat gray waste of ashes," he writes. LeMay, who has been telling people that the atomic bomb is just a bigger bomb, also seems to be impressed. For the newsman's edification, the air force general traces with his finger the shock wave generated by the blast. "It was quite a piece of work," says LeMay, with a tone of professional admiration.

But then Murphy does a double take:

> I suppose I half expected to be shown a scene of destruction of planetary proportions, at least a mighty crater. But the more I studied the photograph the more I realized that it was not markedly different from the vertical photographs of many other bombed out Japanese cities which I have seen here in the Marianas during the last five weeks.

Murphy expresses his surprise to LeMay. The general coolly explains that in a successful incendiary attack on a Japanese city, which is largely built of wood and paper, "nothing survives." If scattered fires can be merged into one giant conflagration, the city burns to the ground, leaving "only a cold, dead half-tone effect on the photograph," writes Murphy. But the atomic bomb, which destroys by shock wave, left some buildings standing, says LeMay, using a term from elementary physics, because of "some quirks in the curve of pressure."

✳ ✳

"I had a rather sharp little attack at five o'clock in the morning," Stimson writes in his diary on Wednesday, August 8. He has had a heart attack, a small one, but a warning. He knows he cannot continue in his job for much longer. He intends to tell the president he needs to step down as soon as possible.

But first he needs to show the president the photographs. Just before he gets into his car to head over to the White House, Bob Lovett hands him a photo of post-atomic Hiroshima, flown all the way from the Mariana Islands, a nearly eight-thousand-mile, thirty-plus-hour trip.

In the Oval Office with Stimson, Truman inspects the photo, which shows a barren gray landscape, something like the inside of an emptied ashtray. The air force has identified and numbered various bridges, warehouses, terminals, and Japanese army buildings that were destroyed.

For his diary that night, Stimson records, in his formal style:

> I showed the President the teletype report from Guam showing the extent of the damage; also the Wire Service bulletin showing the damage as reported by Tokyo at 9 a.m. August 8. I showed him the photograph showing the total destruction and also the radius of the damage which Mr. Lovett had brought us from the Air Corps just before I went. He mentioned the terrible responsibility that such destruction placed upon us here and himself.

Just two days before, Harry Truman had been aboard the *Augusta*, on the last leg of his voyage back from Potsdam, when a navy captain handed him a message from Stimson reporting the "complete success" of the atomic attack on Hiroshima. At that moment, Truman had been eating lunch with enlisted men in their mess hall. The president jumped to his feet and cried out, "Captain, this is the greatest thing in history!" Then he banged a piece of silverware against a glass and repeated the news to the sailors eating their lunch. They roared with approval.

Soldiers and sailors everywhere reacted joyfully to the news. On Okinawa, where Marines were preparing to storm the beaches at Kyushu, men prayed that the invasion would no longer be necessary.

But now, sitting at the presidential desk on this humid August afternoon, the image of flattened, lifeless Hiroshima still fresh in his mind, Truman begins to ponder his "terrible responsibility." Possibly, if he inspects closely, he notices that of the thirty targets identified in the photo, only four are specifically identified as military. Unlike Curtis LeMay or even Henry Stimson, Truman has little experience looking at photographs of bombed-out cities. But he is entirely familiar with moral ambiguity, and his own ambivalence is creeping in.

Truman is scheduled to give a radio address to the nation in two days' time. Aboard the *Augusta,* he had begun drafting the address. His first draft—written before the dropping of the bomb—closely tracks his July 25 diary entry from Potsdam, in which he called Hiroshima "purely a military target" aimed at "soldiers and sailors" not "women and children." For his radio address, Truman wrote in that first draft, "The world will note that the first atomic bombs were dropped on Hiroshima, which is a purely military base. That was because we did not want to destroy the lives of women and children and innocent civilians."

Whatever Truman may have wished for, the photograph he has just examined tells a different story. He begins to edit his own words. He writes:

> The world will note that the first atomic bomb was dropped on Hiroshima, a military base. That was because we wished in this first attack to avoid, insofar as possible, the killing of civilians.

He corrects "bombs" to "bomb" and removes the "purely" before "military base." The reference to "the lives of women and children" is gone, and he inserts "insofar as possible" before "the killing of civilians." He is hedging, not apologizing, and he goes on to write, "That attack is only a warning of things to come. If Japan does not surrender, bombs will have to be dropped on her war industries and, unfortunately, thousands of civilian lives will be lost."

Still, his firmness is mixed with remorse. A day earlier he received an uncompromising telegram from his old Senate pal, Richard Russell of Georgia:

> Permit me to respectfully suggest that we cease our efforts to cajole Japan into surrendering in accordance with the Potsdam Declaration. Let us carry the war to them until they beg us to accept the unconditional surrender. . . . We should cease our appeals to Japan to sue for peace. The next plea for peace should come from an utterly destroyed Tokyo.

Wrestling with an impossible dilemma, Truman responds:

> I know that Japan is a terribly cruel and uncivilized nation in warfare but I can't bring myself to believe that, because they are beasts, we should ourselves behave in the same manner. . . . My object is to save as many American lives as possible but I also have a humane feeling for the women and children of Japan.

Truman writes this letter at his desk while he is paying personal bills that have stacked up while he was on his month-long journey to Potsdam. He writes a dozen checks, including some for White House groceries ($5.03 to the Metropolitan Poultry Company). He is aware that the air force, if necessary, will drop more than one "S-1" on Japan. But he does not know, because he has not been told, that a B-29 bearing a second atomic bomb is at that moment gearing up on Tinian to fly to Japan.

✳ ✳

General Marshall is concerned that the mood at General Spaatz's headquarters on Guam has grown too triumphant. Spaatz, along with Generals Farrell and LeMay, has given a press conference touting the bomb as the future of airpower. On the late afternoon of August 8, at about the same time President Truman is at his desk paying his bills and writing Senator Russell, the chief of staff of the army sends a "personal eyes only" message to General Spaatz:

> You and General LeMay are being widely quoted in papers all over the United States on your remarks regarding results of such a bomb on landings in Normandy, to the effect that our present army is not necessary for the further prosecution of the war in the Pacific and that an invasion will not be necessary, and that the future of armies has been decidedly curtailed. I wish you would refrain from such comments.

Abashed, Spaatz hastily replies, "eyes only," to Marshall:

> Acknowledge your message which is understood and will be complied with. . . . I do not believe that any statement made by me or LeMay to the press could have been interpreted as to mean that our army is not necessary for further prosecution of the war. My statement apparently misquoted: if such a bomb had been available early in the war it might have shortened the

war by about six months. Sorry this has caused embarrassment. My statements to the press, if any, in the future will be written.

The breast-beating by the air force is not limited to the men in Spaatz's headquarters or at the 509th Composite Group's air base on Tinian. On that same day, August 8 (August 9 on Guam), Spaatz receives a telex from General Norstad, Arnold's assistant chief of staff back in Washington:

> It is understood that the Secretary of War in his press conference tomorrow will release a map or photostat of Hiroshima showing the aiming point and the general area of greatest damage. . . . It is believed here that the accuracy with which this bomb was placed may counter a thought that the CENTERBOARD [A-bomb] project involves wanton, indiscriminate bombing.

A leading historian of strategic bombing, Conrad Crane, will later point out:

> If an atomic bomb dropped on a city could be construed as a method of precision bombing, then the doctrine had evolved to the point where civilian casualties were no longer taken into consideration.

And yet . . . at his headquarters on Guam, General Spaatz is still determined to spare civilians, while at the same time showing the decisive impact of airpower. He wants to stay on the team while honoring his own conscience. It is not an easy task.

At the 509th Composite Group headquarters, General Farrell has formed what he half-jokingly calls the "Tinian Joint Chiefs," along with Capt. Deak Parsons and Rear Adm.

William Purnell, his Manhattan Project compatriots who accompanied him from Los Alamos to Tinian. Spaatz's orders are to visually bomb the four cities on the list as bombs are made available. The second strike is scheduled for August 11, but citing the weather, the "Tinian Joint Chiefs" push the delivery date for Fat Man, the Trinity-style plutonium bomb, up to August 9.* (William Laurence, the *New York Times* reporter embedded in the 509th Group, will later mordantly remark that the weather forecast came "all the way from Potsdam.") There is no talk—on Guam and Tinian or in Washington—of waiting for a Japanese response to the first bomb.

Meanwhile, the "Tinian Joint Chiefs" are already gearing up for a third strike—preferably on Tokyo, which is not on the list (and which Truman had ruled out in his diary note weeks earlier). A third A-bomb could be delivered and made ready as soon as August 20 or so. At 4:26 P.M. Tinian time, on August 9, a cable is sent to General Arnold in Washington:

> In view of the effects at Trinity and Hiroshima which
> far exceeded optimistic expectations, Purnell, Parsons,
> and Farrell believe question of targets should be re-
> viewed immediately. The subject was discussed with
> [Fleet Adm. Chester] Nimitz [commander in chief,
> U.S. Pacific Fleet] and Spaatz today at Guam and both
> concurred in our views expressed below.
>
> Because of great potency targets should where practi-
> cable be at least 3 miles on a side [nine square miles,
> large enough to demonstrate the extent of damage from

---

* The first bomb, code-named Little Boy, was a gun-type device—a uranium projectile was fired into another piece of uranium to create a "critical mass" that would explode. The second bomb, code-named Fat Man, was an implosion-type device—a core of subcritical plutonium was compressed by symmetrical explosive charges to create critical mass.

the blast]. Targets with partially burned-out areas having large remaining population and some industry offer
great possibilities for psychological effects. We consider
the "scare radius" to be at least 10 miles. It is recommended that the War Department should no longer require visual bombing but leave decision to the field
command. We consider remaining approved targets
with exception of Kokura as inadequate or improperly
shaped areas. We do not want to waste any of effects. It
is recommended that the list be revised to include large
cities. It is expressly recommended that the region of
Tokio* be included as a target.

Though the message says that "Spaatz . . . concurred in our
views," that is not entirely correct. General Spaatz is all for
"psychological effects"—for scaring the Japanese into surrender. But he does not wish to drop the bomb on areas "having
large remaining population." Rather, his idea is to drop the
bomb on an area where there is little or no population. In an
oral history for the air force in 1962, Spaatz will tell his inter-
viewers that he might have preferred to drop the bomb "in
the ocean or in some wasteland," where people could "see the
effect" without being killed by it.

But in August 1945, with his colleagues determined to hit
a city, he knows that is not possible. So he looks for a compromise. "I thought that if we were going to drop the atomic
bomb, drop it on the outskirts—say in Tokyo Bay—so that
the effects would not be as devastating to the city and the
people," Spaatz will recall in his 1962 oral history. "I made this
suggestion over the phone between the Hiroshima and Nagasaki bombings and I was told to go ahead with our targets."

There is no record to shed more light on Spaatz's sugges-

* As Tokyo was sometimes spelled in military communiqués.

tion, probably made by radio phone to Groves and Arnold, or the response from Washington. Dropping an A-bomb into Tokyo Bay might have created a radioactive tidal wave, hardly what Spaatz was intending. But Spaatz's aim was not just to use the A-bomb to end the war. It was also to end the American firebombing of Japanese cities.

8.

Denial

"Fire every damn flare in the airplane!"

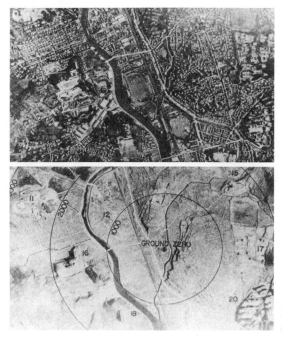

Nagasaki before and after the atomic bomb.

Tokyo
Tinian and Okinawa Islands
August 6–9, 1945

THE FIRST REPORTS TO REACH TOKYO ON AUGUST 6 are sketchy. Telegraph and phones lines to Hiroshima are severed. But trains are being diverted from Hiroshima, and rumors start to reach Tokyo about a momentous calamity to the south. At six P.M., more than nine hours after the atomic bomb exploded, Domei, the state-run news service, seeking to tamp down alarm, broadcasts a brief item:

> A few B-29s hit Hiroshima city at 8:20 a.m. August 6, and fled after dropping incendiaries and bombs. The extent of the damage is now under survey.

At dawn the next day, the deputy chief of the army general staff, Lt. Gen. Torashiro Kawabe, receives a dispatch from Second Army headquarters, or its remnants, that is one sentence long:

> The whole city of Hiroshima was destroyed instantly by a single bomb.

General Kawabe is familiar with Japan's effort, abandoned because it was too difficult and would take too long, to build an atomic bomb. He guesses that the Americans succeeded. But he has not given up hope that Japanese spirit will defeat American science.

At the same time, Foreign Minister Togo is awakened by an official at the state-run news service, which has picked up on shortwave radio Truman's speech announcing to the world the first use of the atomic bomb. Togo reads the translation:

> We have spent two billion dollars on the greatest scientific gamble in history—and won. . . .
>
> It was to spare the Japanese from utter destruction that the ultimatum of July 26 was issued at Potsdam. Their leaders promptly rejected that ultimatum. If they do not now accept our terms they may expect a rain of ruin from the air, the likes of which has never been seen on earth.

Truman's speech is censored by the government, which wants to keep the Japanese people in the dark for as long as possible. But Togo sees an opportunity to win over his mulish fellow leaders, and he prevails on Prime Minister Suzuki to call an emergency meeting of the cabinet. At the meeting, Togo says that "atomic bombs may trigger revolutionary changes in the war"—negating armies altogether—and warns that other cities may now expect Hiroshima's fate. He is hoping to give the military a face-saving excuse to surrender.

But General Anami, the war minister, scoffs. It is too soon for talk of peace, he says. There is no proof that the bombs, or bomb, are atomic. Truman's speech is propaganda, or a trick, he says, bluff and seemingly confident as ever. He assures his colleagues that the army is looking into the situation.

Anami is hiding his own worries. In his private diary for that day, he admits that the Americans have used an atomic bomb, and that he is consulting scientists about the implication of uranium bombs. With his bluster, he appears to be playing for time and putting on a brave front to keep up morale and preserve his credibility with the military diehards. With Anami, it is hard to divine his true motivations; possibly he does not know them himself.

To visit the scene in Hiroshima, an army inspection team is assembled, including Yoshio Nishina, the country's leading nuclear scientist. But at an air base outside Tokyo, the nine-man team of scientists and military officials is delayed; American fighter planes are in the air along the route south and west toward Kyushu. Finally, late in the day on August 7, a small scout plane makes its way to the bombed-out city. Landing on a crude strip just before dusk, the advance team is startled to see no trace of roads, just a vast wasteland, with tufts of grass flattened and burned a reddish color.

Disembarking, the scientists and military men are greeted by a Japanese air force officer who is a strange and grisly sight.

Half his face is burned and blistered; half looks perfectly normal. Ever the good soldier, the officer exclaims, "Everything that is exposed gets burned, but anything that is covered slightly will escape. Therefore it cannot be said that there are no countermeasures!" In the days ahead, some army experts will recommend wearing white clothes to shield against atomic blasts.

"The day began hot and clear," Dr. Michihiko Hachiya writes in his diary on August 8 in Hiroshima. More than 90 percent of Hiroshima's doctors have been killed, but Dr. Hachiya is doing the best he can at the scorched, miserably overcrowded Hiroshima Communications Hospital, fifteen hundred meters from ground zero of the blast. He is beginning to see that dozens of his patients have bloody diarrhea. Hachiya wonders if a dysentery outbreak has already begun. He does not know that he is seeing the first symptoms of radiation sickness. He writes:

> Towards evening, a light southerly wind blowing across the city wafted to us an odor suggestive of burning sardines. I wondered what could cause such a smell until somebody, noticing it too, informed me that the sanitation teams were cremating the remains of people who had been killed. Looking out, I could discern numerous fires scattered around the city. Previously, I had assumed the fires were caused by burning rubble. . . . To suddenly realize these fires were funeral pyres made me shudder, and I became a little nauseated.

On the morning of August 8, Foreign Minister Togo seeks an audience with the emperor. He wants to enlist his August

Mind in the cause of peace. At 3:55 that afternoon, as air raid sirens sound around Tokyo, Togo is escorted to a new bomb shelter, built for the Imperial General Headquarters on the palace grounds, that is deeper than the emperor's customary shelter beneath the *obunko*. There Hirohito waits, petrified, though trying hard not to show it.

Japanese air defenses have picked up a radio signal used by the American air force's 509th Composite Group—the unit that destroyed Hiroshima. Could Tokyo be the next target? Hirohito's suspicion and distrust of his own military is growing. The fragmentary information he has been told about Hiroshima has come not from his military aide-de-camp but from members of his entourage who are gathering rumors and secondhand reports. Every hour or so, the emperor has been asking for updates on Hiroshima. Just a few minutes ago, a more disturbing—and solid—report has arrived that Nishina, the government's chief nuclear scientist, has determined that Hiroshima was destroyed by an atomic bomb.

Togo can see that Hirohito is afraid that the next atomic bomb will be aimed at him. The fear does not appear to be unreasonable. American firebombs have already rained onto his palace grounds, so why should he be spared the bigger bomb?

The gruff foreign minister does nothing to ease the worries of the emperor. He reports that American and British broadcasts are "most enthusiastically" repeating news of the atomic bomb. We have reached a "turning point," says Togo—a turning point that can be used to end the war, provided, of course, that the emperor system, the *kokutai,* is retained. Togo warns that atomic bombs will continue to fall unless Japan does something.

"That is just so," replies Emperor Hirohito. "We must not miss a chance to terminate the war." Hirohito tells him to communicate his wishes to Prime Minister Suzuki, who at this stage is still more afraid of Japan's military fanatics than the B-29s.

Togo rushes from the palace to the official residence of the prime minister, urging him to call a meeting of the Big Six. Suzuki agrees, and his aides begin calling the other four, the war and navy ministers and the army and navy chiefs of staff. The word comes back: they are "unavailable." One minister reports that he is busy with "more pressing business." Togo does not record his reaction to such a preposterous excuse. By now, he is accustomed to living in a world of unreality. In truth, though he is more clear-headed than the others, he is suffering from his own delusions.

Still clinging to the hope that Russia could be an intermediary for peace, Togo sends off a pleading cable to the long-suffering Ambassador Sato in Moscow, asking if the emperor's emissary, Prince Konoe, can obtain an audience at the Kremlin:

> We must know the Soviets' attitude immediately.
> Therefore, do your best to obtain their reply immediately.

If only, Togo believes, or imagines, Prince Konoe can reason with Stalin and Molotov, the Russians will see a role for themselves thwarting American domination of East Asia.

The reply comes at five P.M. Moscow time (eleven P.M. Tokyo time) on that Wednesday evening, August 8. Sato is shown into Foreign Minister Molotov's office. Cutting off the small talk, Molotov reads Sato a short, prepared statement that ends:

> The Soviet Government declares that from tomorrow, that is from August 9, the Soviet Union will consider itself in a state of war against Japan.

His voice dripping with sarcasm, Sato thanks Molotov for his efforts to achieve peace.

It is now just past midnight in Manchuria. Already thousands of Red Army troops are pouring across the border, firing their weapons. Some members of Japan's once-proud Kwantung Army in Manchuria do the heretofore unthinkable: they surrender. Knowing no Japanese, the Soviet troops, all veterans of the European war, shout *"Hände hoch!"* (Hands up!) in German. Before long, hundreds of thousands of Japanese soldiers will surrender. Most will be made slave laborers by the Russians. More than 100,000 Japanese soldiers and settlers will disappear or die.

Fat Man weighs over five tons. The plutonium core at its center is warm to the human touch. The bomb is painted bright yellow, and on the nose, someone has stenciled "JANCFU," for "Joint-Army-Navy-Civilian F(oul)-up." It is just a cheeky joke, but Fat Man's delivery is star-crossed.

In a Quonset hut on Tinian, the crew of *Bockscar,* the B-29 that will drop Fat Man, has its final briefing at twelve-thirty A.M. on August 9, at about the time the first Soviet tanks are smashing through the Japanese lines in Manchuria. Assistant flight engineer Ray Gallagher is feeling low. He thinks that the second time around, the Japanese will be waiting to shoot down B-29s bearing A-bombs.

The flight commander, Maj. Charles Sweeney, has a dilemma. A good Catholic, he has been to confession, where he is mildly flummoxed that he cannot confess to what he is confessing about (top secret). A less ethereal problem is that a fuel pump on *Bockscar*'s auxiliary fuel tanks is stuck, and there is no time to swap in a new one. Bad weather is closing in; lightning flashes already light the sky. Sweeney talks to Tibbets, his boss as commander of the 509th, who tells him the auxiliary tanks are primarily for ballast anyway. Sweeney decides that he has enough fuel in the main tanks to go ahead. He feels the pressure to match Colonel Tibbets's flawless mission in *Enola Gay*.

Bockscar plunges and bounces as it skirts thunderheads on the way to Japan. At seven A.M., as the sun breaks through the towering cumulus clouds, a red light suddenly flashes on the box monitoring Fat Man's fusing and firing circuits. The light indicates that the bomb is fully armed, raising the risk that it could detonate in flight. Lt. Phil Barnes, the bomb's electronics officer, furiously studies his wiring diagrams, then removes the outer casing on the box to examine the switches. Incredibly, given the care that has gone into preparing the bomb, someone has set two switches in the wrong position. Trying hard to stay calm, Barnes resets the switches; the warning light goes out.

At nine A.M., circling over the island of Yakushima, *Bockscar* is supposed to rendezvous with two other B-29s. The one carrying the measurement instruments shows up; the one carrying the cameras does not. The photo plane is circling at the wrong altitude, nine thousand feet too high. Breaking radio silence, the camera plane calls the air base at Tinian to ask, "Has Sweeney aborted?" and "Is *Bockscar* down?" The transmission is poor, and all that the control tower on Tinian can hear is, "*Bockscar* down." Listening, General Farrell vomits.

Arriving at the target city, Kokura, forty-five minutes late at ten-forty-five A.M., Major Sweeney looks down and sees nothing but smoke and haze. A weather plane has earlier reported the skies to be clear over target, but smoke has drifted in. The day before, some two hundred of General LeMay's

B-29s burned the neighboring city of Yahata. The orders are to drop the bomb visually; no radar allowed. "No drop, I can't see the target," calls out the bombardier, Kermit Beahan. Sweeney circles and decides to take another pass. Still "no drop." Then another try. By now, flak is starting to climb toward *Bockscar,* and the radioman picks up traffic suggesting that the Japanese are launching fighters.

Sweeney banks away and makes for the "secondary" target, Nagasaki. The port city on the west coast of Kyushu is sometimes called the San Francisco of the Orient; it is an old trading city with a large Catholic population. It is only a half hour away, but *Bockscar* is down to its last two hours of gas. The crew is growing jittery. At 11:32, Lt. Fred Olivi, the third pilot, writes in his diary:

> Reducing power to save gas—wonder if the Pacific will be cold? Our chances of ditching are—good!!

Nagasaki is covered with clouds. Major Sweeney is in a bind. He can't safely make an emergency landing with the fully armed Fat Man. He can't ditch the plane with the bomb on board. But he doesn't want to waste the bomb by dropping it in the ocean.

Navy commander Fred Ashworth, the weaponeer, who uneasily shares authority with Major Sweeney, announces that they will have to disregard orders and drop the bomb by radar. There is enough fuel remaining for only one run. At the last moment, from the plexiglass nose cone, Bombardier Beahan cries out, "I see it! I got it!" Through a break in the clouds, he has spotted a stadium that he recognizes from aerial photographs of Nagasaki. The plane has passed the original aiming point, the heart of the city, and is now over the Urakami industrial valley. At 12:02 P.M., Beahan yells the traditional "bombs away," and Fat Man tumbles out. The bomb explodes forty-seven seconds later, more than a mile off the original target, but directly over the Mitsubishi armaments plant that produced the torpedoes used in the attack on Pearl Harbor. "It was a boiling cauldron," writes Lieutenant Olivi. "Salmon pink was the predominant color that I remember, but there were all kinds of damn colors in there."

Just before the bomb exploded, Olivi was thinking that "we were going to kill a lot of civilians, women, children, and elderly people," he writes in his diary. As *Bockscar* heads for home, Olivi thinks again about "killing the people." He doesn't "dwell on it," because "I thought if they would have had it [the bomb], they would have dropped it on us."

As soon as Major Sweeney leaves the Japanese coast, he sends out a "Mayday" call in case he has to ditch the plane. No one is listening; because after the earlier, garbled call from the camera plane suggesting that the mission had been aborted, the rescue planes and submarines along the way had headed back to base.

Sweeney knows that *Bockscar* lacks the fuel to make Tinian, so he steers for Okinawa, a closer island but at the outer limit of the plane's range. With fuel gauges showing empty, *Bockscar* reaches the field at Okinawa, but the control tower does not respond—the controllers are in the midst of landing B-24s and B-25s from a bombing raid. The runway is crowded with planes.

"Fire every damn flare in the airplane!" shouts Sweeney. The different-colored flares signal various emergencies— wounded on board, low on fuel, mechanical problems. Lieutenant Olivi sticks the flare gun out of the porthole on the top of the fuselage and fires flares, one after another.

Worried he will run out of gas at any moment, Sweeney comes in at 150 mph, much faster than normal. The number-two inboard engine sputters and dies. The plane lands and slews toward a stand of B-24s; Sweeney wrestles with the controls and stomps the brakes. *Bockscar* veers, slows, stops. They have thirty-five gallons of gas in the tanks, down from more than seven thousand.

Major Sweeney, so exhausted he can barely stand, commandeers a jeep with the weaponeer, Commander Ashworth, and heads for the communications office to cable General Farrell back at the air base on Tinian. The communications office tells him they are too busy to send his message. Ashworth sternly demands to see General Doolittle. The hero of the first bombing attack on Japan, Lt. Gen. James "Jimmy" Doolittle, is now the commander of the Eighth Air Force, which has been transferred from the European theater to begin operations against Japan from Okinawa.

Ashworth is granted an audience with the formidable Doolittle. In the general's tent, Ashworth lays out the target maps and points to the designated aiming point, in the heart of downtown Nagasaki, and then to where the bomb actually hit, up in the valley by the Mitsubishi plant. After studying the maps for a moment, General Doolittle says, "General Spaatz will be much happier the bomb went off over the industrial part of the city."

Doolittle knows there will be fewer civilian casualties that way. Indeed, as it turns out, Fat Man was almost twice as powerful as Little Boy (20,000 kilotons versus 12,000 kilotons), but it killed about half as many people in the initial blast (35,000 versus 70,000). The hillsides in the Urakami valley contained the blast. In Europe, General Doolittle had strongly shared General Spaatz's desire to minimize civilian casualties.

9.

Sacred Decision

"There is life in death"

Left: Emperor Hirohito in ritual Shinto robes at the time of his enthronement in 1928. *Above:* Hirohito in 1945. He was at once a deity and, until he broke free of it, an instrument of the military.

Tokyo
August 9–10, 1945

AT ABOUT FOUR A.M. ON AUGUST 9, FOREIGN MINIS-ter Togo awakens. Domei, the state-run news agency, is calling with a report of Soviet soldiers and tanks crossing the border from Russia into Manchuria. "Are you sure it's true?" Togo asks. But already he has a sinking feeling. He has been "careless," he will write in his diary. Hoping there was still time to negotiate with the Russians, he has overlooked the hints that the Russians were already readying an attack. As ambassador to Russia before the war, he had helped lay the groundwork for the Soviet-Japanese neutrality pact that is not officially supposed to expire for many months. So he has allowed his faith in his own powers of diplomacy to cloud his judgment, to overcome his original suspicion that the Russians would never be good partners for peace. Togo feels, deeply, that he has let down the emperor.

The Russian invasion of Manchuria should have come as no surprise to the army. There have been plenty of tip-offs about an imminent invasion—not shared with Togo's Foreign Ministry—including reports of Russian soldiers coming east without clothing and gear for winter. Nonetheless, Lt. Gen. Torashiro Kawabe, the deputy chief of the army general staff and the architect of the fight-to-the-finish *hondo kessen* strategy, has been given "a serious jolt [*shogeki*]," he writes in his diary. "The Soviets have finally risen! My judgment has proven wrong."

After he gets over his initial shock, Minister Togo recognizes that Japan must immediately accept the surrender terms of the Potsdam Declaration, with the sole proviso that Japan be allowed to keep its emperor. Yet the military clings to its dark dream. Deputy Chief of Staff General Kawabe writes in his diary: "We must be tenacious and fight on." He immediately begins work on a declaration of martial law throughout Japan. "If necessary," he writes, "we will change the government, and the army and navy will take charge." Japan will become a military dictatorship, a shogunate once more—all in the name of the emperor, naturally.

General Kawabe hastens to General Anami at his office at the War Ministry, a grand art deco–style building on Ichigaya Heights, on a hillside not far from the palace, that has somehow escaped the waves of American firebombers. Anami is full of his usual hearty good cheer. Kawabe knows that he is headed to an emergency meeting of the Supreme War Council—the Russian invasion has put an end to temporizing by the Big Six over the implications of the atomic attack on Hiroshima. Kawabe implores Anami to stand fast against surrender and describes his plan for martial law. Anami does not explicitly endorse Kawabe's plan, but he hardly discourages him, telling him that he understands that Kawabe speaks for the entire general staff—the zealots who run Japan's military machine. Anami reassures the deputy chief of staff that he will resist surrender "at the risk of his life," Kawabe records in his diary.

On the way out the door, Anami says, "If my view [that Japan must fight on] is not accepted, I will resign as army minister and request reassignment to a unit in China." His statement is more portentous than swaggering. If the war minister resigns, the government falls. Then comes martial law, and any hope of a peaceful surrender vanishes.

The Big Six convene at eleven A.M., as it happens, at just about the moment *Bockscar* opens its bomb bay doors over Nagasaki. Without knowing about Nagasaki, Prime Minister Suzuki for once sheds his Taoist passivity and comes right to the point: Japan must accept the Potsdam Declaration, immediately, and end the war.

In the conference room, in a bomb shelter under the War Ministry, no one speaks. Suzuki has been too abrupt; it is very "un-Japanese," as one historian will put it. The room is silent and stifling in the damp August heat. Finally Admiral Yonai, the navy minister, speaks up. "We can't get anywhere by being silent forever," he says.

A once-handsome man, his eyes now pouched with fatigue and whiskey, Yonai lays out the options. Japan could just surrender. Or it could insist on some conditions. The first—and on this one they all agree—would be to insist on the preservation of the *kokutai,* the imperial system. There are three other conditions, which they have all discussed from time to time, aimed at keeping the Americans out of the sacred home islands. The Allies shall not:

Occupy Japan

Conduct war crimes trials

Disarm Japan; rather, the Japanese should do it themselves

There are some nods around the table. To his dismay, Foreign Minister Togo realizes that Admiral Yonai, wittingly or not, is opening a Pandora's box. By offering up the three conditions for "discussion," he is giving the military a self-serving chance to avoid blame for defeat. Not only would the two generals and three admirals around the table escape the harsh judgments of an international war crimes tribunal, but—more fundamentally—they would be able to duck responsibility for defeat. They could preserve the essence of their power—before being reborn, once again, true leaders of a nation under arms in the name of the emperor. A student of the aftermath of World War I, Togo knows that the officers of the German army were able to claim that they were not beaten on the battlefield but "stabbed in the back" by the politicians. The men around the table in the dank bomb shelter on Ichigaya Heights want to perform the same trick—and live on to fight another day, as Hitler was able to do for the Wehrmacht.

Togo is frustrated. Admiral Yonai's real feelings and motivations are hard to discern. By reputation, Yonai is "pro peace," but like Prime Minister Suzuki and even the fearless Togo, he can hear the footsteps of assassins. In any case, Togo feels that he has been undermined by the elusive Yonai, just as he had been back in June when Yonai failed to speak up against the militarists' nihilistic *Fundamental Policy,* a policy to fight to the bitter end. Earlier that morning, speaking privately with Yonai before the Big Six meeting, Togo had won Yonai's assurance—or so Togo had thought—that the navy minister would support him on calling for the acceptance of the Potsdam Declaration. Now Togo feels abandoned.

Togo is enough of a political realist to know that putting conditions on the acceptance of the Potsdam Declaration will be a nonstarter, rejected by Washington out of hand. The Americans and their allies might go along with allowing Japan to keep her emperor, but the Allies would never agree to the other three conditions. The war would just go on—which is precisely what the Japanese militarists want.

General Anami does not pretend otherwise. Surrender is out of the question, he insists. Japan has not lost. "The Hundred Million" can and must fight to the death for the sake of the "Yamato race"—for the mythical essence of the people of Japan.

Togo is skeptical of Anami's bluster. In a private conversation two days earlier—out of earshot of the others—Anami had tacitly conceded to Togo that Japan's defeat was only a matter of time. Now, with the other members of the Big Six as jury, Togo plays cross-examining lawyer, hoping to expose Anami as a poseur. He asks: Does the war minister really believe that Japan can win? Drive the Americans into the sea?

Togo drives home his questions with an almost contemptuous tone. But Anami has an answer—an argument that he has made before, actually, for weeks now—and while bloody-minded, it is not so far-fetched. It is the *shukkettsu* ("bleeding") strategy underlying *hondo kessen,* the decisive battle. Japan does not have to defeat the Americans on the battlefield, just make them bleed—to raise the human cost high enough that the United States, materially strong but spiritually weak, will sue for peace. *Then* Japan can demand conditions. If there is to be an occupation, then at least Japan can insist that Tokyo be spared. If there are war crimes trials, let Japan judge its own. If there is to be disarmament, then let Japan retrieve the weapons of its own troops and protect their honor.

Anami's die-hard talk resonates, especially with the army and navy chiefs of staff. Japan's troops cannot surrender, says General Umezu, the army chief of staff. The word *surrender* is not in their vocabulary. These men have been indoctrinated, he says, with the idea that "if they lost their weapons they should fight with their feet; if they couldn't fight with these, they should bite and if they could not, they should cut out their tongues and kill themselves."

But, Togo counters, what of the atomic bomb? The Americans don't need to invade and fight on the ground. The American president, he points out, has threatened a "rain of ruin"—more atomic bombs—on Japan's cities.

The ghastly experience of Hiroshima might be Togo's trump card, but Admiral Soemu Toyoda, chief of the navy general staff, weighs in. Like Anami and Umezu, he is from the same province on Kyushu; the three men are allied against Togo, whose ancient Korean bloodlines make him suspect. Toyoda, who is familiar with Japan's own stalled program to build an atomic bomb, insists that no nation could have enough uranium to build more than one bomb.

At about this point in the discussion, a little before one P.M., a messenger enters the room and hands Prime Minister Suzuki a piece of paper. He reads aloud:

Nagasaki City was struck this morning by severe attack of Hiroshima type. Damage is extensive.

Surely this is all the proof that Togo needs to win his argument and convince the Big Six to accept the Potsdam Declaration. For all their bravado, the others in the Big Six have been hearing rumors that Tokyo is next on the atomic bomb hit list. An American POW, Lt. Marcus McDilda, has confessed that the B-29s have targeted Japan's capital. In truth, captured after parachuting from a crippled bomber, McDilda is making up stories under harsh interrogation.

General Anami presents McDilda's warning about Tokyo as reliable intelligence. But no matter. Incredibly, Anami goes on to say that America can drop a hundred atomic bombs, and still Japan will never yield. He becomes apocalyptic. "We will find life out of death," the war minister declares. He invokes the image, familiar to anyone listening to state-controlled radio, of Japan as a *gyokusai,* a "shattered jewel." The idea of national suicide, of a Japanese Götterdämmerung, is rendered ethereal, like a falling cherry blossom. Anami asks his colleagues, "Wouldn't it be beautiful?"

Togo pushes back against such morbid fantasies, but the afternoon drags on and the speechifying laps itself. Prime Minister Suzuki puffs on his pipe, sips green tea, and looks distracted and sleepy. Admiral Yonai remains mostly silent. Anami, Umezu, and Toyoda present a united front to demand the three conditions that the Allies will never accept. The Big Six are stalled; consensus, all important to the Japanese and necessary before presenting any decision to the emperor, seems beyond reach.

Later in the afternoon, the Big Six meet with the full cabinet and votes are taken. In the full cabinet, the balance of power shifts: ten of the fifteen members are civilians, not military. Togo collects a majority (including the inscrutable Admiral Yonai) in favor of accepting the Potsdam Declaration, with the proviso of keeping the emperor. But the hard-core military officers around Anami remain obstinately opposed.

Then Saburo Ota, the education minister, asks a question that Togo has been dreading. If the cabinet members cannot reach consensus on such a serious matter, shouldn't they all resign?

This is the moment of truth. If Anami is really serious about fighting to the end, he will seize this moment to bring down the government.* Here is the opening to declare martial law, as Deputy Chief of Staff Kawabe was proposing just a few hours earlier, allowing the army and navy to take over the government and lead Japan's last stand, headquartered, perhaps, in the network of tunnels already dug into the mountains.

But Anami says nothing. He lets the moment pass. Togo can only wonder why, and hope that Anami's fantasies about beautiful dead flowers are just that, and that he does not really mean to bring the government of Japan crashing down on the heads of its people, replaced by rulers bent on national suicide.

At ten P.M., after a day of incessant wrangling and no clear resolution, Togo and Prime Minister Suzuki go to the palace to report to the emperor. Togo is overcome with a sense of shame that he has disappointed his monarch, that he has led Japan down the wrong path with his futile diplomacy with Russia, and that the showy speeches and dithering of the Big Six and the cabinet are no match for the reality of Russian invasion and American A-bombs.

He is deeply gratified to learn that Emperor Hirohito plans to call an imperial conference and urge his government to accept the Potsdam Declaration.

This is unprecedented. Under custom dating back to the

---

* Under Japan's military-dominated system of government, Anami could bring down the government just by resigning himself. The army could then have veto power over any new government, simply by refusing to appoint a new war minister. As a practical matter, if Anami had resigned, Japan would have become a military dictatorship—with Anami as the new *shogun,* like the ruling warlord of feudal Japan.

restoration of his grandfather, Emperor Meiji, the emperor never takes a position at these audiences with his government. He is presented with a consensus decision and silently assents. That way he is protected, kept above politics and never in error.

But now Togo learns from palace officials that the emperor will make a *seidan*—sacred decision—and do it right away. The Supreme War Council has been summoned to meet in the new imperial bomb shelter, under the *obunko,* shortly before midnight.

While immensely relieved, Togo is not entirely surprised. Before the full cabinet met at two P.M., Togo had taken Prime Minister Suzuki aside and—after making sure that no one could overhear—told him that the only way out of a deadlock would be for the emperor to intervene himself. Indeed, Togo has been secretly nurturing the idea of a *seidan,* an imperial intervention, through a network of back channels to the palace. For over a year, as the war worsened, the notion of asking the emperor to break a deadlock with a "sacred decision" has been quietly germinating among the small band of peace-minded civilians, especially in the Foreign Ministry. Togo's predecessor as foreign minister, Mamoru Shigemitsu, first floated the radical proposal with the emperor's privy seal, Marquis Kido, back in 1944. Shigemitsu, who lost a leg in an attempted right-wing assassination plot, is no friend of uniformed fanatics. Kido, as the emperor's political liaison, has been wary of talk of a *seidan*—an enormous risk to the emperor whom the privy seal is sworn to protect. But he too is fed up with the military. And more important, so is Emperor Hirohito.

Kokutai is a word of many meanings, and the emperor has come to embrace a narrow one. To him, what matters most is not preservation of the whole imperial system, with the military as the bedrock. What matters is the *koto*—the preservation of the imperial line. If that means sacrificing the military, so be it. The generals and admirals have not served him well, and they have repeatedly misled him; they do not deserve the emperor's loyalty.

Kido, though worried about his own neck, has helped steer Hirohito toward a kind of personal declaration of independence from the military, without ever putting it quite so baldly. All day long, while Togo has been vainly trying to win over the war hawks on the Supreme War Council, a small, loosely allied group of government officials and imperial advisers has been gently nudging the emperor toward the radical—and brave—step of *seidan*. Most prominent among them is Prince Konoe, the former prime minister and frequent imperial adviser as a member of the *jushin*, the retired statesmen who frequent the palace. Konoe realizes that the atomic bomb and the Soviet invasion are actually "gifts from the gods." They are the perfect excuse to give up before Japan is confronted with what the emperor, his lord keeper of the privy seal, and peers of the realm like Prince Konoe fear even more than their own sometimes insubordinate military: a full-scale revolution of the people.

There are already rumblings of discontent. Kido, in his role of guardian, has been in frequent contact with the *kempeitai* (a more aggressive version of the French gendarmerie, under military control) and the *tokko,* or special higher police (sometimes called the thought police). As food grows scarce and the firebombs fall, ordinary citizens have been scribbling graffiti on the walls of train stations and public bathrooms. One person has written: "I curse the emperor, who brought the tragedy of war upon the people." Another has written: "The emperor should bear responsibility for the war!" Police reports depict how the emperor is belittled as a fool, an idiot, and a spoiled child.

The reports are, in fact, alarmist. The Japanese people are

remarkably quiescent, given their dire straits. But to Hirohito and his followers, accustomed to unquestioning reverence and obeisance, the merest ripples of resentment signal grave danger. The palace has always feared rebellion on the right, from young zealots like the mutinous soldiers who staged the February 26 Incident. Now Hirohito worries even more about unrest on the left, from workers and farmers, inspired by Communists, possibly directed from the Kremlin.

The time to act is now, this night, before an atomic bomb lands on the *obunko,* or the Soviets invade the home islands and spread their poisonous ideology. The Big Six, along with several other imperial advisers and government officials, make their way to the palace's subterranean redoubt, for the midnight audience with the emperor.

One by one the soldiers and statesmen arrive in the imperial garden, where peacocks once roamed and where an August moon still silhouettes the pine trees. They approach a concrete carbuncle in the lush hillside. A chamberlain escorts them down a long passageway, through two sets of steel doors, to a windowless conference room with two long wooden tables. In formal dress, the Big Six sit rigidly still, as mosquitoes whir around them in the dim light.

At 11:55 P.M., wearing the uniform of a marshal of the army, Hirohito enters, small but erect. Prime Minister Suzuki calls on Foreign Minister Togo and War Minister Anami to give their by now well-rehearsed arguments. The room, wood-paneled but spare, is stifling and the mosquitoes are merciless. On and on the debate drones: Togo for peace; Anami for war. Finally, shortly before two A.M., Prime Minister Suzuki rises and apologizes to the emperor for his government's inability to reach a consensus. Then he begins to walk from his chair toward the throne.

"Mr. Prime Minister!" cries General Anami, shocked at Suzuki's apparent effrontery.

Suzuki bows low before the emperor and asks for his "sacred decision."

"Then I will express my opinion," says Hirohito, in his high metallic voice. "My opinion is what the foreign minister said."

Togo feels gratitude wash over him. He began the day—almost twenty-four hours earlier—feeling he had disgraced himself in the emperor's eyes. Now, before his peers in the musty heat of the imperial bomb shelter, he is vindicated.

"My reasons are as follows," says Hirohito, who has rehearsed his speech beforehand with Marquis Kido but still speaks haltingly. "After serious consideration of conditions facing Japan both at home and abroad, I have concluded that to continue this war can mean only destruction for the homeland and more bloodshed and cruelty in the world."

Around the room, men begin to weep. A few prostrate themselves.

The emperor's voice catches, but he continues, and his voice stiffens with anger. He launches into an indictment of the military's many failings, the promises made and not kept. "In past experience, there has always been a discrepancy between the fighting services' plans and results," he says. He can no longer credit the scenario of a "decisive battle."

Hirohito touches his white-gloved hand to his glasses, to wipe away a tear.

"To relieve the people and to maintain the nation, we must bear the unbearable," he says. "I have decided to bring the war to an end immediately."

Can it really be over? Has the end really come? As the weary men file out of the imperial bomb shelter, with dawn but a few hours away, an irate Gen. Masao Yoshizumi, the head of the Military Affairs Bureau, who had attended the imperial conference as a secretary, rushes up to Prime Minister Suzuki, who is bent over, exhausted by the day—and by his own *haragei,* his own waffling and attempts at misdirection. Suzuki had appeared to side with the military, before suddenly switching to Togo's side. "Are you satisfied?" Yoshizumi screams. "Are you happy now? You did not keep your promise, Mr. Prime Minister!"

Suddenly, General Anami sweeps in and puts his arms around General Yoshizumi. "Enough, be quiet, please," he says. "I understand you, Yoshizumi." Firmly but gently, he pulls the angry general away. Anami is playing the peacemaker. Have his fiery speeches all been an exercise in *haragei*? Possibly—but possibly not.

At three A.M., as the full cabinet is assembled to hastily affirm the emperor's "sacred decision," Anami extracts a promise from Suzuki and from Admiral Yonai: to support a continuation of the war if the Allies refuse to recognize "the prerogatives of His Majesty as Sovereign Ruler." That is the one condition the Japanese are attaching to their surrender. It was insisted upon by Baron Kiichiro Hiranuma, the chairman of the privy council, a largely moribund group of elders whose seal is nonetheless necessary for all-important consensus. An arch conservative, Hiranuma wanted to make clear to the Americans that the emperor's power comes from the gods, not from the people, and cannot be circumscribed. The wording is tacked on in the small hours of the morning. It is, in the description of one historian, a ticking time bomb.

Togo is so worn, he can barely speak. His pernicious anemia drains him. He collapses into his chauffeured 1938 Buick limousine and heads to the Foreign Ministry. As the sun rises and air raid sirens wail—American warplanes are back over the city—the streets are empty. The message of the atomic bomb is getting through to ordinary citizens. At the same time, around six A.M., Japan's acceptance of the Potsdam Declaration—with the proviso preserving the prerogatives of the emperor—is cabled to Japan's emissaries in Switzerland and Sweden. It will be transmitted—slowly—through diplomatic channels to the foreign ministries of the Allied capitals, Washington, London, Moscow, and Chungking.

General Anami, who has not slept, looks fresh and relaxed as he strides into the War Ministry bomb shelter at nine-fifteen A.M. Standing at a podium, grasping a riding crop, he tells the gathered crowd of officers about the emperor's *seidan,* his sacred decision. There are cries of "No! No!" Anami says the war is still not over and sternly orders his men to maintain discipline in the ranks. Anyone who disobeys him, he says, will have to do so over his dead body. He slaps his riding crop on the lectern.

In the afternoon, the whole cabinet meets, and the various ministers are stumped over the delicate question of what to tell the public. Finally, they agree that it is better to wait for the Allies' response before saying much of anything. A vague statement is cobbled up. It says, essentially, keep on carrying on.

But meanwhile the true believers at the War Ministry have other ideas. They press General Anami to issue a statement to keep up morale among the troops. Under his name, a fire-breathing "Instruction to the Troops" is released to the press. Invoking a "Holy War," it proclaims: "We are determined to fight resolutely although we may have to chew grass, eat dirt, and sleep in the fields. It is our belief that there is life in death."

Anami is in an awkward position. On the one hand, he has

ordered his men to be disciplined, to do nothing that might upset the course of negotiations. On the other hand, he has apparently signed off on a die-hard vow that could prove deeply meddlesome. At the War Ministry, someone cooks up a convoluted story of an early draft fished out of Anami's wastebasket and published without his knowledge. But the incident suggests that Anami is not quite sure where he stands. Perhaps, he is practicing *haragei* to keep his troops under control. Or perhaps he is still imagining fighting to the death—certainly his own death.

At the Foreign Ministry, Togo realizes that Japan cannot afford to wait while the diplomatic wheels grind. What if America decides to drop a third atomic bomb? On Tokyo? He authorizes his aides to transmit over the open airwaves the Japanese offer to surrender with the sole condition of keeping the emperor. To escape army censors, who monitor short-wave radio, Togo's men transmit in English by Morse code. It is eight P.M. in Tokyo, seven A.M.—thirteen hours earlier—in Washington. In London, where it is noon, Reuters flashes a headline, "WAR IS OVER!" and people dance in Piccadilly Circus. The celebration is premature.

10.

Gambits

"The Superforts are not flying today"

Washington, D.C.
Guam Island
August 10–11, 1945

H ENRY STIMSON IS NOT EXPECTING THE WAR TO END
right away. "Tomorrow, we hope to get off to a long rest to
Highhold and St. Hubert's," he writes in his diary on August 9, after the second A-bomb has been dropped. St. Hubert's, a small town in upstate New York, is home of the
Ausable Club, a retreat for rusticating grandees on a lake in
the Adirondack Mountains. Stimson desperately needs to rest
his ailing heart; he cannot afford to delay. At about seven-
thirty on the morning of Friday, August 10, his car is packed
and waiting at the front door of Woodley to take him and
Mabel to the airport—when the phone rings. It is the Pentagon, with the news, announced "in the clear," as Stimson puts
it, that Japan is offering to surrender.

His vacation "busted," Stimson hastens to his Pentagon office, where he reviews the Japanese surrender. His eye immediately spots the catch: that Japan's acceptance of the
Potsdam Declaration does not "prejudice the prerogatives" of
the emperor as a "Sovereign Ruler." The condition is "the
very single point that I feared would make trouble," he writes
in his diary. At Potsdam, Stimson had urged President Tru-

man and Secretary of State Byrnes to permit Japan to keep its emperor. They had refused. Stimson blames the intransigence of the two former politicians on "the uninformed agitation against the emperor" by their fellow Americans "who know no more about Japan than has been given them by Gilbert and Sullivan's 'Mikado.'" He is especially disappointed that the resistance is led by FDR's reform-minded New Dealers, including two stalwart Yale men at State, Dean Acheson and Archibald MacLeish—"extraordinary men to take such a position," he writes, not in praise.

The secretary of war is summoned to the White House. He arrives to find the president with Byrnes, Navy Secretary James Forrestal, and the president's military adviser, Admiral William Leahy. Byrnes is "troubled and anxious," Stimson records. How, asks the secretary of state, can the president accept a surrender that preserves Japan's emperor after repeatedly declaring that only unconditional surrender will do? Stimson is exasperated by what he regards as a largely rhetorical trap. "Of course, during three years of a bitter war there have been bitter statements made about the Emperor," he records in his diary. "Now they come to plague us."

Stimson is heartened when Admiral Leahy takes "a good horse sense position that the question of the Emperor [is] a minor matter compared with delaying a victory in the war which [is] now on our hands." Addressing Truman directly, Stimson goes a step further. The United States will need the emperor "to save us from a score of Iwo Jimas and Okinawas all over China and the New Netherlands [the Japanese-occupied Dutch East Indies]," he says. The emperor is "the only source of authority in Japan under the Japanese theory of the State." Only the emperor can persuade Japan's troops— five million of them, massed in armies scattered all over Asia—to lay down their arms.

Three days earlier, showing Truman the photographs of

devastated Hiroshima, Stimson had used a patronizing metaphor to argue that "kindness and tact" are the proper way to
deal with the Japanese. "When you punish your dog," Stimson told Truman, "you don't keep souring on him all day
after the punishment is over; if you want to keep his affection,
punishment takes care of itself. In the same way with Japan.
They naturally are a smiling people and we have to get on
those terms with them." The "humane thing," insists Stimson,
would be to stop all bombing, right away.

Truman listened impassively but remained unmoved by the
secretary of war's image of a benevolent, stern-but-trusting
dog owner. Truman's frame of reference is the political machine and the Senate cloakroom, not a gentleman's country
estate. Watchful for the double cross, the president regards
Hirohito as a devious war criminal and the Japanese people as
guileful, which is what he will tell a pair of old Senate colleagues in separate conversations later that day.

Truman is also mindful of the advice of his old Senate pal
Byrnes, who warns that the public will not look kindly on a
president who goes soft in the tough going. (Later that day,
sipping whiskey at "bullbat" time, Byrnes tells an aide that
backing away from unconditional surrender would lead to
the president's political "crucifixion.") By nature a dealmaker—
Joseph Stalin will refer to Byrnes as "the most honest horse
thief I ever met"—Secretary Byrnes proposes a clever face-
saving fix: Let Japan keep its emperor, but make him a glori-
fied figurehead under U.S. control during the occupation.
The secretary of state, who was briefly a justice of the U.S.
Supreme Court before joining FDR's wartime cabinet, goes
off to draft some legal language, to be sent to Japan as a response to its surrender offer:

> From the moment of surrender the authority of the
> Emperor and the Japanese Government to rule the state

shall be subject to the Supreme Commander of the Allied Powers who will take such steps as he deems proper to effectuate the surrender terms. . . .

The ultimate form of government of Japan shall, in accordance with the Potsdam Declaration, be established by the freely expressed will of the Japanese people.

Truman is pleased with this approach—a conditional unconditional surrender, a compromise disguised as an ultimatum. He too knows a shrewd gambit when he sees it. Writing in his diary as he eats lunch at his desk, he translates Byrnes's lawyering into Missouri-style plain speaking: "They wanted to keep the Emperor. We told 'em we'd tell 'em how to keep him, but we'd make the terms." Even Stimson is impressed with Byrnes's artful response, which he calls "pretty wise and careful." Once the Allies sign off (a quick process, though the Russians bridle at giving America total control of occupied postwar Japan), the "Byrnes note" will be transmitted to Tokyo, putting the ball back into Japan's court. Alerted by news accounts of Japan's offer to surrender, a noisy crowd is building in the August heat outside the White House. War's end seems tantalizingly close.

Returning to his office for lunch, Stimson is taken aback when his favorite aide, Jack McCloy, wants to take a harder line—"to force upon Japan through the Emperor a program of free speech, etc., and all the elements of American free government," Stimson records in his diary. "I regarded this as unreal," writes Stimson. He tells McCloy he is overlooking the more urgent necessity. The Russians are racing into Manchuria. Are the Japanese islands next? "I felt it was of great importance to get the homeland into our hands before the Russians could put in any substantial claim to occupy and help rule it," writes Stimson. Already the geopolitical plates are shifting; a Cold War, as it would become known, begins while the hot war still simmers.

At two P.M. the entire cabinet convenes, and Stimson once again argues that the United States should stop all bombardment while awaiting Japan's response to the latest turn of the diplomatic wheel. President Truman refuses to stop all conventional bombing—he wants to keep the pressure on. But he declares that there will be no more atomic bombs without his express approval. Recording the president's remarks in his diary, Commerce Secretary Henry Wallace writes, "He said the thought of wiping out another 100,000 people was too horrible. He didn't like the idea of killing, as he said, 'all those kids.'"

In just two days, the president has come a long way from believing—or at least asserting—that Hiroshima was a military base, and that women and children would somehow be spared. The figure of 100,000 deaths is not mere conjecture. The day before, on August 9, Truman was shown ULTRA intercepts of Japanese cables putting the death toll from the Hiroshima attack at 100,000. Truman had delegated to the military so much authority over the atomic bomb that he wasn't even aware that the second strike was taking place until after it happened. Now, belatedly, Truman is asserting firm presidential control. The "terrible responsibility" alluded to in Stimson's diary entry, after he showed the president photos of Hiroshima, is weighing heavily.

After the cabinet meeting, Truman complains to Henry Wallace that he is suffering from dreadful headaches. "Physical or figurative?" asks Wallace. "Both," replies Truman.

At his headquarters on Guam on August 10 (where the time is thirteen hours ahead of Washington), General Spaatz has been preparing the third atomic strike on Japan. According to the orders he carries in his wallet, his only limitation for a third or fourth strike is the availability of bombs. That morning he received a cable from General Groves that the next atomic bomb would be "ready for delivery on the first suitable weather after 17 or 18 August"—in about a week's time. From the original target list, Kokura and Niigata remain to be bombed. Lt. Gen. Nathan Twining, the new commander of the Twentieth Air Force (replacing LeMay, who has become Spaatz's chief of staff), is also drawing up a list of a half-dozen new cities to propose as suitable atomic bomb targets.

Spaatz wants to drop the third atomic bomb on Tokyo (or "Tokio," as he spells it). The day before, on August 9, he cabled General Arnold in Washington:

> Strongly recommend that the next Centerboard [atomic] target be Tokio. More destruction probably would be obtained from choosing a clean target but it is believed that the psychological effect on the government officials still remaining in Tokio is more important at this time than destruction.

Spaatz knows that Tokyo is already burned out and largely evacuated. He hopes that by dropping an atomic bomb in the vicinity of Tokyo—but not too close to the Imperial Palace—he can send a message to Tokyo's leaders without at the same time killing the imperial household or tens of thousands of civilians. (When he writes of the alternative—the "destruction" obtained from "a clean target"—he is referring to flattening an intact city still teeming with people.)

In February, while he was still commanding the strategic air forces in Europe, Spaatz made a partial exception to his general rule against "area bombing"—indiscriminately bombing cities, as the British were doing every night—to direct a raid against central Berlin. Although he was aware that many civilians would be collateral damage, the intended targets were Hitler's ministries, clustered together in the city center. On February 3, with the skies mostly clear, almost a thousand B-17s rained bombs on the Reich Chancellery, Air Ministry, Foreign Ministry, Ministry of Propaganda, and Gestapo headquarters. The bombs also killed, wounded, or "de-housed" many thousands of civilians living nearby. While Spaatz does not think the war can be ended with one decisive blow at the enemy, he does believe that enemy leaders can be shocked toward submission when the bombs begin to fall on, or near, them. He does not want to kill the emperor or Japan's military leaders; after all, they need to be alive to command their troops to surrender. But he does want the emperor's men to experience, at close hand, the psychological effect of the blinding flash and hellish quake that the surviving residents of Hiroshima were already calling a *pikadon* (*pika*, "flash"; *don*, "boom"). Within the third atomic bomb's "scare radius" of ten miles would be all the leaders deciding Japan's fate.

In Washington, General Arnold cables Spaatz that his recommendation to aim the next "Centerboard" attack at "Tokio" is being considered "at a high level," but then comes the message from General Marshall: the atomic bomb "is not to be released without express authority from the President." For the time being, Spaatz stands down, awaiting further orders from the newly assertive president.

Meanwhile conventional bombing is supposed to go on, as ordered by Truman. But Spaatz is a cautious if not a reluctant warrior. The news that Japan has offered surrender terms is the perfect excuse for him to shift over from LeMay's all-out "area bombing" attacks with incendiaries on Japanese cities— what the pilots call "burn jobs"—back to "precision" attacks on military and industrial targets. The switchover has been anticipated (and subtly conveyed by Spaatz to LeMay over late-night poker games); now, with peace hanging in the balance, this seems like a propitious moment to hold off on the indiscriminate bombing of civilians. Spaatz cables General Arnold:

> Not knowing the extent to which area bombing may complicate the situation, am for the present limiting our operations to attacks on military targets visually. Unless I hear from you otherwise, will continue this policy until it is determined whether or not Japan offer is acceptable.

As it happens, the weather in Japan on August 10 is cloudy over the targets. Precise visual bombing of military targets is impossible, so Spaatz cancels the mission. He puts out a brief, perhaps too brief, statement: "The Superforts [B-29s] are not flying today."

A series of misunderstandings and mix-ups ensues. The press, cooped up and grasping at any sign that the war might be ending, reports that the canceled raid is a peace move. This creates an awkward situation for Spaatz's superiors. A *resumption* of air raids over Japan might now be read as a sign that peace talks have broken down. So a slightly miffed General Marshall cables Spaatz:

> You are quoted in the press with statement that "B-29s are not flying today" which has been accepted generally as positive indication that bombing of Japan has been terminated. . . . This presents very delicate and critical problem to the President. Resumption of bombing would appear to indicate that preliminary negotiations had fallen through giving rise to a storm of publicity and confusing views. Until I can reach the President and Secretary of War in about an hour do not repeat do

not dispatch any more missions but carry out these instructions in such a manner as absolutely to avoid any news item leaking out from Guam, Saipan, or Okinawa. Please make no repeat no further press comments of any kind until given release from here.

This is the second time in three days that the army chief of staff has chided Spaatz for saying either too much or too little to the press. Defensively, Spaatz responds:

Press has no authority to quote any statements from me since I have made none. The official reason for calling off yesterday's operation was weather. We are about to carry out a mission today when your message was received. In view of your instruction will cancel mission. Since my last message to you reference press, have made no statements and intend to make no statements. Anything published is purely conjecture on their part.

Perhaps inadvertently, more out of hesitancy than design, Spaatz from his bungalow on Guam has achieved what Secretary Stimson earlier urged on President Truman in the Oval Office: a cessation of bombing while awaiting further word from Japan. Spaatz's own state of mind at this moment is hard to know with certainty, but clues come from his diary entry for that day, August 11. The bombing of civilians is very much in his thoughts. So is the role of airpower. He has been thinking about writing to Robert Lovett, Stimson's assistant secretary for air and Spaatz's close friend from the early days of the war, to make the case for letting the airmen win the war:

Before news came last night of possible Japanese surrender had intended writing to Lovett repeating my views toward invasion. When the atomic bomb was first discussed with me in Washington, I was not in favor of it just as I have never favored the destruction of cities as such with all inhabitants being killed. It was pointed out to me however that the use of the atomic bomb would certainly mean that an invasion would be unnecessary and that thousands of American lives would be saved. The invasion is still planned in spite of this—and only the surrendering of the Japanese after attacks on their homeland by Air will cancel the invasion.

Spaatz's diary entry, though stiffly and awkwardly written—as if he is justifying his actions for the record—reflects his inner struggle over means and ends in modern war. On August 1, Spaatz had been the one to tell Gen. Douglas MacArthur about the atomic bomb. "This changes warfare," MacArthur had responded. The commander in chief, U.S. army forces in the Pacific theater, may have been thinking about his own thwarted glory—he knew that he, the Hero of Corregidor, would lose the chance to command the greatest invasion in the history of warfare. But MacArthur also understood that the atomic bomb was changing war itself.

Although Spaatz is not a visionary or an optimist, he shares the view of his colleagues in the Bomber Mafia that strategic airpower could change war in a humane way—by eliminating endless, grinding trench warfare and bringing a relatively quick surrender by striking at the enemy's industrial base and economic network. The experience of his aircrews in the treacherous skies over Germany sometimes mocked this dream, but Spaatz still believes that airpower can obviate costly invasions.

The hard part has been to project airpower without killing too many civilians. The atomic bomb makes it almost impossible. Like MacArthur, Spaatz can see his kind of war ending in the flash of an atomic bomb. The two men, West Point classes of 1903 and 1914, are both old soldiers being made obsolete by science. Spaatz has tried to adjust, to find work-arounds, like dropping a bomb in Tokyo Bay, but he knows that atomic war would be total war or the end of war—or maybe just the end.

Spaatz's frustrations come out in a morbid, vexed remark he makes to his aide-de-camp, Maj. Sarah Bagby. Bagby writes her mother, "The boss remarked that after this War is ended we should shoot or kill in some humane way the twenty-five leading scientists in each country."

"This War" is not over, and for all Spaatz knows, it may go on for some time. On August 10, he issues orders to build a hard-stand—basically, a concrete slab—on Okinawa to accommodate the B-29s of the 509th Composite Group. This will give the atomic bombers a second base of attack, closer to Japan. It is to be ready "not later than September 15."

11.

Plots

"What are you thinking of?"

Gen. Korechika Anami
was the war minister and
the most powerful man
in Japan. He wanted to
fight to the bitter end.

Tokyo
August 12–13, 1945

WASHINGTON'S REPLY TO JAPAN'S CONDITIONAL OFFER
to surrender arrives in Tokyo, in Morse code via shortwave radio, shortly before one A.M. on August 12. By dawn
on this day, another sticky, hot August morning in Japan,
Foreign Minister Togo is casting about for Japanese words
that will make the Allies' ultimatum seem more like a polite
request. Still dressed in his kimono at his home on the heights
of Azabu, in one of the few neighborhoods that has not been

firebombed, Togo is huddled with his subordinates, looking for locutions that are, in the manner of the Japanese (if not the blunt Togo), artfully vague.

Unlike Harry Truman, Togo trusts the enemy to carry out the proposed terms of the surrender. He believes Washington will be willing to preserve the emperor, at least as a limited constitutional monarch. At the same time, he knows the hard-liners in his own government will balk at the requirement, inserted by Secretary Byrnes, that the emperor "shall be subject to" the Allied commander of the forthcoming occupation. To purists like Baron Hiranuma, who insisted that any surrender preserve the sovereignty of the crown, the words *subject to* sound like "slave to." At the suggestion of one of his subordinates, Togo looks for a face-saving fudge. The Foreign Ministry will translate "shall be subject to" to read as the somewhat more benign "shall be restricted by." But the foreign minister is just tinkering with words. He fears that if Japan does not move quickly to accept Washington's terms, diplomacy will collapse in inner turmoil, and the war will enter a new, even more lethal stage. Already, Togo has been hearing the rumors of popular rebellion and military coup.

Togo has reason to fear the hard-liners. Zealous young army officers are conspiring to kill him, as well as Privy Seal Kido and Prime Minister Suzuki, in order to "protect" the emperor from what they see as his weak-kneed advisers. Just the day before, after learning of the emperor's "sacred decision," about a dozen officers gathered in the bomb shelter of the War Ministry to plot a coup. Their plan is simple: the Imperial Guard that protects the palace will round up the pro-surrender "Badoglios"—slang for traitors (named after Duke Pietro Badoglio, an Italian general who in 1943 betrayed Mussolini and the Fascist cause)—and the army will declare martial law.

This threat is neither far-fetched nor idle. In the February

26th Incident of 1936, army officers slashed the throat of one imperial adviser and shot two others. One of them was the emperor's grand chamberlain—at the time, Admiral Suzuki. He was spared in a scene that could have happened only in the fever state of 1930s Japan. Surprised by gunmen in his bedroom, Suzuki was shot four times. A mutinous officer bent over to finish him off with a short sword, but Suzuki's wife, Taka, had the extraordinary presence of mind to plead, "Please let me do it if it needs to be done." The officer shrugged, handed her his sword, and left the room to seek other victims. Incredibly, the wife's ruse worked, and Suzuki survived. The February 26, 1936, coup failed because the emperor, for once not enabling the military, ordered the army's senior leaders to stop their men.

The plotters are determined to succeed this time. Their leader is a brash young colonel named Masehiko Takeshita. A headquarters staff officer, not a combat hero, Takeshita commands authority by virtue of his swagger and, more significantly, a fortuitous relationship: his brother-in-law is General Anami, the war minister. Takeshita boasts that he can deliver General Anami to support the coup, and if the war minister is on board, then General Umezu, chief of the army general staff, will surely follow.

In the early afternoon, Takeshita and his would-be insurrectionists go in search of General Anami. They find him in his office, buckling on his sword, preparing to attend an emergency meeting of the cabinet. There is some back-and-forth about moving troops around the city to prepare—just in case—for a military takeover. Takeshita is blunt with his brother-in-law. He shouts that if Anami fails to prevent Japan's surrender, he should commit suicide.

Anami glares back at such impetuousness. He has himself suggested he might take his own life rather than submit to surrender, but he stiffens at Takeshita's taunt. He brusquely says he is too busy to talk. The coup plotters back off, for the moment. They do not get a yes from the war minister. On the other hand, they do not get a no. Anami, it seems, is practicing the stomach art. But what does he really believe?

In all likelihood, Anami himself does not know. In his secret diary, his entries are cryptic and opaque. Like the leaderless samurai in *The Tale of the 47 Ronin,* Anami is torn by conflicting obligations. He has a profound duty to his men, his beloved army. But he has a greater duty to the throne.

Anami has some personal loyalty to Emperor Hirohito. He was, for a brief time before the war, the emperor's aide-de-camp. Just the day before, Hirohito had summoned Anami to the *obunko* to chide him for his defiant proclamation that the army would continue to "chew grass and eat dirt" to fight to the end. Hirohito had been stern, but he had addressed Anami by his name—beseechingly, "Anami, Anami"—not his title, to emphasize the personal tie.

Anami feels affection for Hirohito. And yet . . . perhaps he is not the *right* emperor. Like so many army men of his era, Anami has been deeply influenced by a professor at Tokyo Imperial University named Kiyoshi Hiraizumi. Resentful of corrupt politicians and spineless courtiers, a generation of army officers, including Anami, count as Hiraizumi disciples. Spellbound, they have sat night after night on the hard benches of lecture halls to absorb Hiraizumi's teachings, dubbed "the Green-Green school." Hiraizumi sometimes begins by reading a poem, written by an ancient Chinese patriot shortly before he was executed by Mongol invaders: "Evergreens in the snow are even greener." The message is: purity will shine through. Guard the Imperial Way, the *kokutai,* with your life to ensure its essence.

The convenient—and dangerous—corollary, for an overzealous would-be samurai imbued with the warrior's *bushido* spirit, is that sometimes even the man sitting on the throne is not quite pure enough. Emperor Meiji, the father of the modern Japanese state, had been a great man, but his heir, Emperor Taisho, was a befuddled weakling. Taisho was gently eclipsed by the *genro,* the elder statesmen, to make room for Taisho's son, Crown Prince Hirohito. But perhaps Hirohito himself is not strong enough to stand up to his misguided advisers. Perhaps the military needs to "protect" the emperor by separating him from malign influence. Or possibly the generals and the true believers should look to the royal family to find a better emperor.

Faced with an existential crisis, a dozen princes from the five imperial houses are meeting that day at the palace. Anami decides to quietly approach one of them, Hirohito's youngest brother, Prince Mikasa. In court circles, Mikasa is derided as "the Red Prince" because he has voiced concern for common people. Mikasa is considered a palace outsider, which might make him a perfect candidate to join forces with the army and overthrow his brother.

But at his temporary residence on the burned-out palace grounds, Mikasa greets General Anami with scorn. Ever since 1931, when the army staged a provocation to seize Manchuria from China, the military has disregarded the emperor's wishes, chides Mikasa. The young prince summarily dismisses the war minister. Anami is taken aback; the peremptory rebuff by Mikasa signals that Emperor Hirohito is exercising his authority as head of family, and his family members, even his rebellious younger brother, are rallying to him.

True, Hirohito looks disheveled. Slouched, his voice scratchy, he remains a most unprepossessing emperor. But he has glimpsed a path to survival for himself and his mythic 2,600-year-old throne, a road to surrender, and he knows he will not get there by linking arms with suicidal fanatics in the military. Hirohito is also beginning to detect cracks in the military, a barely perceptible weakening of the will.

Earlier that morning General Umezu, the chief of the army general staff, and Admiral Toyoda, the chief of the navy general staff, approached the emperor to say that their soldiers and sailors were up in arms, that they would never submit to a peace that subordinated their emperor to foreign powers. Hirohito listened. But he sensed a lack of conviction in the speechifying of these two military men, as if their hearts were not in it, as if they were just going through the motions to satisfy their extremist subordinates.

Hirohito has always lived in a surreal world, of peacock feather gathering and tea ceremonies, but bitter experience with the military through a war of annihilation is making him, at last, a realist. That morning his closest adviser, the privy seal Marquis Kido, brought him the text of the Allies' response to his *seidan*, the sacred decision to surrender with the sole proviso that Japan be allowed to keep its emperor. Anxiously, Kido read the language that "the ultimate form of government shall be established by the freely expressed will of the Japanese people." This statement is anathema to the deeply held belief that the emperor's authority comes from the gods, not from the people. But Hirohito waves off Kido's concern. If the people do not want him, says the emperor, it won't matter what the language says.

Through the morning, Foreign Minister Togo has been heartened by reports from the palace that the emperor is willing to accept the American terms and to surrender. Earlier that morning Togo was led to believe that Prime Minister Suzuki was also on board to accept the Allies' terms. But he is disappointed when the full cabinet meets at three P.M.

The prime minister has just conferred with General Anami and Baron Hiranuma, and now the prime minister is waffling—once again. Anami reminded Suzuki that right after the emperor declared his sacred decision in the early hours of August 9, the prime minister promised the war minister that he would agree to fight on if the Allies did not accept the emperor's sovereign rule. Clearly, the Allies did not. The emperor would be "enslaved," argued Hiranuma.

Hiding behind clouds of cigar smoke, endlessly sipping green tea, Admiral Baron Suzuki, the great war hero of long ago, has become a weak reed in his decrepitude, thanks perhaps to the would-be assassin's bullet from the February 26, 1936, Incident that he still carries in his body. Now Suzuki tells the cabinet, "If disarmament is forced upon us, we have no alternative but to continue the war."

This is too much for Togo. Barely stifling his anger, he calls for an adjournment. Then he follows the prime minister into his private office and explodes. "What are you thinking of?" he demands. If Japan rejects the Allied terms, he warns, the Allies will harden their stance, not soften it.

Togo retreats to his own office. Anger gives way to depression. He is thinking of resigning. But working with his loyal and clever deputy, Shunichi Matsumoto, he comes up with one more ploy to try to buy time. Although Japan has learned of Washington's response by monitoring shortwave radio out of San Francisco, the actual formal papers have not arrived yet. When they do finally arrive, says Togo, we will simply pretend that they have not. At about six-thirty that night, the official Washington response, sluggishly winding through diplomatic channels, finally lands at the Foreign Ministry. The Japanese deliberately stamp the documents with the wrong time—twelve hours later, 7:40 A.M. on August 13. The fiction is a feeble one. The Foreign Ministry is running out of tricks.

✳ ✳

By seven A.M. on August 13, General Anami, sharp in his pressed khakis, is already in the office of Marquis Kido, the emperor's political adviser, demanding that the emperor put off the decision to surrender in order to demand better terms.

Kido himself is worried about an assassin's bullet. Walking to the palace, he has seen posters, plastered by members of nationalist secret societies, on the walls of burned-out buildings: "Down with BADOGLIO! Kill Lord Kido!" He has decided to move inside the palace moat, taking a room inside one of the few undamaged buildings.

Kido is brusque with Anami. If the emperor tried to bargain with the Allies, he would look like a "fool or a madman," says the privy seal.

Anami doesn't try to argue. He and Kido know each other from Anami's days as the emperor's aide-de-camp, and there is some mutual respect. But Anami does allow that he is under tremendous pressure at his own headquarters, which, he says, is tense. "You have no idea," says Anami. The war minister could be seeking Kido's sympathy. Or he could be subtly threatening.

At eight-forty-five A.M., the Big Six meet in the basement bomb shelter of the prime minister's official residence. Foreign Minister Togo is relieved to learn that Prime Minister Suzuki has reversed direction yet again and now backs acceptance of the Allied terms. Puffing his cigar, Suzuki is genial, in a Taoist, let-the-gods–decide sort of way. Navy Minister Yonai glowers, but he too has come around to Togo's side. But the other three—War Minister Anami and the two military service chiefs, Umezu and Toyoda—are implacable. They are back to insisting that Japan resist occupation, disarmament, and war crimes trials. "Absurd," scoffs Togo. It's as if the emperor's *seidan* had never happened.

Around and around the argument goes. At one point, the two sides are debating the significance and meaning of editorials in American newspapers, monitored from radio broadcasts. Anami passes around translated copies of a *New York Times* editorial of August 11. A "discredited god," argues the newspaper, is better than a "martyred god," meaning that it is wiser to prop up a figurehead emperor in Japan than to hang him and make him a martyr. "Sacrilegious!" splutters Anami. Togo tries to turn the tables by pointing out that the *Times* editorial proves that the Americans are willing to retain the emperor system. Anami counters with a *New York Herald Tribune* editorial categorically stating that the Supreme Allied commander would "rule" Japan. Togo tries to parry, but he is vexed by the "shall be subject to" language of the American response.

At three P.M. Togo and Anami are still futilely circling each other at a meeting of the full cabinet. But Togo notices something: Anami seems to be losing his zest for the fight. The war minister seems to be in a strange reverie, Togo thinks, as if performing in a dream.

In the ninety-degree heat, the ministers dab at their faces with white handkerchiefs. A break is called. Anami withdraws to the office of the cabinet secretary, Hisatsune Sakomizu, and asks Sakomizu to place a call for him to the War Ministry. Sakomizu makes the phone connection, hands Anami the receiver, and listens while Anami cheerfully tells a subordinate that "the Cabinet meeting is starting to take a favorable turn" and that the other ministers are coming around to the war minister's point of view. Sakomizu is dumbfounded. The reality is the opposite. Only a couple of ministers are now siding with Anami; the others want to make peace.

Sakomizu wonders, What is Anami up to? Is it all elaborate misdirection, deception, *haragei*? Why is he intentionally misleading his subordinates back at the War Ministry? Has Ana-

mi's militant hawkishness all been a charade to keep his troops
in line, to hold off a coup while the government sorts out the
proper response to the Americans? Sakomizu does not ask
Anami, and Anami volunteers nothing. The cabinet meeting
resumes and drones on. Holding out against surrender, Anami
is in the minority, but the war hawks still stand in the way of
a consensus needed to bring a decision to the emperor.

At nine P.M. Togo, deeply exhausted, is debating on and on,
submerged in a bomb shelter made rank by smoke and sweat
in the closed-in humidity. He is belaboring the obstinate
chiefs of staff of the army and the navy, General Umezu and
Admiral Toyoda, trying to convince them that prolonging the
war would be ruinous for the Japanese people, sweeping away
the emperor and all he stands for.

A man in a naval aviator's uniform bursts into the room. It
is Vice Adm. Takajiro Onishi, the first commander of the
kamikaze squadrons that have bedeviled the American fleet
for the past nine months. Onishi is in a tearful rage. He has
just come from pleading with Prince Takamatsu, the emper-
or's younger brother, to continue the war. The prince has
coldly rebuffed the admiral, who is now desperate. He implores the two chiefs of staff to come up with a better plan,
one that will win over the emperor. They need to organize a
massive "special attack corps" to throw itself on the enemy.
"If we are resolute and prepared to sacrifice twenty million
Japanese, victory will be ours!" Onishi cries.

The chiefs of staff of the army and the navy just stare at
him. There is no answer to his fanaticism.*

The military coup plotters have been at General Anami's

---

* After the surrender, Onishi committed *seppuku,* ritual suicide—without
a second to finish him off—and died slowly and painfully.

official residence, a modest wooden house not far from the palace, since about eight P.M. Anami's brother-in-law, Colonel Takeshita, once again laid out the plan: arrest the traitorous "Badoglios"—Togo, Kido, and Suzuki. Order the Imperial Guard to isolate and "protect" the emperor. Command the Eastern Army, sworn to guard Tokyo, to join the coup. Declare martial law and prepare to fight the Allies in one final, decisive battle.

Among the plotters is a young lieutenant named Kenji Hatanaka. Slender, with almost delicate features, he is a passionate disciple of the ultra-nationalist professor Hiraizumi's "Green-Green School." He is also regarded around headquarters as something of a pet to General Anami. Hatanaka is willing to go to extreme lengths to preserve the Imperial Way, including replacing the incumbent on the Chrysanthemum Throne. "Any emperor who does not behave like an emperor doesn't deserve to be called emperor," he declares, spouting a Green-Green mantra.

Hatanaka tells Anami of a rumor of a plot by these "Badoglios" themselves to assassinate the war minister. It's far-fetched, and Anami just laughs him off. As the coup plotters spin out their plans—the uprising is now scheduled for ten o'clock the next morning—the general is warm and avuncular with his fiery young charges.

"Now I know how Saigo felt," says Anami, in a good-natured, if rueful way. The young officers all know the story of Takamori Saigo. Considered the greatest of all samurai at the time of the Meiji restoration in the late 1860s, Saigo reluctantly led a rebellion of noblemen against the Meiji government. When it failed, Saigo committed *seppuku,* or so went the legend. (Gravely wounded in battle, he was decapitated by his own troops; he may or may not have intended to take his own life.)

If this coup now succeeds, General Anami will be the military dictator of Japan and commander of the last battle. But he must take command now, or the coup will not succeed.

Instead, Anami deflects and temporizes. He tells the plotters that the plan needs more work, that the communications are too uncertain. He will think about it some more and give his answer after midnight. At about eleven P.M., he ushers the young officers to the door, telling them to leave in groups of two or three, to be careful because they are being watched by the military police, the *kempeitai*.

After they leave, Anami's staff aide, Maj. Saburo Hayashi, cautions his boss against leading on the young hotspurs. What if he is trying to ride a tiger?

Anami just shrugs.

The sultry night is uneasy. In the small hours of the morning, distant thunder rumbles, and air raid sirens begin to wail.

Is Tokyo Next?

"This man is tottering"

Washington, D.C.
Guam
August 12–14, 1945

T HE FRIENDSHIP BETWEEN HENRY STIMSON AND GEORGE
Patton is curious. The two men are, stylistically at least, op-
posites. General George S. Patton, Jr., is a flamboyant show-
off who wears ivory-handled revolvers on his belt. Stimson is
sternly modest; at his dinner table at Woodley, boasting and
name dropping are frowned upon. Yet Patton and Stimson
share a bond, and they have ever since Patton was an ambitious young aide to Stimson at the War Department during
the Taft administration. Stimson is put off by Patton's swagger, but he admires how Patton's Third Army chased Germany's Panzer divisions all the way back to Bavaria.* Stimson
is a far kinder, more trusting soul than Patton. But like Patton, he is a believer in a basic rule of wartime combat: never
let up.

The first day or two after Japan's surrender offer arrived in
Washington, Stimson had hoped that Japan's resistance would

---

* When General Patton slapped two hospitalized soldiers suffering from
combat fatigue, calling them cowards, Secretary of War Stimson saved his
job.

collapse. "I don't see how the Japanese can hold out," he wrote in his diary on August 11. Satisfied with the Byrnes response to the Japanese peace offer—allowing Japan to keep its emperor, but subject to "the Supreme Commander of the Allied Powers" and ultimately to "the freely expressed will of the Japanese people"—Stimson leaves town. It has been another sleepless, hot night at Woodley, and Stimson is longing for his delayed retreat to the Ausable Club, far up in the cool Adirondacks, to rest his heart.

In Washington, Stimson's men are monitoring developments in Japan. They are reading disturbing cable traffic intercepted by the MAGIC and ULTRA code breakers. Encouraged by Anami's "chew grass, eat dirt" proclamation on August 10, the distant armies of Imperial Japan—in China, Indonesia, and Southeast Asia—are vowing to fight to the death no matter what the politicians are saying in Tokyo. This is precisely the scenario Stimson feared when he warned against having to fight "a score of Iwo Jimas and Okinawas" all over Asia.

What does Stimson make of these ominous developments? His diary, in which he has carefully recorded his daily thoughts for decades, peters out after August 11, when he leaves Washington, sick and spent. He does briefly record that he is under doctor's care, allowed only to walk to the dining room at the Ausable Club and, after a couple of weeks' recovery, take his beloved Mabel on a few discreet paddles in a rowboat around the lake.

Stimson has deputized Jack McCloy as "acting secretary of war," but he is well enough to stay in touch. At ten A.M. on August 13, he calls McCloy. In McCloy's diary, there are signs that Stimson is facing the reality that Japanese hard-liners are still holding out, and that stronger measures—up to and including another atomic bomb—may be required. At six-thirty P.M. George Harrison, Stimson's aide who handles all matters relating to the atomic bomb, calls McCloy to suggest that, as McCloy puts it in his diary, "an ultimatum be issued to Japan stating that immediate acceptance of our peace terms must be forthcoming, otherwise all negotiations—including the Potsdam Declaration—are off and the war goes on." At 7:10 P.M. McCloy telephones Under Secretary of War Robert Patterson "re possible issuance of ultimatum to Japan. Patterson agrees—feels strongly that it should be done." McCloy may be acting on his own initiative, but he has talked to Stimson that morning and will telephone him twice the next day. Harrison is also talking to Stimson, and Harrison's directions to General Groves about the atomic bomb strongly suggest that Stimson, even on his sickbed, is taking a page from the book of unremitting warfare by his friend George Patton.

On August 11, General Marshall had ordered General Groves to halt the process of shipping a plutonium core to Tinian to assemble a third atomic bomb. Now on August 13, Harrison passes word from his boss—from Secretary Stimson— that Groves should resume the chain of delivery of the necessary parts and materials to fashion a third bomb. Harrison tells Groves that, initially, the secretary of war approved of Marshall's order to stop the shipment of bomb parts. But now— after speaking with McCloy—Stimson thinks they should resume. Groves is ready and willing to accommodate the secretary of war; he replies that he can start shipment within two days. An A-bomb can be ready for delivery against Japan in about a week's time.

Stimson's friend and partner, General Marshall, is also mulling over another atomic strike against Japan—indeed, an atomic fusillade. Right after the first bomb was dropped on Hiroshima, in a meeting with Marshall and the army's chief strategic planner, Brig. Gen. George Lincoln, McCloy had raised the question no one else seemed to be asking: "Should we pause before dropping another bomb?" No, said Marshall. "This man," he said, "is tottering. We must push him over." The army chief of staff was not inclined to countermand the formal orders General Spaatz carried in his wallet—bomb Hiroshima first, then the three other targets as bombs "are made ready." Only Truman's direct intervention after Nagasaki put a hold on the atomic bombing—and then only for the time being.

Now, with intelligence signals flashing that Japan is not giving up but digging in, Marshall is pondering, however reluctantly, a dramatic escalation. On August 12, Marshall's chief intelligence adviser, Maj. Gen. Clayton Bissell, predicts that "atomic bombs will not have a decisive effect for the next thirty days," and notes that the Japanese army (unlike the civilian population) has stockpiled enough food and provisions to last another four to six months. In other words, it will take more than mere atomic bombs dropped on cities to make the Japanese surrender. Marshall, the army man, has always felt that bombing from the air and blockading by sea will not be enough, that it will be necessary to send in ground troops. At the same time, he is reading the code breakers' intelligence showing a massive buildup by Japanese forces around the southern beaches of Kyushu, site of the invasion still scheduled for November 1. Marshall is beginning to wonder if American landing forces will have to use atomic bombs as battlefield weapons—like conventional iron bombs or artillery shells, only much, much more powerful.

On the afternoon of August 13, Marshall's chief operations officer, Lt. Gen. John Hull, calls Groves's assistant, Col. Lyle Seeman. Hull begins, "What General Marshall wants to know . . ." and proceeds to ask how many bombs will be ready by November 1 (a "good chance" of seven) and whether they can be used to clear the beachhead of enemy forces. Seeman says that the invading forces may have to be "about six miles away" when the bombs are dropped and will need to wait "a safety factor" of "forty-eight hours" before advancing through the blast area in case one of the bombs is "a dud." Marshall is thinking aloud about using a total of nine bombs to support the beach landings at Kyushu—two for each of three invading armies and as many as three more to destroy Japanese reserves. Remarkably, there is no discussion of the possible dangers to U.S. troops marching through a radioactive battlefield.*

On August 11, *The New York Times* captioned its report on Japan's surrender offer: "GI's IN PACIFIC GO WILD WITH JOY; 'LET 'EM KEEP EMPEROR,' THEY SAY." In Washington, large, expectant crowds began milling about in Lafayette Park outside the White House, waiting for news.

Inside the offices of top policy makers, the wait is excruciating. "Never," Secretary of State Byrnes will later recall, "have I known time to pass so slowly!" President Truman unhappily considers his options. The most persuasive one, it will become apparent, is the one laid out in a cable from General Spaatz on Tinian, recommending dropping an atomic bomb close enough to the Imperial Palace that, without killing the emperor, it shocks Japanese leaders into giving up.

Truman started out as a passenger on the unstoppable train known as "S-1." But lately the decisive Truman—the president who will put a sign on his desk that says "The Buck

---

* General Groves is so determined to downplay what will become known as atomic fallout that in November, when he is testifying to Congress about the by-then obvious lethality of radiation, he will blithely state, "As I understand it from the doctors, it is a very pleasant way to die." (Actually, high doses of radiation cause internal organs to melt; death can be agony.)

Stops Here"—has begun to surface. He stepped in to assert his authority over the bomb after learning about the second strike on Nagasaki. Seeing the aerial photos of a devastated Hiroshima had already given him deep pause. But now he is seriously, if fretfully, thinking of using his authority to order a third strike.

At noon on August 14, the Duke of Windsor, who is visiting Washington during his wartime semi-exile, and British diplomat John Balfour arrive at the White House. Truman tells his British visitors that he has been awaiting word from the American embassy in Bern, Switzerland, the neutral country that Japan uses to send diplomatic messages to the Allies. The recent cables have been disappointing. Truman confesses that the latest Japanese telegram "did not contain the message awaited by the whole world." Ambassador Balfour reports back to London that President Truman "remarked sadly that he now had no alternative but to order an atomic bomb dropped on Tokyo."

By now, Truman has already ordered American forces to resume conventional bombing of Japan, both from carrier-based planes and from the "very heavy bombers," the B-29s loaded with high explosives and napalm. On August 13, the message goes out from Marshall to Spaatz: "Concerning very heavy bomber activities, the President directs that we go ahead with everything we've got." From Washington, General Arnold, whose tone suggests he is practically salivating, gets Spaatz on a "special radio teletype conference" to drive home the message that he wants the air force to put on a spectacular finale:

> FROM ARNOLD: It is desired that you start operations
> with your B-29s against Japan at once. What is the

maximum that you can send out? 1000 looks like a
very good minimum to me. Can you reach it? What
can you do about this at once?

REPLY FROM SPAATZ: We will dispatch at least 900 airplanes. . . .

FROM ARNOLD: Now as to distribution. The maximum
number possible must be sent to Tokyo so as to impress the Japanese officials that we mean business and
are serious in getting them to accept our peace pro-
posals without delay. What number can be used effectively over Tokyo?

REPLY FROM SPAATZ: Tokyo is not a good target except
for the atomic bomb.

In Spaatz's estimation, the imperial Japanese capital is already too burned out to be useful for conventional bombs;
B–29s laden with high explosives and incendiaries are sent to
other targets. But bombs—conventional or atomic—are not
the only way to send the Japanese a message. All along, the air
force has been dropping leaflets on Japanese cities in advance
of bombing them, warning civilians to flee—a merciful act
that not so subtly signals American invincibility. (The flyers
said the Americans would attack *some* of the cities listed,
thereby terrorizing even more people.) On the night of August 13, seven B–29s are loaded up with 5 million four-by-
five-inch blue leaflets printed in Japanese. They say:

To the Japanese people

These American planes are not dropping bombs on you
today. They are dropping leaflets instead because the
Japanese Government has offered to surrender, and
every Japanese has a right to know the terms of that
offer and the reply made to it by the United States

Government on behalf of itself, the British, the Chinese, and the Russians. Your government now has a chance to end the war immediately.

Just before dawn, one of the B-29s flies directly over the Imperial Palace in Tokyo. The leaflets are released in canisters, which open in midair, allowing the leaflets to flutter down. One of them lands in a courtyard, where a chamberlain of the imperial household picks it up and immediately carries it to Lord Kido. The emperor's keeper of the privy seal has been sleeping in a spare bedroom, where, he hopes, no assassin can find him. Kido reads the pamphlet. "One look," he will later recall, "caused me to be stricken with consternation."

13.

To Bear the Unbearable

"Like a mid-summer's night dream"

Surrender ceremony on the USS *Missouri,* September 2, 1945. The Japanese delegation was led by Togo's deputy and replacement as foreign minister, Mamoru Shigemitsu, and Army Chief of Staff Gen. Yoshijiro Umezu.

Tokyo
August 14–15, 1945

LORD KIDO KNOWS RIGHT AWAY THAT THE GAME IS up. For the past several days, the people of Japan have been kept in the dark about their government's anguished internal debate over surrender. Now the silence is broken. The privy seal's sense of alarm only grows as he reads several other leaflets that have drifted down onto the streets of Tokyo—and, he can be sure, many other cities as well. The American propaganda prints, in full, the text of Japan's August 10 offer to surrender with the sole condition of keeping the emperor, and Washington's response, received on August 11, that the emperor must be "subject to" the Supreme Allied commander. Kido knows that these incendiary pieces of paper could spark a coup by dissident army officers, which could erupt into civil war and anarchy. He hastens to seek an audience with the emperor.

In consensus-minded Japan, and especially at the palace, little happens quickly, but Hirohito is aware that time has run out. The emperor has been vitalized by the desire to survive American atomic bombs and the suicidal fanatics in his own army, and he wants to save what is left of his country. He wants to convene the top leaders of government for a second *seidan,* at which he will accept Washington's surrender terms and finally, once and for all, end the war and preserve the nation. Prime Minister Suzuki proposes a meeting to begin in about four hours' time, at one P.M. No, says the emperor. Sooner. Right away. He does not want to give the military time to organize a coup.

Hirohito has been hearing rumors, and they are all true. The plotters are planning to launch their coup at ten A.M.—to cut off the palace, isolate the emperor, arrest the "Badoglios," declare martial law, and fight to the end. There has been some wild talk of storming the *obunko* and killing everyone (except the emperor, who will be "protected") with machine guns before taking their own lives with hand grenades. But the calmer discussion still centers on recruiting War Minister Anami to the cause, in the expectation that the army high command will fall in behind him.

Anami, at this moment, is finishing breakfast with Field Marshal Shunroku Hata, commander of the army for the defense of western Honshu and Kyushu. Hata has just returned from Hiroshima. He reports that white clothes serve perfectly well to protect people from atomic rays and that sweet potato roots are growing healthily just one inch beneath the blasted ground. Anami excitedly exclaims, "You must tell the emperor!"

Reality intrudes when Anami returns to headquarters. His brother-in-law, Colonel Takeshita, and his fellow plotters are buzzing about, but they are suddenly silenced by General Umezu, the army chief of staff, who says, flatly, that he will not support a coup. Umezu tells Anami that launching a coup in defiance of the emperor would just split the army and start a civil war. Anami appears to accept this judgment from "the Iron Mask," an impassive operator known for his unflappability.

That should be the end of it, since the coup cannot succeed without men who report directly to Umezu, including the commanders of the Eastern Army and the Imperial Guard. But then Umezu seems to soften. . . . He suggests he is not *absolutely* opposed to the coup. Or at least that is what Takeshita and his men choose to hear. It is hard to know. Anami himself remains opaque and cheerful.

In makeshift government offices around the burned-out palace this morning, staff are witnessing the strange spectacle of cabinet ministers borrowing neckties, coats, and even pants from their aides in a scramble to don the appropriate formal wear for the hastily arranged audience with the emperor, now scheduled for ten-thirty A.M. Through the vaultlike gates of the *obunko* they go, two dozen once-proud, now-anxious men summoned to surrender an empire that has terrorized Asia and the Pacific for more than a decade. The *obunko* is the only steel-reinforced concrete building on the palace grounds, but its underground shelter might as well be a sauna. In the moist August heat, moisture drips from the walls.

The emperor, dressed in his military uniform, enters; the ministers bow low. Premier Suzuki apologizes, yet again, for a failure to reach consensus. One last time the admirals and generals reprise their arguments to fight to the end, "even at the cost of a hundred million lives" (*ichioku gyokusai,* "death in battle of the hundred million," a common patriotic slogan). The emperor grasps the hilt of his sword and speaks. "I have listened carefully," he says, "but my own opinion has not changed."

Hirohito announces that he "agrees with Foreign Minister Togo" that the Allies will preserve Japan's imperial system. He feels sorry for the military, but the Japanese people must be saved. He quotes from his grandfather Emperor Meiji, who, a half century earlier, at the time of a far lesser humiliation—an intervention by Western powers that forced Japan to give up a peninsula in Manchuria—uttered the words, "We must bear the unbearable." Pointedly, Hirohito adds, "The War and Navy ministers have told me there is opposition within the Army and Navy; I desire that the services also be made to comprehend my wishes." And just to make sure they do not distort his words, he announces that he will go on the radio—unheard of!—to speak to the nation.

The reaction in the room is convulsive. Two ministers slide from their seats onto the floor, gasping and keening. Most weep. As they leave, "each of us in his own thoughts wept again," Togo will recall in his memoirs.

Afterward a lunch of whale meat and black bread is served. No one eats except for Prime Minister Suzuki, who seems surprisingly well rested and robust, despite his old age; Taoist passivity has been good for his constitution.

Anami seems to be in a near-delusional state. He pulls aside his aide, Maj. Saburo Hayashi, into a bathroom and babbles excitedly that there is a U.S. Navy fleet with a huge landing force in Tokyo Bay. If we attack them with everything we have, says the war minister, we will get much better peace terms. Incredulous, Hayashi stares back at his superior. The U.S. Navy force is just rumor, he says.

Anami returns to Ichigaya Heights, where the War Ministry is thronged with agitated officers. Colonel Takeshita is after him to resign from the Supreme War Council, thereby bringing down the whole government and creating a chaotic situation that can be resolved only by a military takeover. For a moment, Anami seems tempted. He says, "Bring me ink and a piece of paper." Then he thinks better of it.

He is—perhaps always has been—committed to the emperor. "The emperor has spoken his decision, and we have no choice whatever to obey it," Anami tells the hotheads surrounding him. He straightens and glowers. "Anybody who disagrees," he says, "will have to do so over my dead body."

The most fervent of the coup plotters, Anami's "pet" disciple Colonel Hatanaka, lets out a wail.

A deep lethargy settles over the war ministry at Ichigaya Heights. Some officers, fearing an imminent attack by American paratroopers, start bonfires in the courtyard and begin burning papers. Others close their doors and open bottles of whiskey and sake while contemplating hara-kiri. The building's guards flee, taking food and clothing with them.

At the prime minister's residence, cabinet members gather to draft the imperial rescript that the emperor will broadcast to the nation.* Anami seems calm and genial again, but other cabinet members eye him warily. They wonder if he won't decide to resign after all and subvert the whole painfully wrought peace process.

The war minister does object to one particular sentence in the draft of the emperor's speech. The emperor is scripted to say, "The war situation grows more unfavorable to us every day." Such a declaration of the obvious might seem unremarkable, considering that in less than a fortnight two of Japan's cities have been wiped out by atomic bombs, while the Russians have sent Japan's army reeling in Manchuria. But Anami objects. The army has not lost, he insists. And in any case, to say so would make a lie out of years of triumphant communiqués to the public and undermine the army's honor.

And so the language is changed to read, "the war situation has developed not necessarily to Japan's advantage." The understatement is almost risible, but it satisfies Anami, and the others do not wish to risk the war minister's dissatisfaction.

Foreign Minister Togo seeks to placate Anami further by drafting a formal note requesting the Allies to let the army of Japan disarm itself, while officers keep their ceremonial samurai swords. Squaring his shoulders, Anami is effusive with Togo. "I am grateful beyond expression," he says. Togo thinks Anami is being "overly polite," as he will later put it in his memoir, but, in any case, he is glad to part with smiles.

General Anami returns to his office and gathers up his belongings, including a short ceremonial sword sheathed in a cherrywood scabbard.

---

* A rescript is a decree written in reply; the concept is that the emperor is always responding to his people's needs.

The writing of the imperial rescript, with the careful, elegant brushwork of the court scriveners, takes hours. Finally, before midnight, the emperor leaves the *obunko* and is driven through the darkened palace grounds to the Household Ministry. An air raid siren has sounded, warning that *teki-san*, "Mr. Enemy," is returning, but the B-29s are firebombing a city sixty miles away.

Hirohito is greeted by engineers from NHK, the government radio network, who will record his message to be broadcast to the nation the next day at noon. In his high-pitched, tremulous voice, the emperor reads the rescript into a microphone. "Was it all right?" he asks. No one has the courage to say that the imperial voice trembled. Hirohito suggests that perhaps his voice was too low. He reads the rescript again, and all express satisfaction, although the emperor has left out a conjunction or two.

After the emperor leaves in his maroon Mercedes limousine, there is a discussion about where to safekeep the recordings overnight. The NHK men do not want the responsibility. It is too dangerous in the Radio Tokyo broadcast building, they say. A court chamberlain puts the two recordings in a cloth bag and returns to the palace. In the empty room set aside for the empress's ladies-in-waiting, he locks the bag in a small safe in a bookshelf, then covers the safe with a pile of papers and books.

Shortly after midnight, the fervent Major Hatanaka and a couple of other die-hard coup plotters arrive at the office of Lt. Gen. Takeshi Mori, the commander of the Imperial Guard. Eyes glistening, Hatanaka implores Mori to join them.

"The all-wise emperor" has been misled by his wicked advisers, says Hatanaka. We must save him and save Japan!

Suitably wary, Mori avoids saying yes or no. He filibusters. He discusses his philosophy of life and talks about taking a walk around the Meiji Shrine. It is sweltering in the small, crowded room, and Hatanaka loses patience. Abruptly, he takes out his service revolver and shoots the startled General Mori, who topples over, dead. Then Hatanaka and another plotter swing their swords and hack off the head of General Mori's son-in-law, who has the bad luck to be visiting.

Hatanaka had wanted Mori to sign "Imperial Guards Division Strategic Order No. 584," which directs the Imperial Guard to occupy the palace to "protect the emperor and preserve the *kokutai*," the imperial system (and the army's privileged status). Now Hatanaka steps over the slain Mori and affixes the general's official seal to multiple copies of the directive.

Back at the palace, the guardsmen dutifully obey their new set of orders. Phone lines are cut. Bayonets are affixed to rifles, and machine guns are placed at the gates and bridges around the palace. The chamberlains are rounded up and interrogated: where is the recording of the emperor's speech? Bravely, the chamberlains refuse to say. Troops begin to search the darkened palace. The emperor is left to sleep.

Colonel Takeshita goes to see his brother-in-law, General Anami, ostensibly to make one last attempt to win his support for the coup. But Takeshita is seized by ambivalence; he is not sure what to say.

He finds Anami in his bedroom, sitting by the mosquito netting over his bed.

The war minister is writing notes. "I'm thinking of *seppuku* [suicide] tonight," says Anami.

"It doesn't have to be tonight, does it?" asks Takeshita.

Anami replies that he cannot bear to hear the emperor's speech in the morning.

The two men drink from a large bottle of sake. Takeshita says, "If you keep drinking like that, won't you flub it up?"

Anami responds that "no man who has reached the fifth order of *kendo* [Japanese fencing] needs to worry about that." Besides, he says, the alcohol will make his blood flow more easily. But just in case his hand slips, he asks Takeshita to act as his second, to finish him off.

Another officer arrives to report that the coup is proceeding, and that the Imperial Guard has occupied the palace. Anami is dismissive; the Eastern Army will snuff out the impudent coup, he predicts.

The two men drink some more. Shortly before dawn, Anami dons a loose shirt of pure white, exposing his belly. He remarks that the emperor gave him the shirt when he was his aide-de-camp. He removes his short sword from its lacquered sheath and plunges it into his abdomen, jerking the blade sideways and upward. Then he takes a dagger and, with his finger, searches his neck to find the artery. He thrusts in the dagger; blood spurts everywhere.

As instructed, Takeshita takes the dagger from the general's hand and, with the dripping blade, administers the coup de grâce to Anami's still-writhing body. Then he drapes Anami's bemedaled uniform over him. He picks up the two notes that Anami has written. One says, "Confident of the eternity of our fatherland, I give my life to atone for great crimes." What crimes is Anami atoning for? To this day, it remains unclear. The other note says, "Having received great favors from the emperor, I have nothing to say in this hour of my death."

Anami came perilously close to instigating, or at least, condoning a coup—unless it was all theater all along. Perhaps Anami practiced the stomach art unto death.*

At the palace, the commander of the Eastern Army, Gen. Shizuichi Tanaka, an Oxford graduate and strict disciplinarian, arrives to restore order. One of the original co-conspirators advises Hatanaka to stand down and all will be forgotten "like a mid-summer's night dream." But Hatanaka is too far gone. He dashes off to the NHK radio studio, wildly brandishing his pistol. The technicians manage to divert him, and finally he wanders outside to the plaza in front of the Imperial Palace to put a bullet in his head.

At about six-thirty A.M., a half hour before his customary rising time, Emperor Hirohito appears in his dressing gown. One of his chamberlains will later insist that the emperor slept through the whole event, but this seems unlikely; another account has him peering out through the shutters as soldiers race about outside. Now, pale and disheveled but resolute, Hirohito asks to address the troops, beseeching, "Don't they understand?" It won't be necessary, he is told. Privy Seal Kido emerges from a basement storage closet, where he has spent the night hiding and wondering if he would be cut down like Lord Kira in *The 47 Ronin*. Beyond the gates of the palace, police guards have fought off rebel soldiers, armed with hand grenades, pistols, and swords, attacking the privy seal's private residence. The coup attempt ends as it began, part tragic farce, part mortal danger.

---

* Anami's bloodstained suicide notes have been preserved at the Yasukuni Shrine and war memorial in Tokyo.

✳ ✳

"To my good and loyal subjects . . ." So begins the Voice of the
Crane, as the emperor is sometimes called, after the sacred bird
that can be heard even when never seen. Few Japanese have
heard the real voice of the emperor, high and wavery, but at
noon on this day, August 15, 1945, millions of loyal subjects are
gathered around communal radios—often the village's only
radio, set outside in a street or park. They were summoned by
a radio announcement at 7:21 A.M. and by the brief churn of
air raid sirens a minute before the appointed noon hour.

Hirohito never uses the forbidden words for "surrender"
(*kofuku* and *kosan*) or "defeat" (*haisen*). After noting—in the
language insisted upon by Anami—that the war situation has
developed "not necessarily to Japan's advantage," the emperor
goes on:

> The enemy has begun to employ a new and most cruel
> bomb, the power of which to do damage is indeed in-
> calculable.

Should Japan continue to fight, he warns, it would "not
only result in the ultimate collapse and obliteration of the
Japanese nation, but also it would lead to the total extinction
of human civilization." The emperor (formally *showa,* meaning "peace") is not only saving Japan; he is saving the world.
"We have resolved to pave the way for a grand peace for all
the generations to come by enduring the unendurable and
suffering what is insufferable."

He sympathizes with his people but warns them to "be-
ware most strictly of any outbursts of emotion" that might
engender "needless complications." They must not fall prey
to "any fraternal contention or strife."

There is quiet across the land. Some people have not un-

derstood the emperor's archaic court Japanese or his circum-
locutions. Radio announcers hastily explain, in ordinary
Japanese, what the emperor has just said. Most people bow to
the radio or wander off in catatonic silence.

Outside the palace, a large crowd gathers, and a few people
shout the old battle cry, "Banzai!"

In Hiroshima at a hospital, Dr. Michihiko Hachiya is astonished when his patients, after listening to the emperor's
speech, burst out in anger. "How can we lose the war? . . .
Only a coward would back out now! . . . I would rather die
than be defeated!" He realizes that his gravely sick and
wounded patients cannot bear the thought that their terrible
suffering has been for naught. The doctor writes in his diary
that night, "The more I thought, the more wretched and
miserable I became."

Japan surrenders in absurdity and futility. But at least the
empire surrenders. One false or unlucky move along the way,
and the whole fragile process to end the war could have col-
lapsed into chaos. The emperor will have to release another
rescript and send princes of the royal house to Japan's far-
flung armies to keep the armies in line. A few defiant *kamikazes* fly final missions. When the first American troops, in full
battle gear, land on the beaches of Japan, they expect to be
confronted by fanatical emperor-worshippers; instead, a few
are reportedly accosted by women who call, "Yoo hoo!"
Mostly the streets are empty of women; false rumors of mass
rape are rampant. In Japan and her conquered territories, well
over 20 million people have died.

At two P.M. on August 15 in Tokyo, the cabinet resigns. Foreign Minister Togo is asked to join a new cabinet that is forming, but he declines. Despite all he has done to avert war in

1941 and to bring peace in 1945, he expects, instead, that he will be charged as a war criminal, simply because he was a responsible government official at the time of Pearl Harbor. He is not bitter. In Japan, it is common, or at least expected, that one takes responsibility for bad outcomes, whether or not one is personally to blame.

No High Ground

"The only way you can make a man trustworthy"

Guam
St. Hubert's, New York
Washington, D.C.
August 15, 1945

A MERICAN BOMBS ARE STILL FALLING ON JAPAN WHEN
Radio Tokyo broadcasts the emperor's speech at noon on
August 15. From Washington, General Arnold has been pushing General Spaatz, at his command post on Guam, to put a
thousand bombers into the air. Spaatz has managed to muster
843 B-29s, including seven from the 509th Composite Group
(each dropping one Pumpkin bomb). The dispatch of another 173 fighter escorts allows the air force publicists to proclaim a thousand-plane grand finale against imperial Japan.

But among airmen and commanders, there is ambivalence
about this last onslaught—12 million pounds of demolition
and incendiary bombs on four military targets and two urban-
industrial areas, destroying half of one city and a sixth of the
other. Aboard at least one B-29 en route to target, the crew
debates what to do when they hear, over the radio, of Japan's
surrender. Should they turn around and drop their bombs
into the sea? Though ordered to proceed, they fly back to
base, claiming mechanical problems.

The day before, by means of a "radio teletype conference,"

Arnold had pestered Spaatz, "Can Doolittle send any [B-29s] out from Okinawa? How many? When?"

Spaatz blandly explained that "Doolittle cannot send planes from Okinawa" because the airdromes are being used for anticipated troop transport to what will soon become Occupied Japan. This is the truth, but not the whole truth. Two days earlier Spaatz had gone to Gen. Jimmy Doolittle, his old friend from Europe, and asked if the Eighth Air Force wanted to get in on the final action. Doolittle declined. He did not want to put his aircrews at risk when Japan was so obviously defeated. Doolittle, a national hero for leading the audacious first air raid over Japan in the early months of the war, has recoiled at end-of-the-war overkill. When, during a discussion of atomic bomb targets among the air commanders, one of them suggests, "Why not Tokyo? Let us drop it on the emperor's palace. That will impress them," Doolittle dryly responds, "Yes, if we do that, who are we going to make peace with?"

Spaatz was one of those commanders urging an atomic bomb on Tokyo—but not on the heart of Tokyo, not on the palace, but rather on the already-burned-out outskirts far from the center, as a demonstration of force. Just before midnight on the fourteenth, in another "radio teletype conference" with General Arnold, Spaatz shows that he too is uneasy about the final spasm of violence against Japan. The transcript of the conversation between Arnold and Spaatz reads:

> ARNOLD: These operations have been coordinated with all my superiors all the way to the top.
> SPAATZ: Thank God.

On these conference calls to Washington from halfway around the world, Spaatz is also communicating with Bob

Lovett, Secretary Stimson's aide and the air force's civilian boss. Spaatz and Lovett grew close when Lovett traveled to Europe to witness the air war from Spaatz's headquarters in England and France. Over the teletype from Guam, Spaatz tells Lovett that the Twentieth Air Force is "one of the best air units that we have had in operation" and urges the assistant secretary of war for air to come out to the Pacific to "see this show before it is broken up."

Lovett responds, "I am stuck here with no immediate prospect of breaking loose so rely on you to seize me high ground." *High ground* is a military term of art; at West Point, army cadets are taught that smart commanders always try to seize the high ground, where they can fire down upon the enemy struggling up the hill. Spaatz jokily replies, "High ground will be seized and, if present strain keeps us, properly fertilized." By "properly fertilized," he is referring to the taste he shares with Lovett for scotch whiskey. But then Spaatz turns "high ground" to make a moral metaphor:

> Have looked at good photos of Hiroshima today. The atomic bomb disposes of all high ground. Hope there is never an occasion to use another.

Henry Stimson learns of Japan's surrender over a "scrambler phone" installed in his cabin at the Ausable Club. Jack McCloy calls to give him the welcome news. That evening, as Henry and Mabel enter the club's dining room, a hearty cheer goes up.

But Stimson is on the "verge of an emotional and coronary breakdown," he writes in his diary. He is racked with anxiety that the bomb he has helped to create will destroy the path to moral progress that has been the lodestar of his long life in service. He knows from talking to Robert Oppenheimer that the atomic bomb dropped on Hiroshima is a firecracker compared to the nuclear bombs that await. He fears that the temptation of science will outrun man's morality and self-control.

In long, anguished conversations with McCloy, who has flown up to join his own family, also staying at the club, Stimson looks for ways to put the genie back in the bottle. The first step is to change his own mind. For months, Stimson has regarded the secret of "S-1" as a "master card" and "royal straight flush" in dealing with the Soviet Union. He hoped to use the threat of the bomb as leverage to force the Russians to liberalize their police state and to join the community of free nations. But when McCloy tells Stimson that Secretary of State Byrnes has been boasting that he intends to go to a forthcoming Allied foreign ministers meeting with the atomic bomb "in his pocket, so to speak," Stimson recoils.

Stimson can be a stiff moralist, but he is not self-unaware, and his religious faith has taught him humility. He has the confidence to be humble: he is—not always but often—able to see arrogance, including his own. He understands that threatening the paranoid Soviets with the bomb will backfire. It will only make Moscow more suspicious, more defensive— more likely to race to build their own doomsday weapon. A costly arms race can be the only outcome, global Armageddon the unacceptable risk.

Stimson is old, he is tired, and with his top-buttoned suits and rigidly correct manners, he is willfully old-fashioned, a throwback to an age that is lost, when cavalrymen rode horses, not tanks, and gentlemen did not swear in the presence of ladies. But he is also a visionary. He understands that the weapons to worry about are less the ones that fell on Hiroshima and Nagasaki than the far deadlier ones, as yet unbuilt, that will threaten every single city and every person in the world. His last official act as an old soldier-statesman will be to try to blunt the horror weapons of the future.

On September 12, back in Washington for his final days in office, Stimson hands Harry Truman a personal letter and a lengthy memorandum. He invokes the code he learned as a college boy and that he has tried to live by in the real world. "The chief lesson I have learned in a long life," he has written the president, "is that the only way you can make a man trustworthy is to trust him; and the surest way to make him untrustworthy is to distrust him and show him your distrust." Stimson proposes to trust the Russians. Instead of wearing the atomic bomb "ostentatiously on our hip" like a western gunslinger, Stimson wants to share the secret of the atomic bomb with America's former ally and future enemy. In effect, Stimson calls for a nuclear freeze; America will stop development on its nuclear weapons while it negotiates with the Russians on an arms control treaty.

Truman, with his capacity to appear to agree without really agreeing, offers Stimson the opportunity to make his case to the full cabinet.

September 21, his seventy-eighth birthday, is Henry Stimson's last day in office. He has served six presidents over almost a half century. There are a cake and songs and a nineteen-gun salute. One hundred twenty generals line up to wish him bon voyage. In the cabinet room, Stimson speaks passionately, without notes. The "future of world peace" depends on international arms control, he says. Otherwise, the development of new weapons might "put an end to the world."

The president and his cabinet listen respectfully to the elder statesman. Stimson is buoyed up. He leaves the room—and Washington, aboard the secretary's private plane, bound for Highhold—convinced that "the President has decided to follow almost exactly my recommendations."

But it is already too late. Truman's administration is in fact divided and uncertain about arms control, as is Truman himself. James Forrestal, the secretary of the navy and the future

secretary of defense, a position created in the 1947 reorgani-
zation of the national security establishment, compares Stimson's idea to appeasing Hitler. Congress is firmly against
sharing the atomic secret with the Russians. At the Pentagon,
the air force is already putting together a list of sixty-six Russian cities targeted for the atomic bomb if World War III
breaks out. Gen. Leslie Groves is starting to talk about a preemptive strike.

In any case, it is highly unlikely that the Kremlin would be
receptive to Stimson's idea, or to any plan that would allow
foreign inspectors to nose around Soviet defense installations.
Stalin has already put his chief of secret police hard at work at
developing the Soviet atomic bomb, whose first test explosion is only four years away, at a test site in Kazakhstan, on
August 29, 1949.

The Cold War deepens. By the summer of 1946, Stimson
himself is doubtful that the Russians can be persuaded to
enter a meaningful arms control regime. In October 1947, he
writes in *Foreign Affairs,* the magazine of the foreign policy
establishment, "I have often said that the surest way to make
a man trustworthy is to trust him. But I must add that this
does not always apply to a man who is determined to make
you a dupe."

Privately, he confides to a friend that "my views have become much more conservative with the passage of the past
two years." It might be necessary, he writes, to "stand by with
all the bombs we have got and can make, and hold ourselves
in readiness until Russia learns to be decent."

It is a long wait. In October 1961, over an island in the
Arctic Ocean, the Russians will detonate a thermonuclear
weapon called *Tsar Bomba.* It is fifty megatons, or about three
thousand times the size of the explosion at Hiroshima. In
1966 the U.S. Navy will launch a new nuclear "boomer" submarine, the USS *Henry L. Stimson,* with sixteen nuclear-

tipped missiles, carrying roughly four hundred times the payload of Little Boy and Fat Man. As secretary of state in 1930, Stimson had called for the abolition of submarines as a devious tool of war. What would he have thought about a submarine, named in his honor, that could kill millions of people, most of them civilians, in one blow?*

In the same *Foreign Affairs* article in October 1947, Stimson writes about the legacy he wishes to leave. He calls for the rebuilding of Europe. He warns that America can never go back to isolationism, can never be "an island to herself." Though there will be setbacks, he writes, "I see no reason for any man to face the American future with any feeling other than one of confident hope."

Stimson's two closest aides, Jack McCloy and Bob Lovett—the men he once jokingly called "the Imps of Satan"—hear the call. McCloy becomes high commissioner of Germany during its postwar rebuilding. The crafty Lovett, working as George Marshall's deputy secretary at the State Department, is crucial to persuading Congress to approve of the Marshall Plan and the Western Alliance (NATO, the North Atlantic Treaty Organization), then serves as secretary of defense during the Korean War. In 1960 Lovett declines President Kennedy's offer to make him secretary of state, defense, or treasury.

During the Cuban Missile Crisis in October 1962, President Kennedy calls on Lovett to advise him. Meeting with JFK's national security adviser, McGeorge Bundy, Lovett spots a photo of Henry Stimson on Bundy's desk. "Mac," says Lovett, "I think the best service we can do for President Kennedy is to try to approach this as Colonel Stimson would." Bundy agrees; Stimson's blend of realism and idealism, diplo-

---

* There is no question of what Stimson, the old Victorian, would have thought about the hatch covers on the launch tubes holding the missiles, each painted with a replica of the logo of the *Playboy* Bunny.

macy and power, will be their "bench mark." Lovett later recalled: "All during the conversation, the old Colonel seemed
to be staring me straight in the face." In the end, President
Kennedy takes a Stimsonian approach to the world's most
dangerous nuclear standoff. The United States demands that
Russia remove its nuclear missiles from Cuba. At the same
time, by removing U.S. missiles from Turkey and Italy, Kennedy allows his Kremlin counterpart, Nikita Khrushchev, to
save face.

The final deal with the Kremlin is secretly negotiated by
McCloy. By firmness and diplomacy, the world avoids a catastrophe far worse than even Hiroshima and Nagasaki.

In Japan in the late summer of 1945, government officials
burn documents that might be used to damn them in war
crimes trials, while soldiers returning to Japan loot the remaining stockpiles of food. Then supplies begin to arrive
from the United States—wheat, flour, corn, sugar, powdered
milk, tins of corned beef, even rice—"like a merciful rain
during a drought," according to one Japanese publication.

On September 27, Emperor Hirohito, wearing the formal
dress of a diplomat, calls on General MacArthur, the supreme
commander, who wears an open-necked khaki uniform, at
MacArthur's Tokyo headquarters near the palace. The two
men stand side by side for a photographer. MacArthur is respectful, but the photograph, printed in every newspaper in
Japan and the United States, makes it obvious who is in
charge.

On December 7, 1947, the sixth anniversary of Pearl Harbor, Hirohito visits Hiroshima and stands on the bridge at the
center of town targeted by the *Enola Gay*. The city has been
largely rebuilt. A band plays, and seventy thousand people

cheer. In October 1975, Hirohito visits the United States, and President Gerald Ford, who served in the navy during the Pacific War, gives a state dinner for the emperor, who expresses "everlasting friendship" with America. In 1978 the emperor learns that the names of fourteen wartime government leaders convicted as Class A war criminals have been added to the war dead honored at Tokyo's Yasukuni Shrine. The emperor never visits the shrine again.

Epilogue

Reckonings

W HEN WORD OF THE SUCCESSFUL ATTACK ON HIRO-
shima reached the scientists at Los Alamos on August 6,
Robert Oppenheimer was greeted at the base theater by a
roaring, foot-stomping crowd. The man who had done more
than any other to create the atomic bomb responded by clasp-
ing his hands over his head, like a boxing champion. At a
celebration party later that evening, a few couples danced,
but others just quietly talked and drank, unsure what to feel.
Off in one corner, Oppenheimer discussed a telex that had
just arrived from Washington with the first damage report.
The chief scientist grew depressed. As he left the party, he
saw a young scientist throwing up in the bushes. He said to
himself: "The reaction has begun."

But it had not, not yet. Most Americans approved of dropping two atomic bombs on Japan; some wished their coun-
trymen had dropped more. Many people—millions of veterans
returning home to their long-awaiting families—were grateful to have avoided an invasion. Their worries focused more

on whether Russia would get the bomb, or on whether they could find a new car or a house, a job or a spouse.

Then, on August 31, 1946, a year after Japan's surrender, *The New Yorker* published an entire issue devoted to an article by war correspondent John Hersey about the day the bomb fell on Hiroshima. Writing in a just-the-facts style, made more chilling by understatement, Hersey told the story, hour by hour, sometimes minute by minute, of six survivors. The details were at once quotidian and ghastly, and Hersey described, for the first time to most readers, the grim effects of radiation poisoning.

The article, entitled simply *Hiroshima,* caused an instant sensation. Radio announcers read all thirty thousand words aloud over the air. Editorial writers urged readers to get the full story, and the mayor of Princeton, New Jersey, urged the town's residents to do likewise. One Princeton resident, Albert Einstein, the scientist who, in 1939, had first alerted President Roosevelt to the potential of an atomic bomb, ordered a thousand copies. Hersey's article did not moralize or sensationalize. The journalist's contribution was to humanize what the air force publicists had always taken pains to keep abstract: civilian death.

James Conant, the president of Harvard University and a key player in the Manhattan Project, followed the Hersey *Hiroshima* furor with alarm. He was particularly bothered by a growing chorus of second-guessing from scientists and intellectuals. These were the people who would teach the next generation, he said, and he worried about weakening the resolve of future Cold War leaders. He also did not want his students to come of age thinking that James Conant—or any of the decent scientists who had worked so long and hard on "the gadget"—were some sort of war criminals. Conant wanted a high-profile, considered response, and he had in mind just the man to deliver it. "There is no one who can do this better than Henry Stimson," the Harvard president wrote to Stimson's former assistant, Harvey Bundy.

In the fall of 1946, Stimson was resting at Highhold, still recovering from a heart attack that had nearly killed him a month after he left Washington. Still, he dutifully took on the assignment. Working with Harvey Bundy's son McGeorge, the old lawyer crafted a masterful brief for the defense.* Like Hersey's *Hiroshima,* it was not tendentious, just a statement of fact. The Japanese had moved close to a million men and thousands of *kamikazes* of one kind or another (plane, torpedo, boat, frogman) into position in anticipation of an American invasion of Kyushu. The cost was projected to be several hundred thousand Americans killed or wounded. Dropping two atomic bombs, wrote Stimson, was "the least abhorrent choice." The article, which appeared in *Harper's Magazine* in the February 1947 issue, carried the cover headline "HENRY L. STIMSON EXPLAINS WHY WE USED THE ATOM BOMB."

The establishment's counterattack was effective. *The New York Times* promoted Stimson's *Harper's* article on its front page, and most of the mainstream media fell in line. Conventional wisdom congealed around Stimson's conclusion—that there really had been no other choice. So remained the narrative until revisionist scholars began poking at some gaps in the story. They noted that Stimson had glossed over his own on-again, off-again campaign to abandon unconditional surrender and allow the Japanese to retain their emperor, and that he omitted altogether the Truman administration's discussion of using the atomic bomb as a lever with the Soviets. Popular opinion about the destruction of Hiroshima and Nagasaki began to swing the other way. People started asking, were two bombs really necessary? And why not, first, a demonstration?

---

* The younger Bundy, at the time a junior fellow at Harvard, visited Highhold to help Stimson write his memoir, *On Active Service.* He was dean of the faculty at Harvard when President Kennedy tapped him to become his special assistant for national security.

From the very beginning, long before the revisionists weighed in, Stimson himself was uncomfortable with his role as Public Defender of the Atomic Bomb. In December 1946, after working up a draft of the *Harper's* essay with Bundy, Stimson wrote his old friend and onetime legal assistant, Supreme Court justice Felix Frankfurter, "I have rarely been connected with a paper about which I have so much doubt at the last moment." Stimson confessed, "I think the full enumeration of the steps in the tragedy will excite horror among friends who theretofore thought me a kindly-minded Christian gentleman but who will, after reading this, feel I am cold-blooded and cruel and different from the man who labored for peace under Mr. Hoover."

Justice Frankfurter read the draft article, slept on it for two nights, and essentially told his old boss to brace up. It was important to combat "sloppy sentimentality," Frankfurter wrote. The article would silence "self-righteous critics." Stimson, who disdained whiners, was duly chastened.

Still, Stimson was further unsettled when former acting secretary of state Joseph Grew wrote him after the publication of the *Harper's* article. Grew, the old Japan hand, reminded Stimson that, back in May 1945, the ex-ambassador to Tokyo had first urged President Truman to offer the Japanese a deal: surrender in exchange for retaining the emperor. Stimson had been sympathetic to Grew's suggestion but decided that the timing was off, that to offer terms too early was to show weakness. Now Grew basically argued that Stimson (and even more so, Grew's successor at State, Secretary Jimmy Byrnes) had blown a chance to achieve peace before dropping the A-bomb. "The atom bomb might never have been used at all," he wrote, and "the world would have been the gainer."

For six months, Stimson did not answer Grew, then sent him an uncharacteristically dodgy reply. But in his memoir, published in 1948, Stimson cryptically foretold what the revisionists would later proclaim, that "history might find that the United States, by its delay in stating its position [that Japan could keep its emperor], had prolonged the war."

In later years, two men who were close to Stimson—McGeorge Bundy and Jack McCloy—would say that they detected more than a few pangs of regret in their beloved Colonel about the decision to drop the atomic bomb. But were Stimson's guilt and anxiety justified?

The short answer is no. It is now clear from the memoirs and records of the men who governed Japan, as well as from the cable traffic between Foreign Minister Togo and Ambassador to Moscow Sato, that the Japanese government was nowhere close to welcoming the terms proposed by Joseph Grew in May 1945. Out of the military's long shadow, Togo might have entertained the offer, and the emperor and his chief advisers, principally Lord Kido, were beginning to look for an alternative to Armageddon. But the Japanese military, who by the Meiji constitution—as well as the threat of terror—actually controlled Japan, were adamant. They were determined to fight a final, all-out "decisive battle" to bleed the invaders until the *Americans* sued for peace. The military wanted not just to keep the emperor but to avoid an Allied occupation, disarmament, and war crimes trials. Notwithstanding their otherworldly death wishes, these men were not utterly deluded. No army has ever tried to land on a shore defended by millions of people so willing to die. Had the United States been forced to invade, the bloodbath would have been unbearable—to the American people, even before the besieged Japanese finally succumbed.

The atomic bombs did save lives. Yet Stimson's article is

wrong in one notable way. In the end, Little Boy and Fat Man probably did not save the lives of American and Allied soldiers because it is highly unlikely that the invasion of Kyushu, scheduled for November 1, would have taken place under the circumstances. According to accepted military doctrine, an amphibious force, to achieve a successful landing, must enjoy a three-to-one manpower advantage over dug-in defenders on shore. As Asia-Pacific War historian Richard Frank has shown, by the beginning of August 1945, MAGIC and ULTRA intercepts revealed that the two-to-one or three-to-one advantage in troops initially enjoyed by General MacArthur's massing invasion force had shrunk to one-to-one or worse. Although MacArthur stubbornly (or blithely) dismissed the intelligence indicating heavy Japanese reinforcements, Admiral King, the chief of naval operations, was fast backing off his provisional approval of an invasion. Even Army Chief of Staff Marshall, while committed to troops on the ground, was anxiously looking for workarounds, including the battlefield use of multiple nuclear weapons.

Instead of invading Japan, U.S. forces more likely would have starved the Japanese people. General Spaatz's new plan to replace "burn jobs" with precision bombing was aimed at Japan's railroad network carrying rice to the Kanto Plain around Tokyo, where most Japanese live. In August 1945, most Japanese were living off meager diets. By Christmastime, blockaded and strangled, the Japanese would have been starving to death by the millions, though the army, which had stockpiled food, would have starved last. In the most probable scenarios, Japan would have plunged into chaos and civil war—with opportunistic pot-stirring by the Russians, who invaded Sakhalin and the Kuril Islands north of Japan in late August and entertained larger ambitions, including a zone of occupation in the home islands, until Truman pressured them to back off. As soon as the American occupation began, the supreme commander, General MacArthur, delivered thousands of tons of food to the badly malnourished Japanese.

The atomic bombs not only saved many thousands and possibly millions of Japanese lives, they saved the lives of even more Asians beyond Japan. Under the unforgiving rule of the Imperial Japanese Army, Chinese, Southeast Asians, and Indonesians were dying at the rate of perhaps 250,000 a month. Had the war dragged on, it is horrific to imagine the dystopia that would have engulfed vast areas from Manchuria to Borneo. At admittedly terrible cost, the atomic bombs averted a far greater catastrophe. It is also likely that it took both atomic bombs—as well as a Soviet invasion of Manchuria—to shake the Japanese military's fanatical resolve and finally convert the emperor to the cause of peace, as well as his own self-preservation.

Possibly, one bomb was enough to persuade the emperor, but it took at least two to make the Japanese military realize that the threat of more bombs offered a face-saving excuse to surrender—a "gift from the Gods."* It is even more certain that a demonstration of the atomic bomb, if it was even practical, would have failed to impress the likes of General Anami. Though he got a hint from the intercepted cable traffic, Henry Stimson had no way of knowing the extent of Japanese intransigence. He may have imagined there were more

---

* The Japanese military knew from its own failed attempt to build an atomic bomb that even a single bomb required a fantastic and time-consuming effort. After grudgingly conceding that Hiroshima had been destroyed by an atomic bomb, some Japanese military leaders argued that the Americans could not possibly build more. Nagasaki showed them otherwise. Any delay in delivering that second bomb would have strengthened the hand of fanatics and possibly tipped the delicate balance against peace. As it was, the Americans in early August had only had two usable bombs, with a third coming later in the month.

"submerged liberals" than Foreign Minister Togo and a hand-
ful of peace-minded bureaucrats. But history has proved him
right that only a strong shock could make the Japanese surrender.

Stimson never lost his faith in what he called the Law of Moral
Progress—his belief that mankind was on a path from tyranny
to freedom, albeit with a few switchbacks. In war crimes trials, Secretary of War Stimson saw an opportunity to outlaw
war itself. As a federal prosecutor, he had used conspiracy laws
to reach corporate bosses who did not personally commit
crimes like fraud but who ran criminal enterprises that did. At
the Nuremberg war crimes trials in Germany, which began in
November 1945, Stimson's approach paid off. The criminal
syndicate that ran Nazi Germany really was a conspiracy, and
it kept records, including precise accountings of the Final Solution that resulted in the Holocaust that killed 6 million Jews.

The legal conspiracy approach was questionable when applied to Japan's wartime leaders. By contrast, local war crimes
trials were straightforward. After about fifty military tribunals
all over Asia, nearly a thousand Japanese army officers were
executed for specific atrocities, up to and including cannibal-
ism. But the main war crimes trial, the International Military
Tribunal for the Far East, held in Tokyo over more than two
years stretching into 1948, was on less solid ground. In a massive courtroom carved out of the old War Ministry at Ichigaya
Heights (with air conditioning installed), twenty-five senior
Japanese officials were tried for "crimes against peace." The
hope was to put the world on notice that the international
community would not tolerate wars of aggression—as opposed to defensive wars.

At the outset, the Americans decided to spare the emperor,
not just because his role in prosecuting the war was murky,

but also because Hirohito was needed as a symbol of stability; without the emperor as unifying figurehead, General MacArthur and his staff feared, Japan might collapse into a famine and chaos that would be exploited by Communists.

To the Japanese, the proceedings in Tokyo had a strong whiff of "victors' justice." The Japanese defendants in the dock could argue, with some merit, that they were being prosecuted because they had lost. The Japanese also argued that they were the victims of white man's justice, since almost all the judges were white men from colonial powers like Britain and its commonwealth, France, and the Netherlands, as well as the United States.*

The charge of conspiracy was a stretch: all the defendants were in the dock for a conspiracy to wage "aggressive war" that allegedly began in 1928 and ran until 1945—whether they were in the government or not.

Henry Stimson once compared the Japanese to "Dr. Jekyll and Mr. Hyde"—most of them intelligent and law abiding, until transformed into monsters, like the character in Robert Louis Stevenson's novella about the outwardly good doctor who drinks serum that makes him evil. Shigenori Togo never drank the potion, but he got swept in with the Mr. Hydes. He was not sent to the gallows, the fate of seven other defen-

---

* To be sure, crying "racism" was not exactly unimpeachable testimony, coming from the Japanese. The rigidly proud members of the "Yamato Race" viewed Chinese and Koreans—and certainly white people—as lesser beings, spiritually and physically deficient. Indeed, the Japanese were slow to develop radar in part because they prized their sharp night vision. In truth, each side brutally dehumanized the other. The British commander in Burma, Field Marshal Viscount William Slim, for instance, described the Japanese soldier as "the most formidable fighting insect in history."

dants, but he was sentenced to twenty years in prison, largely because as foreign minister at the time of Pearl Harbor, he did not resign from the government to stop the surprise attack.*

In five days of testimony, Togo tried to argue that he had seen no choice but to support the war, once his sincere and persistent efforts at diplomacy had failed. Resigning his post as foreign minister would have made no difference, he argued, and he was probably right. The war hawks would have just found a more pliant foreign minister.

During his days in court, Togo was consoled by the presence of his wife, Edy, and their daughter, Ise. They were quietly relieved when he was not sentenced to hang, like Prime Minister Tojo and others who led Japan into war. But Togo's family was allowed to visit him only twice a month in Sugamo prison, where Togo remained ill and largely alone.

He did not complain; indeed, after his sentencing, he seemed spiritually renewed. Instead of playing cards with the other inmates, he read ancient literature and composed poetry, examining mankind and looking forward to a day when the best of East and West would fuse into one civilization. He wrote Edy, in her native German, "Just like you, I am mentally strong. I have very often met this kind of dangerous situation. Even if I am compelled to end my life, my mind will not be disturbed. I will have a peaceful mind."

Drawing on his memory and testimony from the war crimes trials, he wrote his memoirs. He did not make excuses for his mistakes, but remained reverential to the emperor throughout, as well as forgiving of his nemesis General Anami. When his family visited him in prison in mid-July 1950, he handed them a stack of notebooks. The last paragraph reads:

---

* Togo was one of the fourteen "Class A war criminals" whose names were added to the list of honored war dead at Yasukuni Shrine in 1978.

Vividly before my eyes is the scene of the Imperial
Conference at which the Emperor decided for surrender, and my feeling of then returns to me: that while
the future of Japan is eternal, it is a blessing beyond
estimation that this most dreadful of wars has been
brought to a close, ending our country's agony and saving millions of lives; with that my life's work has been
done, it does not matter what befalls me.

Two weeks later, on July 23, 1950, Togo, aged sixty-seven,
died of a heart attack.

Riddled with arthritis, crippled by heart disease, Henry Stimson could no longer ride. He tried mounting a wooden horse,
to strengthen his limbs, but it was no use. On October 20,
1950, three months after Togo's death, Stimson, aged eighty-
three, also died of a heart attack. He was holding Mabel's
hand at the time, and he called out her name. At dinner,
Mabel continued to set a place for her husband.

Tooey Spaatz served briefly as the chief of the newly independent U.S. Air Force. He resisted the calls of some, like
General Groves, for a preventive attack on Russia, and if war
were to break out, he opposed the first use of nuclear weapons. When he retired, he turned down jobs in the defense
industry, in order to play cards and fish. He went on hunting
trips with his old flying buddies but did not carry a gun and
instead became an avid bird watcher. Increasingly, he had
trouble sleeping. At the end of his life, he drew close to his
granddaughter, Katharine, who was, like him, strong-willed

but reticent. He called her into his study one day and held her hand as he talked—for the first time in his life, he said—about the wrongness and folly of using nuclear weapons. He gave a familiar mournful sigh, she recalled—she had heard that sigh before, as her grandfather tried fitfully to doze in the afternoons. He seemed very sad.

Spaatz died of a stroke on July 14, 1974, at eighty-three, and was buried with full honors at the U.S. Air Force Academy, which he had helped to establish.

It is ironic that, of these three men, only the one on the losing side appeared to die in peace. Perhaps that is because Togo's overwhelming concern was to stop the killing and to save lives—to preserve the emperor, yes, but also to save all of Japan from apocalyptic suffering. Stimson and Spaatz were faced with the more anguishing conundrum of killing people—many, many thousands of people—to save many more people. Their job was made much harder by the death wish of intransigents like General Anami.

Because he believed—almost religiously—that civilization was morally perfectible, and that he was, by fortune of birth and education, obliged to lead, Stimson agonized to the end. He worried that the temptation of science—specifically the efficacy of the nuclear weapons he had helped to create— would outrun man's ability to make moral choices. Worn by time, he sometimes seemed to stagger under an impossible weight. Spaatz, by contrast, had a far more modest view of his own role, and he had the hard comfort of a soldier's duty. By day, this was usually enough. But, as he wrote his wife from his headquarters in Europe, he would worry, as he lay awake in the small hours past midnight, about the bombs he had loosed raining down on families not unlike his own. No wonder, as his own death approached, he could not sleep, but sometimes emitted a doleful sigh.

It is hard to imagine the pressure that these men faced in the spring and summer of 1945. The surrender of Japan came at a high cost. Decision makers on both sides engaged in wishful thinking and psychological denial, and peace of mind was hard for the victors to find. But Japan did surrender before hundreds of thousands—probably millions—more lives were lost. Stimson, Spaatz, and Togo gave mightily of themselves to bring peace, and at last they succeeded.

Acknowledgments

My interest in Japan's surrender, as well as the decision to drop the atomic bomb, is personal, as it is for many children of World War II veterans. For a long time, I believed that, had the United States not dropped atomic bombs on Hiroshima and Nagasaki, I might never have been born.

During World War II, my father, Evan W. Thomas II, was a junior-grade lieutenant in the U.S. Navy aboard an LST (Landing Ship, Tank). After service in Europe, including the D-Day landings, his ship was scheduled to head for the Pacific for the invasion of Japan. My mother went to visit him before he shipped out. She told her mother, "I hope I get pregnant." In her diary, her mother wrote, "I hope she doesn't." My grandmother was afraid my father would not make it back.

So in August 1945, when my family heard news of Japan's surrender, they rejoiced along with many others. My father, and thousands like him, would live.

It's a dramatic and familiar tale, but like many war stories, it glosses over more complicated truths. The actual story, I came to realize, is more surprising.

I want to thank the people who helped me to focus on and understand three characters who faced nearly impossible dilemmas in the summer of 1945.

I am grateful to Shigenori Togo's twin grandsons, Kazuhiro and Shigehiko, for sharing their research and memories with me. Kazu, who was himself a longtime Japanese foreign service officer, made available to me an unpublished paper he had written on Foreign Minister Togo's role in the surrender that included excerpts of his grandfather's private diary. The paper was translated for me by Brian Walsh, a Princeton Ph.D. who teaches international affairs at Kwansei Gakuin University in Japan and is a scholar, particularly, of the immediate postwar era in Japan. Brian carefully read my manuscript; his help and friendship have been invaluable. I was introduced to Brian by his former Princeton professor Paul Miles, a retired U.S. Army colonel who taught military history at West Point and Princeton for many years and who has long been a friend and adviser to me. Brian, in turn, led me to other scholars of the fall of the Japanese Empire: Peter Mauch of Western Sydney University, Roger Brown of Saitama University, and Shibayama Futoshi of Kwansei Gakuin University.

I am grateful for the advice and guidance of a number of other World War II historians. Rich Frank, the leading scholar of what he has correctly renamed the Asia-Pacific War, has been a wise and generous guide. Alex Wellerstein's research on what Truman knew—and didn't know—about the bombs and their targets was fascinating to me. I learned much about the complex politics of surrender from talking to Marc Gallicchio and reading his perceptive study *Unconditional.* Many thanks to Sheldon Garon for allowing me and my wife to attend an academic conference on Hiroshima's legacy, held at Princeton in the fall of 2015, that featured a range of experts including Wellerstein, Jeremy Yellen (insightful on the specter of revolution in Japan), and Sean Malloy, the leading scholar on Henry Stimson and the bomb. (Papers for the conference were later published as *The Age of Hiroshima,* edited by Michael D. Gordin, author of the valuable *Five Days in August,* and G. John Ikenberry.) Thanks, too, to Noriko Kawamura of Washington State University, author of *Emperor Hirohito,* for sharing with me her sympathetic insights about the emperor's role.

My happiest discovery was to learn, from a mutual friend,

that Katharine "Tatty" Gresham was writing a book about her grandfather, General Spaatz, whose understated leadership has been overlooked by historians. Tatty shared not only her draft manuscript but also letters and entries from her grandfather's war diary. I was educated about U.S. strategic bombing in World War II by two gifted experts at the Army War College, Tami Biddle and Conrad Crane. They vetted the manuscript, and Con Crane introduced me to Trevor Albertson, who has taught at the Air Force Command and Staff School and helped me understand the record of the often-misunderstood General Curtis LeMay. Thanks, too, to Jonathan Fanton, author of a fine dissertation on the clever but elusive Robert A. Lovett, and to Anne Karalekas, author of a forthcoming biography of Lovett, for talking with me.

My friend Al Kilborne, a gifted history teacher at Washington's Maret School—housed in the mansion that was, when Stimson lived there, known as Woodley—encouraged me and helped me empathize with the somewhat austere Colonel. Al introduced me to Eleanor Perkins, the last surviving family member to have really known Stimson. I enjoyed sharing Stimson stories with Ted Aldrich, who has written a joint biography of Stimson and George C. Marshall, *The Partnership,* published in 2022.

At the National Archives, thanks to Eric Van Slander for leading me to the war crimes trials and prison records of Shigenori Togo. As always, I am grateful to my friend Michael Hill, a master researcher; Mike, my wife, Oscie, and I have become a team over the years, enjoying many discoveries and many laughs. In Japan, Hideko Takayama, who became not just an enormous help but a good friend to Oscie and me when we were working on my earlier book *Sea of Thunder,* chipped in by reading a Japanese-language biography of General Anami by Fusako Tsunoda. My friend Jon Meacham brought me to Random House after we worked together for many years at *Newsweek*. How much I have enjoyed the pleasure of his company, and that of his wonderful family, too.

I am blessed to have an editor, Kate Medina, and an agent, Amanda Urban, who deserve to be the legends they are. At Random House, Kate's assistant, Louisa McCullough, is a joy to work with. I am grateful to the many pros at Random House, including Michael Hoak, Steve Messina, Ralph Fowler, Rebecca Berlant, Richard Elman, and Stacey Stein. Once again, Carol Poticny provided expert help with the photos. A shout-out, too, to Douglas Hallett, who brings his good lawyer's eye to my manuscripts.

My partner in all things, my beloved wife, Oscie, shaped (and whittled and refined) this book from beginning to end. Our daughters, Louisa and Mary, are an everlasting source of delight and wisdom.

Evan Thomas
Washington, May 2022

Bibliography

Addison, Paul, and Jeremy A. Crang. *Firestorm: The Bombing of Dresden, 1945.* London: Pimlico, 2006.

Aldrich, Edward Farley. *The Partnership: George Marshall, Henry Stimson, and the Extraordinary Collaboration That Won World War II.* Lanham, Md.: Stackpole Books, 2022.

Alperovitz, Gar. *The Decision to Use the Atomic Bomb.* New York: Vintage Books, 1995.

—————. "Was Harry Truman a Revisionist on Hiroshima?" *SHAFR Newsletter,* June 1998.

Alperovitz, Gar, Robert Messer, and Barton Bernstein. "Marshall, Truman, and the Decision to Drop the Bomb." *International Security* 16, no. 3 (Winter 1991–92).

Alvarez, Luis W. *Adventures of a Physicist.* New York: Basic Books, 1987.

Arnold, H. H. *Global Mission.* New York: Harper & Bros., 1949.

Asada, Sadao. "The Shock of the Atomic Bomb and Japan's Decision to Surrender: A Reconsideration." *Pacific Historical Review* 67, no. 4 (November 1998).

—————. Review of Hasegawa's *Racing the Enemy,* Hasegawa's response, and Asada's response to Hasegawa. *Journal of Strategic Studies* 29, no. 1 (February 2006): 169–79.

Atkinson, Rick. *The Guns at Last Light: The War in Western Europe, 1944–1945.* New York: Henry Holt, 2013.

Baime, A. J. *The Accidental President: Harry S. Truman and the Four Months That Changed the World.* New York: Houghton Mifflin, 2017.

Barrett, David Dean. *140 Days to Hiroshima: The Story of Japan's Last Chance to Avoid Armageddon.* New York: Diversion Books, 2020.

Benedict, Ruth. *The Chrysanthemum and the Sword: Patterns of Japanese Culture.* New York: Houghton Mifflin, 1946.

Bernstein, Barton. "American Foreign Policy and the Origins of the Cold War." In *Politics and Policies of the Truman Administration,* ed. Barton Bernstein. Chicago: Quadrangle Books, 1971.

—————. "The Atomic Bombings Reconsidered." *Foreign Affairs* 74, no. 1 (January–February, 1995).

—————. "Looking Back: Gen. Marshall and the Atomic Bombing of Japanese Cities," Arms Control Association, January 28, 2004, armscontrol.org/act/2015-11/features/looking-back-gen-marshall-atomic-bombing-japanese-cities.

—————. "The Making of the Atomic Admiral: 'Deak' Parsons and Modernizing the U.S. Navy," *Journal of Military History* 63, no. 2 (April 1999).

—————. "The Perils and Politics of Surrender: Ending the War with Japan and Avoiding the Third Atomic Bomb." *Pacific Historical Review* 46, no. 1 (February 1977), 1–27.

—————. "Roosevelt, Truman, and the Atomic Bomb, 1941–1945: A Reinterpretation." *Political Science Quarterly* 90, no. 1 (Spring 1975).

—————. "Seizing the Contested Terrain of Early Nuclear History: Stimson, Conant, and Their Allies Explain the Decision to Use the Atomic Bomb." *Diplomatic History* 17, no. 1 (Winter 1993).

—————. "Truman and the A-Bomb: Targeting Noncombatants, Using the Bomb, and Defending the 'Decision.'" *Journal of Military History* 62, no. 3 (July 1998).

—————. "Writing, Righting, or Wronging the Historical Record: President Truman's Letter on His Atomic-Bomb Decision." *Diplomatic History* 16 (1992).

Beschloss, Michael. *The Conquerors: Roosevelt, Truman, and the Destruction of Hitler's Germany.* New York: Simon & Schuster, 2002.

Biddle, Tami Davis. "Dresden 1945: Reality, History, and Memory." *Journal of Military History* 72, no. 2 (April 2008).

—————. "On the Crest of Fear: V-Weapons, the Battle of the Bulge, and the Last Stages of World War II in Europe." *Journal of Military History* 83, no. 1 (January 2019).

—————. *Rhetoric and Reality in Air Warfare: The Evolution of British and American Ideas in Strategic Bombing, 1914–1945.* Princeton: Princeton University Press, 2002.

Bird, Kai. *The Chairman: John J. McCloy and the Making of the American Establishment.* New York: Simon & Schuster, 1992.

—————. *Color of Truth: McGeorge Bundy and William Bundy, Brothers in Arms.* New York: Simon & Schuster, 2000.

Bird, Kai, and Martin Sherwin. *American Prometheus: The Triumph and Tragedy of J. Robert Oppenheimer.* New York: Vintage, 2005.

Bix, Herbert. *Hirohito and the Making of Modern Japan.* New York: HarperCollins, 2000.

————. "Japan's Delayed Surrender: A Reinterpretation." *Diplomatic History* 19, no. 2 (Spring 1995).

Bland, Larry, ed. *The Papers of George Catlett Marshall,* vol. 5. Baltimore: Johns Hopkins University Press, 2003.

Blume, Lesley M. M. *Fallout: The Hiroshima Cover-Up and the Reporter Who Revealed It to the World.* New York: Simon & Schuster, 2020.

Bonnett, John. "Jekyll and Hyde: Henry Stimson, '*Mentalité,*' and the Decision to Use the Atomic Bomb on Japan." *War in History* 4, no. 2 (April 1997).

Borneman, Walter. *The Admirals: The Five-Star Admirals Who Won the War at Sea.* New York: Little, Brown, 2012.

Brinkley, Alan. "The Good Old Days" (review of Hodgson's *The Colonel*). *New York Review of Books,* January 17, 1991.

Brooks, Lester. *Behind Japan's Surrender: The Secret Struggle That Ended an Empire.* New York: McGraw-Hill, 1968.

Brower, Charles. "Sophisticated Strategist: General George A. Lincoln and the Defeat of Japan, 1944–45." *Diplomatic History* 13, no. 3 (July 1991).

————. *Defeating Japan: The Joint Chiefs of Staff and Strategy in the Pacific War, 1943–1945.* New York: Palgrave Macmillan, 2012.

Brown, Daniel James. *Facing the Mountain: The True Story of Japanese American Heroes in World War II.* New York: Viking, 2021.

Brown, Roger. "Desiring to Inaugurate Great Peace: Yasuoka Masahiro, Kokutai Preservation, and Japan's Imperial Rescript of Surrender." Presentation to the Japanese History Study Group of the Institute of Social Sciences at Tokyo University, September 30, 2004, courtesy Roger Brown.

Bundy, McGeorge. *Danger and Survival: Choices About the Bomb in the First Fifty Years.* New York: Vintage Books, 1998.

Butcher, Harry C. *My Three Years with Eisenhower.* New York: Simon & Schuster, 1946.

Butow, Robert J. C. *Japan's Decision to Surrender.* Stanford, Calif.: Stanford University Press, 1954.

Byrnes, James F. *All in One Lifetime.* New York: Harper & Brothers, 1958.

Cary, Otis. "The Sparing of Mr. Stimson's 'Pet City.'" *Japan Quarterly* 22, no. 4 (October–December 1975).

Chase, James. "A Pragmatic Idealist" (review of Hodgson's *The Colonel*). *New York Times,* October 21, 1990.

Christman, Al. *Target Hiroshima: Deak Parsons and the Creation of the Atomic Bomb.* Annapolis, Md.: Naval Institute Press, 1998.

Christopher, Robert C. *The Japanese Mind*. New York: Fawcett, 1983.

Clodfelter, Mark. *Beneficial Bombing: The Progressive Foundations of American Air Power, 1917–1945*. Lincoln: University of Nebraska Press, 2010.

Compton, Arthur Holly. *Atomic Quest: A Personal Narrative*. London: Oxford University Press, 1956.

Conant, Jennet. *Man of the Hour: James B. Conant, Warrior Scientist*. New York: Simon & Schuster, 2017.

—————. *Tuxedo Park: A Wall Street Tycoon and the Secret Palace of Science That Changed the Course of World War II*. New York: Simon & Schuster, 2002.

Coox, Alvin. *Japan: The Final Agony*. New York: Ballantine Books, 1970.

Coster-Mullen, John. *Atom Bombs: The Top Secret Inside Story of Little Boy and Fat Man*. Privately published by the author, 2015.

Craig, Campbell, and Sergey Radchenko. *The Atomic Bomb and the Origins of the Cold War*. New Haven, Conn.: Yale University Press, 2008.

Craig, William. *The Fall of Japan*. New York: Galahad Books, 1967.

Crane, Conrad. *American Airpower Strategy in World War II: Bombs, Cities, Civilians, and Oil*. Lawrence: University Press of Kansas, 2016.

Craven, Wesley Frank, and James Lea Cate, eds. *The Army Air Forces in World War II*, vol. 5, *The Pacific: Matterhorn to Nagasaki, June 1944 to August 1945*. Chicago: University of Chicago Press, 1953.

Dalton, Kathleen. *Theodore Roosevelt: A Strenuous Life*. New York: Vintage, 2004.

Davis, Richard G. *Bombing the European Axis Powers: A Historical Digest of the Combined Bomber Offensive, 1939–1945*. Maxwell Air Force Base, Ala.: Air University Press, 2019.

—————. *Carl A. Spaatz and the Air War in Europe*. Washington, D.C.: Center for Air Force History, 1993.

Dobbs, Michael. *Six Months in 1945: FDR, Stalin, Churchill, and Truman—From World War to Cold War*. New York: Knopf, 2012.

Donovan, Robert. *Conflict and Crisis: The Presidency of Harry S Truman, 1945–1948*. New York: W. W. Norton, 1977.

Doolittle, James H. *I Could Never Be So Lucky Again*. New York: Bantam Books, 1991.

Dower, John W. *Embracing Defeat: Japan in the Wake of World War II*. New York: W. W. Norton, 1999.

—————. *War Without Mercy: Race and Power in the Pacific War*. New York: Pantheon, 1986.

Drea, Edward. *In the Service of the Emperor: Essays on the Imperial Japanese Army.* Lincoln: University of Nebraska Press, 1998.

————. *Japan's Imperial Army: Its Rise and Fall, 1853–1945.* Lawrence: University Press of Kansas, 2009.

————. *MacArthur's Ultra: Codebreaking and the War Against Japan, 1942–1945.* Lawrence: University Press of Kansas, 1992.

————. "Previews of Hell: Intelligence, the Bomb, and the Invasion of Japan." *American Intelligence Journal* 16, no. 1 (Spring–Summer 1995).

Fanton, Jonathan. "Robert Lovett: The War Years." Ph.D. diss., Yale University, 1978.

Feis, Herbert. *Japan Subdued: The Atomic Bomb and the End of the War in the Pacific.* Princeton, N.J.: Princeton University Press, 1961.

Ferrell, Robert H. *Dear Bess: The Letters from Harry to Bess Truman, 1910–1959.* New York: W. W. Norton, 1983.

————. *Harry S. Truman: A Life.* Columbia: University of Missouri Press, 1994.

————. *Harry S. Truman and the Cold War Revisionists.* Columbia: University of Missouri Press, 2006.

Forrest, Jerome. "The General Who Would Not Eat Grass." *Naval History* 9, no. 4 (July–August 1995).

Frank, Richard. *Downfall: The End of the Imperial Japanese Empire.* New York: Penguin, 1999.

————. "Ketsu Go." In Tsuyoshi Hasegawa, ed., *The End of the Pacific War: Reappraisals.* Stanford, Calif.: Stanford University Press, 2007.

————. *Tower of Skulls: The History of the Asia-Pacific War, July 1937–May 1942.* New York: W. W. Norton, 2020.

Gallicchio, Marc. "After Nagasaki: General Marshall's Plan for Tactical Nuclear Weapons in Japan." *Prologue* (Winter 1991).

————. *Unconditional: The Japanese Surrender in World War II.* New York: Oxford University Press, 2020.

Gardner, Lloyd. "Unconditional Surrender: The Dawn of the Atomic Age." In Dale Carter and Robin Clifton, eds., *War and Cold War in American Foreign Policy, 1952–1962.* New York: Palgrave Macmillan, 2002.

Gentile, Gian. "Shaping the Past Battlefield 'For the Future': The United States Strategic Bombing Survey's Evaluation of the American Air War Against Japan." *Journal of Military History* 64, no. 4 (October 2000).

Giangreco, D. M. "'A Score of Bloody Okinawas and Iwo Jimas': President Truman and Casualty Estimates for the Invasion of Japan." *Pacific Historical Review* 72, no. 1 (February 2003): 93–132.

————. *The Soldier from Independence: A Military Biography of Harry Truman*. Minneapolis: Zenith, 2009.

Giovannitti, Len, and Fred Freed. *The Decision to Drop the Bomb*. New York: Coward-McCann, 1965.

Gladwell, Malcolm. *The Bomber Mafia: A Dream, A Temptation, and the Longest Night of the Second World War*. New York: Little, Brown, 2021.

Gordin, Michael D. *Five Days in August: How World War II Became a Nuclear War*. Princeton, N.J.: Princeton University Press, 2007.

Gordin, Michael D., and G. John Ikenberry. *The Age of Hiroshima*. Princeton, N.J.: Princeton University Press, 2020.

Gordin, Michael D., et al. Roundtable on Tsuyoshi Hasegawa, *Racing the Enemy: Stalin, Truman, and the Surrender of Japan*. H-Diplo, January 16, 2006, https://issforum.org/roundtables/PDF/Gordin-Hasegawa Roundtable.pdf.

Green, Bob. *Duty: A Father, His Son, and the Man Who Won the War*. New York: William Morrow, 2000.

Gresham, Katharine. *General Tooey*. Unpublished manuscript.

Groves, Leslie M. *Now It Can Be Told: The Story of the Manhattan Project*. New York: Harper & Brothers, 1962.

Hachiya, Michihiko. *Hiroshima Diary: The Journal of a Japanese Physician, August 6–September 30, 1945*. Chapel Hill: University of North Carolina Press, 1955.

Ham, Paul. *Hiroshima and Nagasaki: The Real Story of the Atomic Bombings and Their Aftermath*. New York: St. Martin's, 2014.

Hamby, Alonzo. "Harry S. Truman: Insecurity and Responsibility." In Fred Greenstein, ed., *Leadership in the Modern Presidency*. Cambridge, Mass.: Harvard University Press, 1988.

————. *Man of the People: A Life of Harry S. Truman*. New York: Oxford, 1995.

Hansell, Heywood S. *The Strategic Air War Against Germany and Japan: A Memoir*. Washington, D.C.: Office of Air Force Studies, 1986.

Hasegawa, Tsuyoshi, ed. *The End of the Pacific War: Reappraisals*. Stanford, Calif.: Stanford University Press, 2007.

————. *Racing the Enemy: Stalin, Truman, and the Surrender of Japan*. Cambridge, Mass.: Harvard University Press, 2005.

Hastings, Max. *Retribution: The Battle for Japan, 1944–1945*. New York: Vintage, 2007.

Hata, Ikuhiko. *Hirohito: The Showa Emperor in War and Peace.* Kent, Conn.: Globe Oriental, 2007.

Heinrichs, Waldo. *American Ambassador: Joseph Grew and the Development of the United States Diplomatic Tradition.* New York: Oxford University Press, 1966.

Heinrichs, Waldo, and Marc Gallicchio. *Implacable Foes: War in the Pacific, 1944–1945.* New York: Oxford, 2017.

Hersey, John. *Hiroshima.* New York: Knopf, 1946.

Hershberg, James G. *James B. Conant: Harvard to Hiroshima and the Making of the Nuclear Age.* Stanford, Calif.: Stanford University Press, 1993.

Hodgson, Godfrey. *The Colonel: The Life and Wars of Henry Stimson, 1867–1950.* New York: Knopf, 1990.

Holloway, David. *Stalin and the Bomb.* New Haven, Conn.: Yale University Press, 1994.

Hotta, Eri. *Japan 1941.* New York: Vintage, 2014.

Ienaga, Saburo. *The Pacific War, 1931–1945: A Critical Perspective on Japan's Role in World War II.* New York: Pantheon, 1978.

Iokibe, Makato. "American Policy Towards Japan's 'Unconditional Surrender.'" *Japanese Journal of American Studies,* no. 1 (1981).

Isaacson, Walter, and Evan Thomas. *The Wise Men: Six Friends and the World They Made.* New York: Simon & Schuster, 1986.

Jordan, David M. *Robert A. Lovett and the Development of American Air Power.* Jefferson, N.C.: McFarland & Co., 2019.

Jordan, Jonathan W. *American Warlords: How Roosevelt's High Command Led America to Victory in World War II.* New York: New American Library, 2015.

Kawamura, Noriko. *Emperor Hirohito and the Pacific War.* Seattle: University of Washington Press, 2015.

Kelly, Cynthia, ed. *The Manhattan Project: The Birth of the Atomic Bomb in the Words of Its Creators, Eyewitnesses, and Historians.* New York: Black Dog, 2007.

Kelly, Jason. "Why Did Stimson Spare Kyoto from the Bomb? Confusion in Postwar Historiography." *Journal of American–East Asian Relations* 19 (2012).

Kido, Koichi. *The Diary of Marquis Kido, 1931–1945: Selected Translations into English.* Frederick, Md: University Publications of America, 1984.

Kiyotada, Tsutsui, ed. *Fifteen Lectures on Showa Japan: Road to the Pacific War in Recent Historiography.* Tokyo: Japan Publishing Industry Foundation for Culture, 2016.

Knebel, Fletcher, and Charles W. Bailey II. *No High Ground: The Complete Eye Opening True Story of the First Atomic Bomb.* New York: Harper & Brothers, 1960.

Kort, Michael. *The Columbia Guide to Hiroshima and the Atom Bomb.* New York: Columbia University Press, 2007.

Koshiro, Yukiko. *Imperial Eclipse: Japan's Strategic Thinking About Continental Asia Before August 1945.* Ithaca, N.Y.: Cornell University Press, 2013.

Kozak, Warren. *LeMay: The Life and Wars of General Curtis LeMay.* Washington, D.C.: Regnery, 2009.

Krauss, Robert, and Amelia Krauss, eds. *The 509th Remembered: A History of the 509th Composite Group as Told by the Veterans That Dropped the Atomic Bombs on Japan.* Privately printed, 2005.

Kunetka, James. *The General and the Genius: Groves and Oppenheimer: The Unlikely Partnership That Built the Bomb.* Washington, D.C.: Regnery, 2015.

Lanouette, William. *Genius in the Shadows: A Biography of Leo Szilard, the Man Behind the Bomb.* New York: Skyhorse, 2013.

Larrabee, Eric. *Commander in Chief: Franklin Delano Roosevelt, His Lieutenants, and Their War.* Annapolis, Md.: Naval Institute Press, 1987.

———. "Why We Dropped the Bomb." *Civilization,* January–February 1995.

Laurence, William L. *Dawn over Zero.* New York: Knopf, 1947.

Leahy, William D. *I Was There: The Personal Story of the Chief of Staff to Presidents Roosevelt and Truman.* New York: McGraw-Hill, 1950.

LeMay, Curtis, with MacKinlay Kantor. *Mission with LeMay: My Story.* New York: Doubleday, 1965.

Lifton, Robert Jay, and Greg Mitchell. *Hiroshima in America: A Half Century of Denial.* New York: Avon Books, 1995.

Maddox, Robert. *The United States and World War II.* New York: Routledge, 1992.

Malloy, Sean. *Atomic Tragedy: Henry L. Stimson and the Decision to Use the Bomb Against Japan.* Ithaca, N.Y.: Cornell University Press, 2008.

———. "'A Very Pleasant Way to Die': Radiation Effects and the Decision to Use the Atomic Bomb Against Japan." *Diplomatic History* 36, no. 3 (June 2012).

———. "'The Rules of Civilized Warfare': Scientists, Soldiers, Civilians, and American Nuclear Targeting, 1940–1945." *Journal of Strategic Studies* 30, no. 3 (June 2007).

Mauch, Peter. " 'Our Islands Are Being Violated One After the Other': Emperor Hirohito's Prayerful Reports to His Imperial Ancestors, October 1937–August 1945." *Japan Studies Review* 23 (2019).

————. "The Showa Political Crisis, July 1940: The Imperial Japanese Army Courts a Breach with Its Sovereign." *War in History* 27, no. 4 (2019).

McCullough, David. *Truman.* New York: Simon & Schuster, 1992.

McNamara, Craig. *Because Our Fathers Lied.* New York: Little, Brown, 2022.

Mets, David R. *Master of Airpower: General Carl A. Spaatz.* Novato, Calif.: Presidio Press, 1988.

Miles, Paul. "Marshall as a Grand Strategist." In Charles Brower, ed., *George C. Marshall: Servant of the American Nation.* New York: Palgrave Macmillan, 2011.

Miller, Donald L. *Masters of the Air: America's Bomber Boys Who Fought the Air War Against Nazi Germany.* New York: Simon & Schuster, 2006.

Miller, Richard Lawrence. *Truman: The Rise to Power.* New York: McGraw-Hill, 1986.

Minohara, Tosh. " 'No Choice But to Rise': Togo Shigenori and Japan's Decision for War." In Masato Kimura and Tosh Minohara, eds., *Tumultuous Decade: Empire, Society, and Diplomacy in 1930s Japan.* Toronto: University of Toronto Press, 2013.

Miscamble, Wilson D. *The Most Controversial Decision: Truman, the Atomic Bombs, and the Defeat of Japan.* New York: Cambridge University Press, 2011.

Morison, Elting E. *Turmoil and Tradition: A Study of the Life and Times of Henry L. Stimson.* New York: Atheneum, 1960.

Newman, Robert. "Hiroshima and the Trashing of Henry Stimson." *New England Quarterly* 71, no. 1 (March 1998).

————. *Truman and the Hiroshima Cult.* East Lansing: Michigan State University Press, 1995.

Nolan, James L., Jr. *Atomic Doctors: Conscience and Complicity at the Dawn of the Nuclear Age.* Cambridge, Mass.: Harvard University Press, 2020.

Norris, Robert S. *Racing for the Bomb: The True Story of General Leslie R. Groves, the Man Behind the Birth of the Atomic Age.* New York: Skyhorse, 2002.

O'Brien, Phillips Payson. *The Second Most Powerful Man in the World: The Life of Admiral William D. Leahy, Roosevelt's Chief of Staff.* New York: Dutton, 2019.

Oi, Mariko. "The Man Who Saved Kyoto from the Atomic Bomb." BBC News, August 9, 2015.

O'Reilly, Bill. *Killing the Rising Sun: How America Vanquished World War II Japan.* New York: Henry Holt, 2016.

Pacific War Research Society. *Japan's Longest Day.* Tokyo: Kodansha, 1965.

Pellegrino, Charles. *To Hell and Back: The Last Train from Hiroshima.* New York: Rowman & Littlefield, 2015.

Pringle, Henry. "The Laird of Woodley." *New Yorker,* October 4, 1930.

Ralph, William. "Improvised Destruction: Arnold, LeMay, and the Fire-bombing of Japan." *War in History* 13, no. 4 (2006).

Reston, James. *Deadline.* New York: Random House, 1991.

Rhodes, Richard. *The Making of the Atomic Bomb.* New York: Simon & Schuster, 1986.

Robertson, David. *Sly and Able: A Political Biography of James F. Byrnes.* New York: W. W. Norton, 1994.

Roll, David L. *George Marshall: Defender of the Republic.* New York: Dutton Caliber, 2019.

Rovere, Richard. "The American Establishment." *Esquire,* May 1962. Reprinted in *Wilson Quarterly,* Summer 1978.

Ruoff, Kenneth J. *Japan's Imperial House in the Postwar Era, 1945–2019.* Cambridge, Mass.: Harvard University Asia Center, 2020.

Sayle, Murray. "Sex Saddens a Clever Princess." Japan Policy Research Institute Working Paper no. 66, April 2000.

Schmitz, David F. *Henry L. Stimson: The First Wise Man.* Wilmington, Del.: Scholarly Resources, 2001.

Sherry, Michael S. *The Rise of American Air Power: The Creation of Armageddon.* New Haven, Conn.: Yale University Press, 1987.

Sherwin, Martin J. *Gambling with Armageddon: Nuclear Roulette from Hiroshima to the Cuban Missile Crisis.* New York: Knopf, 2020.

————. *A World Destroyed: Hiroshima and the Origins of the Arms Race.* New York: Vintage, 1987.

Shoji, Junichiro. "The Japanese Termination of War in WWII: The Significance and Causal Factors of 'The End of War.'" *International Forum on War History: Proceedings* (2015).

Sigal, Leon V. *Fighting to the Finish: The Politics of War Termination in the United States and Japan, 1945.* Ithaca, N.Y.: Cornell University Press, 1988.

Spector, Ronald. *Eagle Against the Sun: The American War with Japan.* New York: Free Press, 1985.

Stimson, Henry. "The Challenge to Americans." *Foreign Affairs* 26, no. 1 (October 1946).

——. "The Decision to Use the Atomic Bomb." *Harper's Magazine,* February 1947.

——. *My Vacations.* Privately printed, 1949.

——. "The Nuremberg Trial: Landmark in the Law." *Foreign Affairs* 27, no. 2 (January 1947).

Stimson, Henry, and McGeorge Bundy. *On Active Service in Peace and War.* New York: Harper & Brothers, 1947.

Sweeney, Charles W. *War's End: An Eyewitness Account of America's Last Atomic Mission.* New York: Avon, 1997.

Tamon, Suzuki. "Emperor Hirohito's 'Sacred Decision' and the Political Process of Japan's Surrender." In Tsutsui Kiyotada, ed., *Fifteen Lectures on Showa Japan: Road to the Pacific War in Recent Historiography.* Tokyo: Japan Publishing Industry Foundation for Culture, 2016.

Thomas, Evan. *Sea of Thunder: Four Commanders and the Last Great Naval Campaign, 1941–1945.* New York: Simon & Schuster, 2006.

Thomas, Gordon, and Max Morgan Witts. *Enola Gay.* New York: Stein & Day, 1977.

Tibbets, Paul W. *The Tibbets Story.* New York: Day Books, 1981.

Togo, Kazuhiko. "Foreign Minister Togo's Bitter Struggle." Unpublished manuscript.

Togo, Shigenori. *The Cause of Japan.* New York: Simon & Schuster, 1952.

Toland, John. *The Rising Sun: The Decline and Fall of the Japanese Empire, 1936–1945.* New York: Modern Library, 1970.

Toll, Ian. *Twilight of the Gods: War in the Western Pacific, 1944–1945.* New York: W. W. Norton, 2020.

Truman, Margaret, ed. *Where the Buck Stops: The Personal and Private Writings of Harry S. Truman.* New York: Time Warner, 1989.

Walker, J. Samuel. *Prompt and Utter Destruction: Truman and the Use of Atomic Bombs Against Japan.* Chapel Hill: University of North Carolina Press, 1997.

Walker, Steven. *Shockwave: Countdown to Hiroshima.* New York: HarperPerennial, 2005.

Walsh, Brian. "Japanese Foreign Ministry's Document Destruction Order of 7 August 1945." Research Note. *Journal of American–East Asian Relations* 26 (2019).

Weigley, Russell F. *Eisenhower's Lieutenants: The Campaign of France and Germany, 1944–1945.* Bloomington: University of Indiana Press, 1990.

Weisman, Steven R. "Japan's Imperial Present." *New York Times Magazine,* August 26, 1990.

Wellerstein, Alex. "The Kyoto Misconception: What Truman Knew, and Didn't Know, About Hiroshima." In Michael Gordin and John Ikenberry, eds., *The Age of Hiroshima* (Princeton, N.J.: Princeton University Press, 2020).

————. "A 'Purely Military' Target? Truman's Changing Language About Hiroshima." *Restricted Data,* January 19, 2018, nuclearsecrecy .com.

————. "Tokyo v. Hiroshima." *Restricted Data,* September 22, 2014, nuclearsecrecy.com.

Werrell, Kenneth P. *Blankets of Fire: U.S. Bombers over Japan During World War II.* Washington, D.C.: Smithsonian, 1996.

Wetzler, Peter. *Imperial Japan and Defeat in the Second World War.* London: Bloomsbury Academic, 2020.

Wortman, Marc. *The Millionaires' Unit: The Aristocratic Flyboys Who Fought the Great War and Invented American Air Power.* New York: PublicAffairs, 2006.

Wyden, Peter. *Day One: Before Hiroshima and After.* New York: Simon & Schuster, 1984.

Yellen, Jeremy. "The Specter of Revolution: Reconsidering Japan's Decision to Surrender." *International History Review* 35, no. 1 (2013).

Yoshida, Shigeru. *Memoirs.* Boston: Houghton Mifflin, 1962.

Notes

List of Abbreviations

AHF	Atomic Heritage Foundation, atomicheritage.org
Bundy File	Harrison Bundy, Files Relating to the Development of the Atom Bomb, 1942–46, Records of the Chief of Engineers, NA II
HSTL	Harry S. Truman Library and Museum, TrumanLibrary .gov
LOC	Library of Congress
McCloy Papers	John J. McCloy Papers, Amherst College Library
NA II	National Archives, College Park, Md.
NSA	National Security Archive, George Washington University, nsarchive.gwu.edu
Spaatz Papers	Carl Spaatz Papers, LOC
Stimson File	Records of the Office of the Secretary of War, Top Secret Correspondence, 7/1940–49/1945, NA II
Stimson Papers	Henry Lewis Stimson Papers, Yale University Library

Introduction: The Dilemma

xi *"We were going to live"*: Paul Fussell, "Thank God for the Atomic Bomb," *New Republic,* August 1981.

xii *popular currency:* For polling on public attitudes, see Bruce Stokes, "70 Years After Hiroshima, Opinions Have Shifted on Use of Atomic Bomb," Pew Research Center, August 5, 2015.

xiii *actors caught in a dilemma:* Many commentators attribute moral confusion and hypocrisy to the decision to drop the bomb. This charge is often leveled at Henry Stimson, a central figure in this book. Biographer Godfrey Hodgson labeled Stimson "morally perplexed and intellectually confused." Hodgson, *Colonel,* 337. See also Sherry, *Rise of American Air Power,* 269. For a more sympathetic and, I believe, accurate analysis, focusing on Stimson's "psychology of combat," which emphasized seizing the initiative and never letting up, see Bonnett, "Jekyll and Hyde." Bonnett also astutely observes, "As far as he [Stimson] was concerned, living with moral ambiguity was part of the job" (196). According to many commentators, racism may have been a factor, although not a determinative one for the leaders involved. Bernstein, "Atomic Bomb Reconsidered," notes that "the earlier moral insistence on noncombatant immunity crumbled during the savage war" and adds: "It may have been easier to conduct this new warfare outside Europe and against Japan because its people seemed like 'yellow sub-humans' to many rank-and-file American citizens and many of their leaders" (140). On the other hand, the bomb was built in a race against the Germans' own nuclear program, and had it been ready in time to use against Germany, I have no doubt the United States would have used it. I. I. Rabi, one of the scientists who worked on the bomb, said that if the bomb had been ready six months earlier, "Roosevelt would have had to use it against Berlin. It would have been criminal not to." Newhouse, *War and Peace in the Nuclear Age,* 42. In September 1944, when Col. Paul Tibbets was given command of the 509th Composite Group that dropped the bomb, he was instructed to prepare for simultaneous bomb drops on Germany and Japan. "General Paul Tibbets: Reflections on Hiroshima," Voices of the Manhattan Project, National Museum of Nuclear Science & History (1989).

xiii *the word* **decision**: It is hard to overstate the level of controversy among historians over the decision to drop the bomb, starting with whether there even was a "decision." Especially in 1995, at the time of the fiftieth anniversary of Hiroshima, historians waged an intense debate over the question of why the United States used the bomb. See J. Samuel Walker, "Recent Literature on Truman's Atomic Bob Decision: A Search for the Middle Ground," *Diplomatic History* 29 (April 2005): 311–34. The classic revisionist is Gar Alperovitz (see his updated *Decision to Use the Atom Bomb*); the leading postrevisionists are Barton Bernstein, author of numerous academic articles; Tsuyoshi Hasegawa (*Racing the Enemy*); and most persuasive to me, Richard Frank (*Downfall*). A thorough recent narrative treatment, drawing on Frank as well as Lester Brooks (*Behind Japan's Surrender*), is David Dean Barrett's *140 Days to Hiroshima*. An excellent current website on all things atomic is Alex Wellerstein's *Restricted Data* blog, nuclearsecrecy.com. Extensive atomic bomb documents are digitized by the National Security Archive (nsarchive.gwu.edu), the Atomic Heritage Foundation (atomicheritage.org), and the Truman Library (Trumanlibrary.gov). A good summary of "The Debate Over the Japanese Surrender," with an interview of the leading historiographer of the bomb, J. Samuel Walker, can be found at AHF. A balanced approach to the "complexity, the uncertainty, the sheer messiness of policy making"—and to the difficult moral choice—is Miscamble, *Most Controversial Decision.*

xiii *"psychic numbing":* The concept comes from Dr. Robert J. Lifton. See Lifton and Mitchell, *Hiroshima in America.* The best illustration is the quote attributed to Stalin, "One death is a tragedy; a million deaths is a statistic." For an interesting study of a man who repressed his emotions in a good cause—"Deak" Parsons, the armorer on the *Enola Gay*—see Bernstein, "Making of the Atomic Admiral."

xiii *"If you kill enough":* Kozak, *LeMay;* LeMay, *Mission with LeMay.* For a vivid recent portrait, see Gladwell, *Bomber Mafia.*

xiv *a dozen hospital ships:* By the end of World War II, the United States had fifteen hospital ships in the Pacific. "Benevolence in Tokyo Bay: the USS Benevolence (AH-13)," National World War II Museum, nationalww2museum.org.

xiv *fudge the numbers:* Heinrichs and Gallicchio, *Implacable Foes,* 478. Meeting with President Truman on June 18, General Marshall estimated about thirty-one thousand casualties—killed and wounded—in the first thirty days of the invasion of Kyushu, code-named Operation Olympic. Many scholars now believe that number was lowballed by about a factor of ten. "The evasive and in some cases deliberately misleading manner in which the president's advisers dealt with the casualty projections is troubling to say the least," write Heinrichs and Gallicchio. "The most that can be said of this effort to attach the number to the proposed invasion is that it demonstrated that Marshall was prepared to massage the figures in order to gain approval for OLYMPIC."

xiv *"Mr. President, I feel":* Bird and Sherwin, *American Prometheus,* 332. Oppenheimer was frustrated that Truman did not seem to grasp where nuclear technology was heading. Oppenheimer's conflicted passions are at the heart of two Pulitzer Prize–winning books, Bird and Sherwin's biography and Rhodes's *Making of the Atomic Bomb.*

xiv *"like a little boy":* Newman, *Truman and the Hiroshima Cult,* 43.

Truman went to great lengths to defend his role and sometimes exaggerated it. From Hasegawa, *Racing the Enemy*:

> Referring to this directive [to drop the A-bomb], Truman later noted in his memoirs: "With this order the wheels were set in motion for the first use of an atomic weapon against a military target. I had made the decision. I also instructed Stimson that the order would stand unless I notified him that the Japanese reply to our ultimatum was acceptable." This three-sentence paragraph is full of truths and half-truths. The atomic bomb was not targeted specifically "against a military target." The order was to prepare not only a single "atomic weapon" but also "additional bombs." But the most important point is that Truman did not issue any order to drop the bomb. In fact, he was not involved in this decision but merely let the military proceed without his interference. (152)

According to Malloy, *Atomic Tragedy*: "Truman's later recollections of the deliberations on the atomic bomb at Potsdam are so filled with errors as to be virtually useless" (216n54). On Truman's need to show himself in control, see Gordin, *Five Days in August*:

> Truman's need to be in control of events, or to be perceived in control of them, is a theme that runs through almost all biographical studies of him and his personality. See, for example, Alonzo L. Hamby, "Harry S. Truman: Insecurity and Responsibility," in Fred I. Greenstein, ed., *Leadership in the Modern Presidency* (Cambridge, Mass.: Harvard University Press, 1988), 41–75, on 55; idem, "An American Democrat, A Re-Evalution of the Personality of Harry S. Truman," *Political Science Quarterly* 106 (1991): 33–55; Barton J. Bernstein, "Writing, Righting, or Wronging the Historical Record: President Truman's Letter on His Atomic-Bomb Decision," *Diplomatic History* 16 (1992): 163–73, on 172; and Sherwin, *A World Destroyed*, 147–48. (164n37)

See also Bernstein, "Truman and the A-Bomb," for an overview of Truman's role.

xv **Henry L. Stimson:** His diaries and papers are at the Yale University Library and at LOC (on microfilm). The most thoroughgoing, insightful scholar on Stimson is Sean Malloy (*Atomic Tragedy*). Malloy suggests that Stimson missed opportunities both to end the war before using nuclear weapons and to achieve arms control. I agree that Stimson, elderly and worn, was not always at the top of his game in this period, but I am more sympathetic to him given the difficulty of his situation—the near impossibility of dealing with either the Japanese or the Russians. Stimson was engaged in a real-time balancing act and in the end was right to believe that only a real shock would bring the Japanese leaders to their senses. For a persuasive discussion of Stimson's realism and idealism, see Chase, "Pragmatic Idealist."

xvi *Gen. Carl "Tooey" Spaatz:* His papers, including a war diary, are in LOC. I am indebted to his granddaughter, Katharine Gresham, for sharing a draft of her forthcoming biography of General Spaatz, *General Tooey,* which includes letters that are not in his papers at the LOC.

xvii *Emperor Hirohito remains:* For his role, compare the revisionist view in Bix, *Hirohito,* and the defense of Hirohito in Kawamura, *Emperor Hirohito.* For the need to critically examine the testimony of Japanese officials, see Asada, "Shock of the Bomb." At a conference on the atomic bomb at Princeton in October 2015, Yukiko Koshiro, a leading Japanese scholar (*Imperial Eclipse: Japan's Strategic Thinking About Continental Asia Before August 1945*), told me that the testimony of some court defenders, like Lord Kido, the keeper of the privy seal, was useless. I disagree with this assessment but heed the caution.

xvii *Foreign Minister Shigenori Togo:* His memoir is *Cause of Japan.* His grandsons Kazuhiko Togo and Shigehiko Togo shared portions of his diary and correspondence with me. Kazu Togo also gave me a monograph he wrote about his grandfather, translated for me by Dr. Brian Walsh, adjunct professor of International Studies at Kwansei Gakuin University in Japan.

Chapter 1: Sleepless

Stimson's diaries are in Stimson Papers.

3 *resolute personal integrity:* Malloy, *Atomic Tragedy,* 5; Hodgson, *Colonel,* 17.

3 *"stood outside":* On Stimson's investment wealth, see Stimson and Bundy, *On Active Service,* 108; Conant, *Tuxedo Park,* 72.

4 *colonial administrator:* Stimson and Bundy, *On Active Service,* 138.

4 *Stimson bought Woodley:* Morison, *Turmoil and Tradition,* 254; Stimson and Bundy, *On Active Service,* 160.

4 *Stimson cannot sleep:* On Stimson's insomnia, see Morison, *Turmoil and Tradition,* 72.

5 *on the day of Pearl Harbor:* Jordan, *American Warlords,* 4.

5 *His mother died:* Stimson and Bundy, *On Active Service,* xii; Morison, *Turmoil and Tradition,* 21.

5 *Phillips Academy in Andover:* See Frederick Allis, Jr., *Youth from Every Quarter: A Bicentennial History of Phillips Academy* (Andover, Mass.: Phillips Academy, 1979).

5 *hunting grizzly bears:* Morison, *Turmoil and Tradition,* 71; Stimson, *My Vacations,* 1.

6 *"the only way you can make a man":* Isaacson and Thomas, *Wise Men,* 181.

7 *"reading other gentlemen's":* Stimson and Bundy, *On Active Service,* 188; Hodgson, *Colonel,* 203.

7 *MAGIC and ULTRA:* Frank, *Downfall,* 104–5.

7 *to ban submarines:* Malloy, *Atomic Tragedy,* 13, 33.

8 *"chasing a vagrant sunbeam":* On Stimson's dislike of FDR's deviousness, see Stimson and Bundy, *On Active Service,* 376; Hodgson, *Colonel,* 231. In 1941 FDR had appointed Stimson his secretary of war, less to gain his advice than to use Stimson, a respected Republican, as a cover against inquiring congressmen. FDR made his own policy and left various other jobs to Stimson. One of them was to keep Congress from meddling with the secret atomic bomb project. When FDR died, Stimson became, in effect, in charge of the bomb and the crash education of Harry Truman.

8 *"Why, you old Republican":* Bird, *Chairman,* 120.

9 *She was wounded:* Mabel was depressed by the prolonged engagement. See Morison, *Turmoil and Tradition,* 45–49.

9 *"New England conscience on legs":* Ibid., 84.

9 *hates to be physically touched:* Ibid., 25.

10 *blamed him for his mother's death:* Ibid., 19.

10 *"he never slumped:"* Eleanor Perkins (Stimson's niece), interview by author.

10 **Marshall and Stimson:** Stimson and Bundy, *On Active Service*, 442–43.

10 **door between their adjoining offices:** Jordan, *American Warlords*, 39.

11 **"the Imps of Satan":** Isaacson and Thomas, *Wise Men*, 192–95.

11 **McCloy and Lovett great authority:** On Stimson's warm relationship with his aides, see Stimson and Bundy, *On Active Service*, 340–44; Malloy, *Atomic Tragedy*, 43.

12 **Allied firebombing of this ancient:** On the bombing of Dresden, see Crane, *American Airpower Strategy*, 159; and Miller, *Masters of Air*, 444. Biddle, "On the Crest of Fear," offers useful context. Addison and Crang, *Firestorm*, is the best recent compendium study of Dresden. The classic treatment is Frederick Taylor's *Dresden* (reprint New York: HarperPerennial, 2005). An excellent overview is Biddle, "Dresden 1945."

12 **"the least Prussianized part":** On Stimson's pressure for an investigation of Dresden, see Bland, *Papers of Marshall*, 5:79–80.

13 **"dehousing":** "Having one's house demolished is most damaging to morale," wrote Winston Churchill's science adviser, Lord Cherwell, formerly Dr. Adolphus Lindemann, in "Dehousing Memorandum," March 1942. Ham, *Hiroshima and Nagasaki,* 50. The British, again without irony, believed that bombing a population would have a profound economic effect since workers would be displaced and disoriented if not killed outright. Tami Biddle, interview by author.

14 **"dipping down":** Stimson and Bundy, *On Active Service*, 453.

15 **"the Yale Unit":** Wortman, *Millionaires' Unit*, 46.

15 **Stimson depends on Lovett:** Stimson and Bundy, *On Active Service*, 468. Stimson told Lovett, "The next time anyone asks you what your authority is, you just tell them that whatever authority the Secretary of War has, you have." Fanton, "Robert Lovett," 56. Recommending Lovett for a decoration after the war, Stimson wrote, "He has truly been my eyes, ears, and hands in respect to the growth of that enormous airpower which had so astonished the world." "Decorations for Civilian Officers in the War Department," Stimson File, NA II.

15 **break civilian morale:** On Lovett's wish to break German morale, see Fanton, "Robert Lovett," 145; Isaacson and Thomas, *Wise Men*, 205–9; and "Army's Lovett," *Time*, February 9, 1942. Lovett affected a gallows humor. After being shown photographs of a British urban

area attack, Lovett wrote to a British air marshal on the joint staff, "I have studied the pictures with great interest and, I confess, some of the sadistic barbarism that I was joking about last night." Lovett to W. L. Welsh, June 30, 1943, Papers of the Assistant Secretary of War for Air, Secret File, NA II.

15 *Lovett, though a civilian:* Jordan, *Robert Lovett,* 94.

16 *"Tube Alloys":* Hyde Park Aide-Memoire, September 1944, AHF.

16 *"the dire," "the dreadful":* Malloy, *Atomic Tragedy,* 49; Lifton and Mitchell, *Hiroshima in America,* 118.

16 *secretary of war first learned of S-1:* Stimson and Bundy, *On Active Service,* 612–13.

17 *aim the first atomic bomb at Japan:* Malloy, *Atomic Tragedy,* 57. Leslie R. Groves, "Policy Meeting" (memorandum), May 5, 1943, Top Secret, Doc. 3, Atomic Bomb and the End of World War II, NSA. Note, however, that when Colonel Tibbets was given command of the 509th Composite Group in September 1944, he was told to prepare to bomb both Germany and Japan.

17 *keep the money flowing from Congress:* Stimson and Bundy, *On Active Service,* 614.

17 *"a most thorough and searching":* On Stimson's conversation with Bundy on March 5, see undated memo, Bundy File, NA II. Stimson felt the war had so degraded and brutalized the public that a spiritual revivalist "who had balanced judgment and tolerance" like Brooks was called for: "The Secretary said that it ought almost to be a man"—Bundy crossed out "an evangelist"—"who could touch the souls of mankind and bring about a spiritual revival on Christian principles. The Secretary said that as a result of the emotions stirred by the war the world had never been in a worse condition to handle the impact of this discovery." In a Columbia oral history in 1960, Harvey Bundy was defensive about Stimson and the bomb. He said Stimson was "horrified" by the firebombing of Tokyo but the United States had "passed the point of no return" and had to demonstrate "the sheer destructive power" of the bomb to avoid a bloody invasion and force Japan's surrender. Harvey Bundy oral history, Oral History Program, Columbia University.

18 *Phillips Brooks:* Dalton, *Theodore Roosevelt,* 18.

18 *technical capacity to do evil:* On weighing science and morality, see Malloy, *Atomic Tragedy,* 39. As a law student at Harvard before the

turn of the century, Stimson had been drawn to the lectures of the philosopher John Fiske. Fiske preached that man was on a trajectory toward freedom and away from tyranny, and Stimson became a believer in what he called the Law of Moral Progress. Fiske also preached that "the Anglo-Saxon race" was superior—an indefensible article of faith in the pseudo-science of the time shared by Harvard grads and future statesmen including Theodore Roosevelt—and thereby had an obligation to uplift other ("lesser") races. The secretary of war viewed himself as an "old abolitionist" but balked at integrating the armed forces, saying the country was not ready. (Indeed, he refused to even meet with civil rights leaders arguing for integration.) For Stimson's racial attitudes, see Hodgson, *Colonel,* 130–371, 134, 171–72, 249–50, 259–60, 372–73. "Stimson's convictions were those of a northern conservative born in the abolitionist tradition. He believed in full freedom, political and economic, for men of all colors; he did not believe in the present desirability, for either race, of social intermixture." Stimson and Bundy, *On Active Service,* 461. Stimson has been properly criticized for his role in the forced relocation of over one hundred thousand Japanese-Americans on the West Coast during the paranoid post–Pearl Harbor atmosphere of early 1942. In his diary on February 27, 1942, he wrote that the mass internment was being justified "on the ground that their racial characteristics are such that we cannot understand or trust even citizen Japanese. The latter is a fact but I'm afraid it will make an awful hole in the constitution." For a lawyer—a former U.S. attorney—and a self-conscious Christian, the internment of Japanese was a moral failure. The only explanation, though not a good excuse, is wartime expediency.

19 ***Atrocity stories:*** Stimson kept in his own files two photographs of Japanese soldiers with swords raised, about to behead kneeling, blindfolded, and bound POWs. The covering note says, "Local natives corroborated that the beheading of American aviators is a regular ritual." "Memorandum for the Commanding General, Army Air Forces, May 23, 1944," Stimson File, NA II.

19 ***war weariness is settling:*** Biddle, "On the Crest of Fear"; Heinrichs and Gallicchio, *Implacable Foes,* 422–23.

20 ***"Well, I have been responsible":*** Harvey Bundy, "Remembered Words," *Atlantic Monthly,* March 1957.

20 **about** not **using the bomb:** Stimson and Bundy, *On Active Service*, 613. A leading postrevisionist historian of the bomb, Robert Maddox, wrote, "There was no debate over whether to use the bomb when it became available; the question was how." Maddox, *United States and World War II*, 305. Barton Bernstein points out that on March 3, when Bundy wrote Stimson proposing language for a presidential statement, he spoke of when the bomb would be used, not whether. Bernstein, "Truman and the A-Bomb," 549, and Bernstein, "Atom Bomb Reconsidered," 138–39.

20 **"On his knees":** Hodgson, *Colonel,* 332. In response to the revisionist criticism that the decision to drop the bomb was made "thoughtlessly, by default," one scholar, Robert Newman ("Hiroshima and Trashing Stimson," 21), has noted:

> By my count, between 5 March 1945 and the Hiroshima bombing on 6 August, Stimson recorded in his diary face-to-face discussions about the atom bomb with:

Harvey Bundy, assistant to the secretary of war, on	32 days
George Harrison, assistant to the secretary of war, on	26 days
President Truman, on	14 days
Army chief Marshall, on	12 days
John McCloy, assistant secretary of war, on	8 days

21 **"They had my ulcers":** Craig McNamara's *Because Our Fathers Lied,* his memoir of his father, tells the full story. General Groves, who slept easily, never spoke to his wife, Grace, about the bomb. But she suffered a "nervous breakdown," apparently caused by her mother's death but conceivably exacerbated by what psychiatrists would later call "projective identification." See Bernstein, "Reconsidering the 'Atomic General.'" See also John Burton, "Understanding Boundaries: What Is Projective Identification?" *Psychology Today,* June 24, 2021.

22 **jellied gasoline called napalm:** On LeMay and the firebombing of Japanese cities, see Ralph, "Improvised Destruction"; Gladwell, *Bomber Mafia;* and Crane, *American Airpower Strategy,* 167–86. For a detailed discussion of firebombing, see Wellerstein, "Tokyo v. Hiroshima." For the actual bombing report, see Headquarters XXI Bomber Command, "Tactical Mission Report, Mission no. 40 Flown 10 March 1945," n.d., Secret, Doc. 8, NSA.

23 *terror bombing of cities:* On Stimson's assertion that U.S. policy was not to inflict terror bombings on civilians, see Malloy, *Atomic Tragedy,* 63. The bombing of Japanese cities was not literally terror bombing, in the sense that the motivation was not to terrorize civilians by killing them. Rather, the goal was to knock out Japan's economy and military production. But because bombing was imprecise, the air force had to burn down large urban areas to destroy the factories within. This was not LeMay's idea alone. Trevor Albertson, a historian of airpower who taught at the air force's Command and Staff College at Maxwell Air Force Base, has examined the cable traffic in the spring of 1945 between Twentieth Air Force chief of staff Gen. Lauris Norstad in Washington and LeMay on Guam, laying out the industrial targets to be hit by LeMay's bombers. The Twentieth Air Force was directly commanded by the chief of the air force, General Arnold. Since Arnold was recovering from a heart attack at the time, Robert Lovett was effectively Norstad's boss. Trevor Albertson, interview by author.

24 *Highhold, his estate:* Stimson and Bundy, *On Active Service,* xxii; Stimson, *My Vacations,* 170. In a passage of *My Vacations* that is pure Stimson, he attributes the relative modesty of Highhold to his caretaker, John Culleton, an Irish immigrant: "Highhold is the expression of John's personality rather than that of anyone else." Stimson, unaware that he is describing a level of gentility far beyond hiring a society architect or decorator, goes on to recount:

> When he [John] found that I was fond of riding and missed it in the work of a law office, he used to meet me in the evening at the station with both horses saddled and with leather puttees under his arm with which to transform me into a horseman, and together we galloped home over the intervening wood roads and farmlands to my immense satisfaction.
>
> John had no idea of an "estate" or formal gardening or any of the things that the wealthy people of that date were putting their money into on Long Island.

25 *"In March he":* Stimson and Bundy, *On Active Service,* 632.

Chapter 2: Target Practice

Stimson's diaries are in Stimson Papers.

28 *"if you ever pray":* McCullough, *Truman,* 346–53.

29 ***Truman and Stimson are:*** Bernstein, "Roosevelt, Truman," 36.

29 **an ardent New Dealer:** Hamby, *Harry Truman,* 14, 221, 306.

29 *"nuisance and a pretty":* McCullough, *Truman,* 291.

30 **Leslie Groves is not used:** For descriptions of Groves, see Norris, *Racing for the Bomb,* 2, 5, 11, 123, 196, 241–42; and Bernstein, "Reconsidering the 'Atomic General.'"

31 *"Don't try to tell me":* Gen. Leslie Groves, interview, pt. 9, Voices of the Manhattan Project, National Museum of Nuclear Science & History, AHF.

31 **Groves and his Target Committee:** Malloy, *Atomic Tragedy,* 56–62; Notes on Initial Meeting of Target Committee, May 2, 1945, Top Secret, Doc. 9, NSA; and Maj. J. A. Derry and Dr. N. F. Ramsey to Gen. L. R. Groves, "Summary of Target Committee Meetings on 10 and 11 May 1945" (memorandum), May 12, 1945, Top Secret, Doc. 11, NSA.

33 *"Owing to the spread":* Ibid., 51–52; Bernstein, "Atom Bombings Reconsidered," notes, "So far as the skimpy records reveal, no member of the Target Committee chose to dwell on this matter. They probably assumed that the bomb blast would claim most of its victims before the radiation could do its deadly work" (141). General Groves cleverly compartmented the scientists at the University of Chicago's Met Lab, who did worry about the effects of radiation, from the scientists at Los Alamos, who were primarily concerned with producing a deliverable bomb. When Oppenheimer warned about the effects of radiation, he was concerned with protecting the airmen in the plane delivering the bomb. J. R. Oppenheimer to Brigadier General Farrell (memorandum), May 11, 1945, Doc. 10, NSA.

One scientist—the head of the Met Lab at Chicago—did directly confront the moral issues. Arthur Compton, a Nobel laureate advising the Interim Committee, wrote on May 28 that dropping the A-bomb "introduces the question of mass slaughter, really for the first time in history. It carries with it the question of possible radioactive poison over the area bombed. Essentially, the question of use . . . of the new weapon carries much more serious implications than the introduction of poison gas." But Compton's concerns seem not to have registered deeply with his colleagues on the scientific panel advising the Interim Committee. Bernstein, "Atomic Bombs Reconsidered," 143. Likewise, a group of scientists under Nobel Prize winner James Franck, out of the University of Chicago's labs, objected to dropping the bomb essentially on humanitarian grounds and proposed a noncombat demonstration. Arthur B. Compton to secretary of war (memorandum), enclosing "Memorandum on Political and Social Problems," from Members of the Metallurgical Laboratory of the University of Chicago, June 12, 1945, Secret, Doc. 22, NSA. Niels Bohr, a leading physicist, tried to take their views to Stimson in late June, but Stimson refused to see him. It was too late; the decision had been made. Harvey Bundy oral history, Columbia University; Compton, *Atomic Quest,* 234–35; Hodgson, *Colonel,* 326. An excellent analysis on the radiation question is Malloy, "'Very Pleasant Way to Die.'" Malloy puts much of the onus on Oppenheimer for simply not wanting to deal with the poisonous effects of radiation.

34 *"they were all interested in":* Gen. Leslie Groves, interview, pt. 4, Voices of the Manhattan Project, National Museum of Nuclear Science & History, AHF.

35 **made a conscious decision:** On the decision not to bomb concentration camps, see Beschloss, *Conquerors,* 63–67, 88–89. Bird, *Chairman,* shows that Stimson was copied on relevant correspondence (215).

36 *"It's a superb record":* Jordan, *Robert Lovett,* 97.

36 **ran out of incendiaries:** LeMay, *Missions,* 368.

36 **magazine called** Impact: Crane, *American Airpower Strategy,* 97–99.

36 *"marvelous":* Malloy, *Atomic Tragedy,* 54; Stimson diary, entries for September 7, 1942, and October 15, 1943; Stimson to Spaatz, February 13, 1945, Stimson File, NA II. Spaatz sent Stimson the photo album two days after the air force conducted its first real urban area attack, in the British manner, on Berlin on February 3. Spaatz to Stimson, February 5, 1945, Stimson File, NA II. The Berlin attack, conducted in clear skies, was aimed, roughly speaking, at government buildings in central Berlin, but it killed thousands of people. Clodfelter, *Beneficial Bombing,* 175, claims as many as 25,000 deaths,

but it is probably more accurate to say that U.S. forces projected 25,000 casualties (dead and wounded) and the Germans reported a much lower figure, 2,895 dead (and 120,000 made homeless). Conrad Crane and Tami Davis, interviews by author.

37 *"The moral position":* Malloy, *Atomic Tragedy,* 106; John McCloy diary, entry for May 21, 1945, McCloy Papers. Barton Bernstein has made an interesting argument that General Marshall missed an opportunity to raise his concerns with Truman. Bernstein, "Looking Back."

38 *The killing of civilians is much:* Stimson was influenced by a letter from atomic scientist Oswald Brewster ("the letter of an honest man," Stimson wrote) raising serious moral issues. See O. C. Brewster to President Truman, May 24, 1945, with note from Stimson to Marshall, May 30, 1945, attached, Secret, Doc. 14, NSA.

38 *"General Marshall said he thought":* John McCloy, "Memorandum of Conversation with General Marshall," May 29, 1945, Top Secret, Doc. 17, NSA.

39 *"General LeMay made it clear":* "Tokyo Erased," *New York Times,* May 30, 1945. The extensive damage is described in Kido, *Diary,* entry for May 25, 1945.

40 *"such areas are small":* Malloy, *Atomic Tragedy,* 106. See generally Malloy, "'Rules of Civilized Warfare'"; and "Minutes of Third Target Committee Meeting," May 28, 1945, Top Secret, Doc. 15, NSA.

40 *"Well, your report is":* Giovannitti and Fried, *Decision to Drop the Bomb,* 40. See also Groves, *Now It Can Be Told,* 271–76.

41 *"will leave no question about":* On Stimson and Kyoto, see Cary, "Sparing of Kyoto." Stimson, who visited the city at least three times in the late 1920s, apologetically asked McCloy, "Would you consider me a sentimental old man if I removed Kyoto from the target cities from our bombers?" (340). But Kelly, "Why Did Stimson Spare Kyoto," argues that the more hard-nosed side of Stimson wanted to spare the city for strategic reasons—to reduce Japanese antipathy to the United States in the postwar rivalry with the Soviet Union.

42 *"Will you please inform":* Malloy, *Atomic Tragedy,* 109.

43 *"three winners of the Nobel Prize":* On the Interim Committee meeting, see Rhodes, *Making of Atomic Bomb,* 642–51; Compton, *Atomic Quest,* 238–39; "Notes of the Interim Committee Meeting," May 31, 1945, Doc. 18, NSA.

44 *James "Jimmy" Byrnes:* Robertson, *Sly and Able,* 396–99. Leo
Szilard, an early and brilliant atomic scientist who traveled to
Byrnes's home in South Carolina to lobby against using the bomb,
wrote that Byrnes told him he wanted to use it as leverage against
the Russians.

45 *"the appalling lack of conscience":* "Stimson and the Atomic Bomb,"
Andover Bulletin, Spring 1961.

47 *doubletalk:* Ham, *Hiroshima and Nagasaki,* 155–60; Hodgson, *Colonel,* 322. The committee had crossed a moral Rubicon, while not
wishing to recognize it. Bernstein, "Atomic Bombings Reconsidered":

> Directed by Stimson, the committee was actually endorsing
> terror bombing—but somewhat uneasily. They would not focus
> exclusively on a military target (the old morality), as Marshall had
> recently proposed, nor fully on civilians (the emerging morality).
> They managed to achieve their purpose—terror bombing—
> without bluntly acknowledging it to themselves. All knew that
> families—women, children, and, even in the daytime, during the
> bomb attack, some workers—dwelled in "workers' houses."
> (144)

48 *He stays quiet:* Malloy, *Atomic Tragedy,* 117; Malloy, " 'Rules of Civilized Warfare,'" 500.

50 *"pretty thin veneer":* Frank, *Downfall,* 67. See also Crane, *American
Airpower Strategy,* 175–77, and Sherry, *Rise of American Air Power,*
286. Crane directed me to the recent research of Trevor Albertson,
a former U.S. Air Force officer and instructor at the Air Command
and Staff College at Maxwell Air Force Base. Albertson has re-
viewed all the once-classified bombing records of the Twentieth Air
Force and concluded that LeMay's bombers were aiming at Japan's
economy, not its citizenry. My own research in Stimson's files at the
National Archives supports Albertson's view. General Arnold followed up his meeting with Stimson on June 1 by sending Stimson
briefing papers showing a large amount of industrial activity in the
cities subjected to firebombing. "Memo from Arnold to Stimson,
Subject: Incendiary Attacks by the 20th Air Force" ("further to our
discussion on the subject of incendiary attacks"), June 2, 1945, in
three tabs: "Chart showing the disposition of Japanese industry; a
map showing the location of the principal cities subject to incendi-

ary attack; a statement of the 33 industrial targets and general description on their industrial content."

Stimson's only response was to remove Kyoto from the target list—for conventional as well as atomic bombing. Eaker to Stimson, June 11, 1945, Stimson File, NA II.

51 *"highly pleased":* "Memorandum of Conference with the President," June 6, 1945, Top Secret, Doc. 21, NSA.

51 **grim irony:** Lifton and Mitchell, *Hiroshima in America,* 133.

51 **cog in the Kansas City machine:** McCullough, *Truman,* 185, 221; Hamby, *Harry Truman,* 158–59; Miller, *Truman,* 164, 223, 239, 245, 255.

52 *"I preferred to use a big gun":* Stimson and Bundy, *On Active Service,* 35.

52 *"Our demand has been":* McCullough, *Truman,* 359.

53 **polls show that:** Heinrichs and Gallicchio, *Implacable Foes,* 505.

53 **claims to have never surrendered:** Frank, *Downfall,* 35.

54 **Grew, of Groton and Harvard:** Heinrichs, *American Ambassador,* 3–19. During his time as ambassador, Grew had grown close to some liberal-minded Japanese officials. When American firebombs hit the upper-class neighborhood of Yamanote in Tokyo, where many of his friends lived, Grew exclaimed "we can't waste any more time." Iokibe, "American Policy," 46.

54 *"the prince of appeasers":* Dean Acheson's nickname for Grew. Gallicchio, *Unconditional,* 34. Acheson was one of the pro-reform New Dealers at the State Department who believed that Japan essentially had to start over, eliminate the emperor system, and embrace democracy. His zeal overlooked what Grew correctly understood, that for the Japanese, surrender discussions were a nonstarter without some provision to keep at least a constitutional monarch. The Japanese were so dug in that any appeal to reason would almost certainly have failed. Still, as some historians argue, America might look better in the light of history if it had tried.

54 **Captain Truman:** Giangreco, *Soldier from Independence.*

55 *"Okinawa from one end of Japan to the other":* Feis, *Japan Subdued,* 11; see also Giangreco, "'Score of Bloody Okinawas.'" There has been an enormous controversy among scholars over casualty estimates. See Newman, "Hiroshima and Trashing Stimson," 26–28.

55 **On June 18 he summons:** Heinrichs and Gallicchio, *Implacable Foes,* 5, 24, 430, 476–507; "Minutes of Meeting Held at the White House," June 18, 1945, Top Secret, Doc. 26, NSA.

56 **Adm. William Leahy, a crusty:** Leahy not only opposed an invasion, he also opposed dropping the atomic bomb. He later wrote, "My own feeling was that in being the first to use it, we had adopted an ethical standard common to the barbarians of the Dark Ages." Leahy, *I Was There,* 513. Leahy had been FDR's main military adviser, but his status was diminished under Truman, who looked more to Byrnes, Stimson, and Marshall. It is an interesting historical counterfactual to wonder what might have happened if FDR had lived and listened more closely to Leahy than Truman did. For a provocative discussion of Leahy's role, see O'Brien, *Second Most Powerful Man,* 334–59. See also Leahy, *I Was There,* and Walter Borneman's considered treatment of Leahy in *Admirals.*

56 **former president Hoover:** Giangreco, " 'Score of Bloody Okinawas,' " 104, 107.

57 **"Really, we should have":** On McCloy's role, see Bird, *Chairman,* 246; and "McCloy on the A-Bomb," in Reston, *Deadline,* 494–502. For McCloy's exaggerations, see Isaacson and Thomas, *Wise Men,* 295n775; Gallicchio, *Unconditional,* 58.

58 **final show of force:** Stimson listened to Grew, but he was persuaded by Marshall and the joint chiefs that to concede on the emperor before Japan surrendered would only embolden the Japanese militarists to fight to the end—as they had on Okinawa and Iwo Jima. Newman, "Hiroshima and Trashing Stimson," 22.

58 **"Japan is susceptible to reason":** Stimson, "Memorandum for the President: Proposed Program for Japan," July 2, 1945, Stimson Papers. Stimson's working papers on the question of unconditional surrender (in the file marked "Japan" in Stimson File, NA II) show his close personal attention to the question of keeping the emperor and his struggle—and uncertainty—over timing. In a typed draft of his "Memo for President: Proposed Program for Japan," he inserted by hand (with numerous erasure marks), after a section proposing a surrender-or-else ultimatum, "I personally think that if in saying this we should add that we do not exclude a constitutional monarchy under the present dynasty, it would substantially add to the chances of acceptance." The memo continues in almost tortured

prose to weigh the timing of threats and actions against Japan, including dropping the atomic bomb, which he awkwardly alludes to:

> Success of course will depend on the potency of the warning which we give her. She has an extremely sensitive national pride and, as we are now seeing every day, when actually locked with the enemy will fight to the very death. For that reason the warning must be tendered before the actual invasion has occurred and while the impending destruction, though clear beyond peradventure [doubt or chance], has not yet reduced her to fanatical despair. If Russia is a part of the threat, the Russia attack, if actual, must not have progressed too far. Our own bombings should be confined to military objectives as far as possible.

Chapter 3: The Stomach Art

60 *"rice-plant mounds"*: Coox, *Japan: Final Agony*, 28.

61 *Togo is an unlikely leader:* Kazuhiko Togo and Shigehiko Togo (Togo's grandsons), interviews by author. Togo's record is extensively preserved in his POW 201 file for the Tokyo War Crimes trials, preserved at Records of the Supreme Commander for the Allied Powers, Legal Section, Administration Division, POW 201 File, 1945–52, NA II. A biographical report by the Department of State Interim Research and Intelligence Service, Research and Analysis Branch, describes, too harshly, his prickly personality—and the very qualities that allowed him to defy the militarists in his own government:

> His predominant traits, according to source, are "evasiveness, pugnacity, and a total blindness towards any side of a question except his own." Mr. Grew describes TOGO as being "grim, unsmiling, and ultra-reserved." "He speaks English well enough," the former Ambassador observes, "but talks so low that few can understand him." Another observer calls him "a very ugly man with a disagreeable manner," but possessing "undeniable ability."

Records of General Headquarters, Far East Command, Supreme Commander Allied Powers, Central Command, 8132nd Army Unit, Sugamo Prison, NA II.

62 *envied Americans their sense:* Togo, *Cause of Japan*, 11, 14.

62 *"taciturn, expressionless"*: Brooks, *Behind Japan's Surrender*, 38.

62 *"not just as a statesman"*: Togo, *Cause of Japan*, 35. Togo was ordered home from Moscow in August 1940; the pact was not actually signed until April 1941. But the work was Togo's. In his toast, Molotov appreciated Togo's unbending qualities: "In my public life of many years, I have never known any man who insists so earnestly and so frankly as Mr. Togo on what he believes to be right."

62 *strenuously opposed going to war*: Minohara, "'No Choice,'" 258–71.

63 *moving one's furs and jewels*: Frank, *Downfall*, 5.

63 *study of fallen nations*: Brooks, *Behind Japan's Surrender*, 38.

63 *watching the cherry blossoms*: Tamon, "Hirohito's 'Sacred Decision,'" 259.

63 *Suzuki was once*: Brooks, *Behind Japan's Surrender*, 30–33.

64 *"I think we can carry on"*: Togo, *Cause of Japan*, 269.

65 **haragei**: Butow, *Japan's Decision*, 71; Drea, *In the Service*, 202; Giovannitti, *Decision to Drop the Bomb*, 43; Sigal, *Fighting to Finish*, 47.

65 **giri**: Benedict, *Chrysanthemum and Sword*, 43, 99, 101, 137, 167, 193, 199–205.

67 **gekokujo**: Drea, *Japan's Imperial Army*, 174.

67 *"government by assassination"*: Butow, *Japan's Decision*, 179; Drea, *In the Service*, 186. The phrase comes from the original source: Hugh Byas, *Government by Assassination* (New York: Knopf, 1942).

69 *"A tragedy of timidity"*: Stimson and Bundy, *On Active Service*, 220–81.

69 *charnel house*: Newman, *Truman and Hiroshima Cult*, 138, quoting historian Gavin Daws. See also Drea, *In the Service*, 214. The Chinese called Japan's pacification program "the Three Alls: Kill All, Burn All, Loot All." For a history of racial animosity and war crimes by a leading (but critical) Japanese historian, see Ienaga, *Pacific War*.

70 *gun muzzle*: Walker, *Shockwave*, 159.

70 *"the Ivory Mask"*: Drea, *In the Service*, 195.

70 *Adm. Mitsumasa Yonai*: On Yonai and Toyoda, see Brooks, *Behind Japan's Surrender*, 50–54. Toyoda joined the Big Six in early June.

70 *Gen. Korechika Anami*: Drea, *Japan's Imperial Army*, 219; Hastings, *Retribution*, 453; Brooks, *Behind Japan's Surrender*, 49. Anami's title was generally translated as "war minister" in the American press,

tracking the American custom, "secretary of war." The Japanese term, *rikugunsho,* translates more accurately as "army minister."

71 ***his overextended forces were outflanked:*** Frank, *Tower of Skulls,* 212–13.

71 ***"end the war" sentiments:*** Butow, *Japan's Decision,* 75.

71 ***Togo has hope for Anami:*** Togo, *Cause of Japan,* 304.

72 ***persuade the other members:*** Hasegawa, *Racing the Enemy,* 72. Togo credited "one of the military members." Togo, *Cause of Japan,* 283.

72 ***"spirit" of the Japanese:*** Butow, *Japan's Decision,* 79.

72 ***Japan's economic condition:*** Toland, *Rising Sun,* 116, 838–39.

72 ***meetings on May 11, 12, and 14:*** Barrett, *140 Days to Hiroshima,* 51– 60; Togo, *Cause of Japan,* 284–88. Koshiro, *Imperial Eclipse,* makes the interesting argument that most historians have overestimated the shock of the atomic bomb and failed to see the importance that Japanese policy makers attached to working with Russia to create a Eurasian stronghold against Anglo-American influence.

74 ***"Even if the Japanese":*** Toland, *Rising Sun,* 749.

75 ***"a split personality":*** Kazuhiko Togo, "Foreign Minister Togo's Bitter Struggle," quoting Togo diary for June 6, 1945.

75 ***"unbroken for ages":*** Bix, *Hirohito,* 39, 171, 349.

76 ***suicidal* tokko *tactics:*** Wetzler, *Imperial Japan,* 73.

76 ***kamikazes:*** Bix, "Japan's Delayed Surrender," 214.

76 ***sanctioned the use of poison gas:*** Bix, *Hirohito,* 372.

76 ***executed three of eight:*** Kawamura, *Emperor Hirohito,* 116.

76 ***"Isn't there some way":*** Bix, *Hirohito,* 464; Wetzler, *Imperial Japan,* 25–26.

76 ***fireflies:*** Kawamura, *Emperor Hirohito,* 128.

76 ***Walt Disney cartoons:*** Bix, *Hirohito,* 453.

76 ***take a concubine:*** Ibid., 271.

77 ***"So they have finally done it":*** Kawamura, *Emperor Hirohito,* 63.

77 ***spending nights in the shelter:*** Peter Mauch, interview by author. Dr. Mauch is a modern Japanese historian and senior lecturer at Western Sydney University.

77 ***The May firebombing:*** Coox, *Japan: Final Agony,* 24–35.

78 ***deep in the mountains:*** Drea, *In the Service,* 286; Tamon, "Hirohito's 'Sacred Decision,'" 261.

78 ***His own mother:*** Mauch, "'Our Islands,'" 76.

79 ***ride the tiger:*** Kawamura, *Emperor Hirohito,* 101–2; Drea, *In the Service,* 178.

79 *"The progress of the war"*: Kido, *Diary,* entry for June 8, 1945.

79 *soap is scarce:* Hastings, *Retribution,* 45.

80 *"Draft Plan"*: Hasegawa, *Racing the Enemy,* 101; Kawamura, *Emperor Hirohito,* 158; Butow, *Japan's Decision,* 113.

80 *"Of course, very good"*: Butow, *Japan's Decision,* 72.

81 *"That! It is all right!"*: Togo, *Cause of Japan,* 293.

81 *old automobile engines:* Shoji, "Japanese Termination," 66.

81 *"approves of the steps"*: Togo, *Cause of Japan,* 297.

82 *On June 22 Hirohito:* Butow, *Japan's Decision,* 119–20; Hasegawa, *Racing the Enemy,* 106; Hata, *Hirohito,* 57.

82 *Malik ducks:* Butow, *Japan's Decision,* 121–23.

83 *send Prince Konoe:* Hasegawa, *Racing the Enemy,* 121.

83 *"His Majesty the Emperor"*: MAGIC Diplomatic Summary, no. 1204, July 12, 1945, in Kort, *Columbia Guide,* 279–80. Several of these MAGIC decrypts (including July 13 and 17) are in NSA, Docs. 39B, 41, 42. The American code breakers were also breaking the codes of their Allies and other nations, including France, Portugal, Turkey, Saudi Arabia, Czechoslovakia, Switzerland, Italy, and Peru, among others.

83 *"academic fine phrases"*: Kort, *Columbia Guide,* 280–81.

84 *"We are unable to consent"*: Ibid., 284–85.

84 *nowhere near surrender:* Frank, *Downfall,* 85–86, 184–85.

84 *Anami insists that Japan has not:* Butow, *Japan's Decision,* 125–27.

84 *Ketsugo Sakusen:* Frank, *Downfall,* 85–86; 184–85.

85 *THERE ARE NO CIVILIANS:* Ibid., 188.

85 *"given" to the people:* Gallicchio, *Unconditional,* 25.

86 *makes perfect sense:* Frank, "Ketsu Go," 80.

86 *shukkettsu:* Drea, *In the Service,* 246.

Chapter 4: The Patient Progresses

Stimson's diaries are in Stimson Papers.

88 *raped his daughters:* Dobbs, *Six Months,* 286–95.

89 *"the war weariness"*: On the Weckerling document, see Frank, *Downfall,* 218–38; Drea, *In the Service,* 210; Gallicchio, *Unconditional,* 100.

90 *"Now I am become Death"*: Rhodes, *Making of Atomic Bomb,* 668–77.

90   *"The Secretary cut a gay caper"*: Bird, *Chairman,* 251; John McCloy diary, entry for July 16, 1945, McCloy Papers. See Harrison to secretary of war, July 17, 1945, Telegram War [Department] 33556, Top Secret, Doc. 45, NSA; Gen. L. R. Groves to secretary of war, "The Test" (memorandum), July 18, 1945, HSTL. Harrison's cables to Stimson are also in Bundy File, NA II.

90   **Stimson wants to take advantage:** Stimson to Byrnes, enclosing memorandum to the President, "The Conduct of the War with Japan," July 16, 1945, Top Secret, Doc. 37, NSA.

91   *"conniving":* Newman, *Truman and Hiroshima Cult,* 14.

91   **the Saltonstalls, the Peabodys:** Bix, "Japan's Delayed Surrender," 199.

91   **Stimson as well was impressed:** Though Stimson once remarked that he found the "Japanese citizen" untrustworthy on racial grounds, he was impressed by Japan's Westernized diplomats whom he encountered at peace conferences in the late 1920s and early '30s. He certainly has more faith than Truman that the Japanese can be made trustworthy. Stimson and Bundy, *On Active Service,* 224–25.

92   **the Pendergast machine:** For a comparison of Truman and Stimson's views, see Gallicchio, *Unconditional,* 208–13: Hamby, *Harry Truman,* 327, 331; Newman, "Hiroshima and Trashing Stimson," 22.

94   **Stimson sees Russian repression:** Stimson and Bundy, *On Active Service,* 638. On Stimson's ambivalence about trusting the Russians, see the excellent analysis by Malloy, *Atomic Tragedy,* 35, 69–86, 102–3, 109–12, 131–34, 145–57, 163–66, 169–80.

94   *"He threw me out":* Isaacson and Thomas, *Wise Men,* 300.

95   *"Dearest little Misty":* Stimson to Mabel, July 20, 1945, Stimson Papers.

95   *"Patient progressing rapidly":* Rhodes, *Making of Atomic Bomb,* 686. See Gen. L. R. Groves to secretary of war, "The Test" (memorandum), July 18, 1945, Top Secret, Doc. 46, NSA.

95   *"pet city":* Harrison to Stimson, July 21, 1945, War 35987, Bundy File, NA II.

96   **Groves has added Kokura:** Malloy, "'Rules of Civilized Warfare,'" 501.

96   **LeMay has proposed Nagasaki:** Craven and Cate, *Army Air Forces,* 5:710.

96   *"where, why, and what effects":* Arnold diary, entries for July 22, 23,

24, 1945, Henry Arnold Papers, LOC; Arnold, *Global Mission,* 589. Stimson pressed Arnold, according to Arnold's diary:

> July 23—Conference with Secretary of War re ultra bombing effort and its results on Japanese desire for peace. Surrounding communities, other nations, psychological reactions of Japanese. Effect of weather and topography. Sent a radio to Spaatz.

The next day he wrote again:

> Secretary of War came to see me re ultra Super Bombing. I told him to wait until I heard from Spaatz.

This was the more aggressive Prosecutor Stimson of prior years, digging down through the bureaucracy. But it was too late to be asking these questions. Stimson signed off on the order to Spaatz to drop the bomb the next day, July 25.

97 ***Stalin is impassive:*** Dobbs, *Six Months,* 329–30.

97 ***"subject to suitable":*** Frank, *Downfall,* 220.

99 ***"We have discovered the most terrible":*** McCullough, *Truman,* 440.

100 ***Truman was misled:*** Wellerstein, "Kyoto Misconception." Truman's Potsdam diary, entries for July 16, 17, 18, 20, 25, 26, and 30, are at Doc. 47, NSA.

100 ***"Hiroshima (population 350,000)":*** Malloy, " 'Rules of Civilized Warfare,' " 503; Marshall to Handy, July 22, 1945, Handy to Marshall, July 24, 1945, both in Bundy File, NA II; Jack Stone to Henry Arnold, "Groves Project," July 24, 1945, HSTL.

101 ***only about 10 percent will:*** Bernstein, "Reconsidering the 'Atomic General,' " 905. Rich, *Downfall,* 287, uses a much higher figure—military dead as high as twenty thousand, slightly more than a quarter.

101 ***"You judge it; I can't":*** McCullough, *Truman,* 440.

101 ***murky and disputed:*** Truman claimed, in a 1953 letter to the official historian of the army air forces, James Cate, that on July 25, General Marshall told him that the invasion would cost "at a minimum one quarter of a million casualties, and might cost as much as a million." Craven and Cate, *Army Air Forces,* 5:712–13. But Truman's recollections in the letter are self-serving and questionable.

101 ***On July 27:*** On Eisenhower and Stimson, see Alperovitz, *Decision to Use the Bomb,* 353–58. For skepticism, see Frank, *Downfall,* 332n; and

Barton Bernstein, "Ike and Hiroshima: Did He Oppose It?" *Journal of Strategic Studies* 10 (Spring 1987): 377–89. John Eisenhower, interview by author for *Ike's Bluff*.

Chapter 5: Prompt and Utter

104 ***"We call upon":*** For the Potsdam Declaration, see Kort, *Columbia Guide*, 226.

104 ***"Behold the frog":*** Benedict, *Chrysanthemum and Sword*, 216.

105 **honne:** Hotta, *Japan 1941*, 241.

105 ***Overcome with a mixture:*** On Togo and Pearl Harbor, see ibid., 269–71; Togo, *Cause of Japan*, 45–224. Minohara, " 'No Choice' " explains why Togo did a volte-face from opposing the war to backing it. Togo's hope was to put off a decision to go to war by working out a modus vivendi, called Plan B, that would pull some Japanese troops from Southeast Asia in exchange for a three-month pause on America's oil embargo. After the Japanese intercepted some Chinese cable traffic, Togo—mistakenly—thought the Americans were answering his modus vivendi proposal with one of their own. Thus, he was shocked and devastated by Hull's hard-line stance. There is an eerie similarity between Togo's wishfulness about the progress of diplomacy in November 1941 with his similarly too-hopeful belief that the Russians might act as an intermediary in August 1945.

106 ***"the Hero wronged":*** Hotta, *Japan 1941*, 271.

106 ***"Following are our terms":*** On Togo's reading of the Potsdam Declaration, see Togo, "Bitter Struggle"; Togo, *Cause of Japan*, 311–12.

106 ***"or else" ultimatum:*** Frank, *Tower of Skulls*, 223.

107 ***Three Sacred Treasures:*** Dower, *Embracing Defeat*, 290.

108 ***obscure word* mokusatsu:** Butow, *Japan's Decision*, 142–47; Brooks, *Behind Japan's Surrender*, 160–64; Hasegawa, *Racing the Enemy*, 165–74. The *mokusatsu* story is often presented as a tragedy of errors, a misunderstanding, and a missed opportunity. Brian Walsh, a scholar of Japan's surrender who teaches at Kwansei Gakuin University in Japan (and was translator and analyst for the author), argues convincingly that *mokusatsu* was not in any way mistranslated. Rather, every member of the Big Six, save Togo, was determined to reject the Potsdam Declaration. Not even Togo was ready to accept it as written.

108 ***Togo is furious:*** Togo, *Cause of Japan*, 312–14.

109 **Togo gamely, stubbornly:** America's code breakers tracked his futile progress. See "Magic"—Diplomatic Summary, War Department, Office of the Assistant Chief of Staff, G-2, no. 1221 (July 29, 1945), no. 1222 (July 30, 1945), no. 1225 (August 2, 1945), no. 1226 (August 3, 1945), no. 1227 (August 4, 1945), no. 1228 (August 5, 1945), Top Secret Ultra, Docs. 53–56, NSA.

Chapter 6: A Bucket of Tar

112 **No record that President Truman:** On July 30, Stimson's aide Harrison cabled Truman that the time for dropping the bomb was approaching so rapidly that the president needed to sign off on a statement for release to the press. On July 31, Truman wrote, in his personal hand, "Suggestion approved. Release when ready but not sooner than August 2." McCullough, *Truman,* 448. He is referring to a press release.

112 **Spaatz wants it in writing:** Knebel and Bailey, *No High Ground,* 95, 124–26; Gordin, *Five Days in August,* 50. A series of cables between Handy and Marshall led up to Spaatz's order: see "Framing the Directive for the Nuclear Strikes," Docs. 60a–d, NSA.

113 **"You know something, Tooey":** Mets, *Master of Airpower,* 333.

113 **felt the need to step in:** Drew Middleton, "Boss of the Heavyweights," *Saturday Evening Post,* May 20, 1944.

113 **"own man":** Mets, *Master of Airpower,* 2.

113 **"clean sleeve":** Davis, *Spaatz and Air War,* 4.

114 **a small, rickety biplane:** Carl Spaatz oral history, September 27, 1968, USAF Oral History Program, Spaatz Papers.

114 **two German Fokkers:** Mets, *Master of Airpower,* 35.

114 **Bomber Mafia:** Gladwell, *Bomber Mafia,* 49

114 **"a relative term":** Crane, *American Airpower Strategy,* 101.

114 **smart enough to see:** Miller, *Masters of the Air,* 44–45.

115 **bombed Switzerland by mistake:** Crane, *American Airpower Strategy,* 108. In late 1944, using radar, only 5 percent of bombs landed within a mile of the aiming point. Gresham, *General Tooey.*

115 **"tarred":** Davis, *Spaatz and Air War,* 437. In 1962, Spaatz offered a phlegmatic account of his view of precision bombing:

> We always attacked only legitimate military targets with one exception—the capital of a hostile nation. Berlin was the adminis-

trative and communications center of Germany and therefore became a military target. Other than that, our targets were always
military targets. Our stand was that we'd bomb only strategic
targets—not areas. I believed that we could win the war more
quickly that way. It wasn't for religious or moral reasons that I
didn't go along with urban area bombing.

Spaatz, oral history by Gen. Noel Parrish and air force historian Alfred Goldberg, Spaatz Papers. This passage, though widely quoted,
does not fully reflect his actual views. For example, in the summer
of 1944, he blocked Operation Shatter, proposed by his intelligence
staff to break German morale by bombing small cities and towns,
for "humanitarian" reasons. Gresham, *General Tooey.*

115 **using oxen:** Atkinson, *Guns at Last Light,* 353, 358.
115 **Spaatz insisted on visual bombing:** Crane, *American Airpower Strategy,* 83.
115 **"Come on over":** "The Man Who Paved the Way," *Time,* June 12,
1944.
116 **"They all have that":** Ibid.
116 **26,000 airmen died:** Clodfelter, *Beneficial Bombing,* 182.
116 **"the Land of Doom":** Atkinson, *Guns at Last Light,* 350–54, for a
pithy summary. The most vivid overall treatment of the airman's experience in Europe is Miller, *Masters of the Air,* passim.
116 **number of missions to thirty-five:** Mets, *Master of Airpower,* 185.
116 **wall off sentiment or remorse:** Gresham, *General Tooey.*
117 **"Any suggestions you have?":** Ibid.
117 **cable from General Arnold:** Ibid. and Katharine Gresham, interview
by author.
118 **Spaatz's apologies for blowing:** Ibid.
118 **"My one hope":** Gresham, *General Tooey.* Spaatz wrote his wife, "I
do not have many qualms about what I have done in our bombing
when I am fully alert and reasoning well. However sometimes when
I wake up at night I am not so happy." Spaatz to Ruth Spaatz,
April 20, 1945, quoted in Gresham, *General Tooey.* Spaatz usually
sent short letters, typed by his aide Major Bagby, to his family; this
was an unusual, long handwritten letter to his wife. It is not in
Spaatz Papers at LOC.
118 **"Dresden":** Katharine Gresham, *General Tooey,* and interview by

author. For background on Dresden, see Addison and Crang, *Firestorm;* and Biddle, "On the Crest of Fear" and "Dresden 1945."

119 ***Spaatz arrives on the island:*** Spaatz diary, July 29, 1945, Spaatz Papers.

119 ***a whole set of new directives:*** Directive to commanding general, U.S. Army Strategic Air Forces, July 25, 1945, Spaatz Papers; see Frank, *Downfall,* 303–4; Ralph, "Improvised Destruction," 515–16.

119 ***"indigenous food supplies":*** Crane, *American Airpower Strategy,* 182; Newman, *Truman and the Hiroshima Cult,* 16. In a memo sent by Lovett to Stimson on July 31, 1945, Lovett included a study done by the Strategic Bombing Survey that stated, "With sufficient time, Japan's food situation could be made disastrous by a combination of blockade, destruction of nitrogen production, and direct attack on rice production by TN 8 [a chemical weapon available in 1946]. . . . Japan's hope of long term resistance can be eliminated by shortening the period which she has enough food to avoid widespread starvation." But the report concluded: "Japanese rice production is not considered a profitable target in view of currently accepted strategy. It is felt that indigenous food supplies may be very important to the commander in charge of the occupation." Lovett's memo noted that "Spaatz concurs." "Memorandum for Secretary of War," July 31, 1945, Stimson File, NA II.

120 ***"I never got any direct orders":*** Gresham, *General Tooey.*

120 ***Spaatz keeps his own orders:*** Ibid.

120 ***"He looked at me":*** Ibid.

120 ***lead plane, Butcher Shop:*** Tibbets, *Tibbets Story,* 81.

121 ***an RAF officer along:*** Ibid., 93.

121 ***"My anxiety is for":*** Ibid., 99.

122 ***drop a Pumpkin on the grounds:*** This prank may have been more consequential than Tibbets realized. The Japanese were monitoring the radio traffic of the 509th Composite Group. After the 509th dropped an atomic bomb on Hiroshima, its flight patterns took on ominous significance. For Japanese defenders to know that a B-29 from the 509th had targeted the Imperial Palace, if only with a practice bomb, would have added to the terror felt by its denizens, the emperor and his minions.

123 ***On the morning of August 5:*** On the 509th and the flight of the *Enola Gay,* see ibid., 210–27; Thomas and Witts, *Enola Gay,* 206–68;

and Coster-Mullen, *Atom Bombs,* chap. 4. Tibbets says Capt. Deak Parsons yelled "Flak!" but the preponderance of the evidence suggests it was Tibbets. See Coster-Mullen, *Atom Bombs,* 401n118.

124 ***In Hiroshima, about 70,000:*** "How Many Died at Hiroshima?" Atomicarchives.com.

124 ***Spaatz went fishing:*** Spaatz diary, entry for August 5, 1945, Spaatz Papers.

124 ***"How did it go, son?":*** Knebel and Bailey, *No High Ground,* 213.

125 ***the beer is gone:*** Ibid.

Chapter 7: Terrible Responsibility

Stimson's diaries are in Stimson Papers.

129 ***waiting for word:*** Groves, *Now It Can Be Told,* 318–24; Knebel and Bailey, *No High Ground,* 217.

130 ***"I'm glad you said that":*** Groves, *Now It Can Be Told,* 324.

131 ***"Have you any more information?":*** Knebel and Bailey, *No High Ground,* 218.

131 ***"as if swept clean by a terrific":*** Kenny to Spaatz, August 8, 1945, Spaatz Papers. After the bombing, Groves sent Marshall and Stimson an extensive damage report: Gen. L. R. Groves to chief of staff (memorandum), August 6, 1945, Top Secret, Doc. 63, NSA.

132 ***"nothing survives":*** Charles Murphy, undated draft article, Spaatz Papers. The night the bomb was dropped, Murphy had dinner with Spaatz, along with members of three prominent publishing families who owned *The New York Times,* the *Chicago News,* and the *Minneapolis Tribune.* Spaatz diary, August 6, 1945, Spaatz Papers.

133 ***"Captain, this is the greatest thing":*** McCullough, *Truman,* 453.

134 ***thirty targets:*** Lifton and Mitchell, *Hiroshima in America,* 24. Less than 10 percent of the city's manufacturing, transportation, and storage facilities were damaged.

134 ***"The world will note":*** Wellerstein, " 'Purely Military' Target," and Wellerstein, "Kyoto Misconception," 45–48. For Truman's reaction to the news, see Walter Brown diary, entry for August 6, 1945, Doc. 64, NSA. Brown was an aide to Byrnes, traveling back from Potsdam. On August 9, Truman learned from MAGIC intercepts that the Hiroshima bombing killed 100,000 people. "Magic"—Far

East Summary, War Department, Office of the Assistant chief of staff, G-2, no. 507, August 9, 1945, Doc. 74, NSA.

135 *"I know that Japan":* Richard Russell to Harry Truman, August 7, 1945; Harry Truman to Richard Russell, August 9, 1945, HSTL.

135 *paying personal bills:* Baime, *Accidental President,* 344. Truman's views on the bomb continued to evolve. In July 1948, at a meeting to discuss custody of atomic weapons, Lewis Strauss noted, "The President indicated that he was not going to have 'some trigger-happy Colonel' using atomic bombs—and they were not weapons in the ordinary sense, but the liberation of a great natural force which killed women and children and old people indiscriminately." Alperovitz, "Was Truman a Revisionist," 2.

136 *bearing a second atomic bomb:* Wellerstein, "Kyoto Misconception," 49, 324n76.

136 *"You and General LeMay":* Marshall to Spaatz ("personal eyes only"), August 8, 1945, Spaatz Papers.

136 *"Acknowledge your message":* Spaatz to Marshall ("eyes only"), August 9, 1945, Spaatz Papers.

137 *"It is understood":* Norstad to Spaatz (telecon), August 8, 1945, Spaatz Papers.

137 *"If an atomic bomb":* Crane, *American Airpower Strategy,* 186.

138 *"Tinian Joint Chiefs" push:* Gordin, *Five Days in August,* 90; Christman, *Target Hiroshima,* 198–99.

138 *"all the way from Potsdam":* Laurence, *Dawn Over Zero,* 226.

138 *"In view of the effects at Trinity":* Kirkpatrick to Nimitz and Spaatz, August 9, 1945, Spaatz Papers.

139 *"I thought that if we were":* Carl Spaatz oral history, February 21, 1962, USAF Oral History Program, Air Force Historical Research Agency, Maxwell Air Force Base.

140 *to end the American firebombing:* Crane, *American Airpower Strategy,* 188. In his memoir, Stimson observed that one effect of the atomic bombs was to stop the firebombing. Stimson and Bundy, *On Active Service,* 633.

Chapter 8: Denial

141 *The first reports to reach Tokyo:* Walker, *Prompt and Utter Destruction,* 278.

142 *"A few B-29s hit"*: Knebel and Bailey, *No High Ground,* 191.

142 *"The whole city of Hiroshima"*: Butow, *Japan's Decision,* 151.

142 **He guesses that the Americans:** Hasegawa, *End of Pacific War,* 98.

142 *"We have spent two billion"*: Kort, *Columbia Guide,* 230.

143 *"atomic bombs may trigger"*: Asada, "Shock of the Bomb," 486; Hasegawa, *Racing the Enemy,* 184. Hasegawa downplays Togo's desire to end the war. Sigal, *Fighting to Finish,* says Togo talked in a "roundabout way" (237). Togo had met with Anami on the night of August 7, and Anami signaled, unofficially, that he was no longer confident Japan could prolong the war. Kiyotada, *Fifteen Lectures,* 264. See also Kawamura, *Emperor Hirohito,* 164; Bix, "Japan's Delayed Surrender," 210-225; and Shoji, "Japanese Termination," 57–71.

144 *"Everything that is exposed"*: Butow, *Japan's Decision,* 152.

144 *"The day began hot and clear"*: Hachiya, *Hiroshima Diary,* 26–32.

145 *a new bomb shelter:* Tamon, "Hirohito's 'Sacred Decision,'" 264.

145 *Every hour or so:* Asada, "Shock of the Bomb," 487.

145 *"most enthusiastically"*: On Togo's meeting with the emperor, see Togo, *Cause of Japan,* 315; Asada, "Shock of the Bomb," 488; Kido, *Diary,* entry for August 8, 1945; Cabinet Meeting and Togo's Meeting with the Emperor, August 7–8, 1945, Doc. 67A, NSA. Translation of excerpts from Gaimusho [Ministry of Foreign Affairs], ed., *Shusen Shiroku* [Historical Records of the End of the War], annotated by Jun Eto (Tokyo: Ministry of Foreign Affairs, 1952), 4:57–60.

146 *"We must know the Soviets'"*: On Togo's wire to Sato, see Hasegawa, *Racing the Enemy,* 185. See also Admiral Takagi diary, entry for August 8, 1945, Doc. 67B, NSA. The diary entry recounts a conversation with Navy Minister Yonai that captures the mood of the Big Six after Hiroshima and before Nagasaki: Prime Minister Suzuki still talks tough, fearful that any sign of weakness will set off a rebellion by frontline troops. Yonai worries about popular unrest, noting a further cut in the rice ration in Tokyo is scheduled for August 11.

147 **"Hände hoch!"**: Hastings, *Retribution,* 496. The fate of the Kwantung Army and the Japanese settlers in Manchuria under Stalin's rule was particularly awful. See Andrew Barshay, *The Gods Left First: The Captivity and Repatriation of Japanese POWs in Northeast Asia, 1947–1956* (Berkeley: University of California Press, 2013).

147 *"JANCFU":* Toll, *Twilight of Gods,* 711.

147 *Gallagher is feeling low:* Coster-Mullen, *Atom Bombs,* 69.

148 *has been to confession:* Sweeney, *War's End,* 186; Walker, *Prompt and Utter Destruction,* 201.

148 *fuel pump:* Ibid., 204–5.

148 *red light suddenly flashes:* Coster-Mullen, *Atom Bombs,* 72.

148 *"Has Sweeney aborted?":* Toll, *Twilight of Gods,* 715.

149 *"No drop":* Coster-Mullen, *Atom Bombs,* 74.

149 *Sweeney banks away:* Ibid., 76–82.

149 *Navy commander Fred Ashworth:* Fred Ashworth oral history, in Krauss and Krauss, *509th Remembered,* 20; Coster-Mullen, *Atom Bombs,* 82–83. Sweeney told Coster-Mullen that "Spaatz told him that a lot of the top brass breathed easier because they wound up dropping the bomb where they did instead of the original AP [aim point]." Coster-Mullen, *Atom Bombs,* 422.

Chapter 9: Sacred Decision

152 *"Are you sure it's true?":* Hasegawa, *Racing the Enemy,* 197.

152 *"careless":* Togo, "Foreign Minister Togo's Bitter Struggle," and interview by author. *Careless* was also translated as "stupid."

153 *without clothing and gear for winter:* Gallicchio, *Unconditional,* 134.

153 *"a serious jolt":* Hasegawa, *Racing the Enemy,* 200.

153 *"We must be tenacious":* Hasegawa, *End of Pacific War,* 127.

154 *"at the risk of his life":* Asada, "Shock of the Bomb," 492; Hata, *Hirohito,* 59.

154 *"un-Japanese":* Brooks, *Behind Japan's Surrender,* 59.

154 *"We can't get anywhere":* Butow, *Japan's Decision,* 160.

155 *three other conditions:* Hasegawa, *Racing the Enemy,* 203.

156 *Togo had won Yonai's assurance:* Togo, *Cause of Japan,* 316.

156 *Anami had tacitly conceded:* Asada, "Shock of the Bomb," 493. I have relied largely on Asada's rendition of the meeting. There is no one authoritative account of the Big Six and cabinet meetings on August 9. Butow, *Japan's Decision,* 160n65. They began in an atmosphere of "impatience, frenzy, and bewilderment," according to Fujita Hisanori, grand chamberlain to the emperor. Asada, "Shock of the Bomb," 490. Anami's own diary suggests he was not as assured as his bluster made him seem. According to Peter Wetzler, who exam-

ined the diary, Anami wrote "in his Memo on August 9, if the situation of the Imperial House was not properly resolved the Yamato Folk had no choice but 'for the sake of justice [*seigi*] to fight to the end, dying in the name of an eternal cause [loyalty to the nation, *kuni*].' On the same day, 'Accept the three country [Potsdam] proclamation? Go as far as an "honorable death" [*gyokusai*]?'" Wetzler, *Imperial Japan,* 157. It is not clear if he is talking about his own death or the death of the entire nation.

157 *"if they lost their weapons":* Bix, "Japan's Delayed Surrender," 219.

158 *Lt. Marcus McDilda:* Ibid., 492.

158 *"We will find life out of death":* Brooks, *Behind Japan's Surrender,* 67.

158 *Then Saburo Ota:* Ibid., 71.

160 **seidan—***sacred decision:* Hasegawa, *Racing the Enemy,* 203–6; Hasegawa, *End of Pacific War,* 113–45; Kawamura, *Emperor Hirohito,* 155, 161–67; Kido, *Diary,* entries for July 25 ("bearing the unbearable") and August 10, 1945; Butow, *Japan's Decision,* 176; Yellen, "Specter of Revolution," 216–17. It appears that Kido and perhaps even the emperor were initially inclined to go along with Anami and the military on all four conditions, but Shigemitsu and Konoe talked them out of it. Kido, *Diary,* entry for August 9, 1945. Togo acted as a prod to these behind-the-scenes machinations on the afternoon of August 9. In his memoir, he says that before the two P.M. cabinet meeting, he told Suzuki that, given the deadlock, "the only possible solution would be to request an imperial decision; but it was necessary that the Premier take care lest the cabinet be disabled, before that could be done—by the resignation of the War Minister, for instance." Togo, *Cause of Japan,* 318.

161 *a small, loosely allied group:* During most of the war, the so-called Yoshida Anti-War Group, nominally led by former ambassador to London (and postwar Japanese prime minister) Shigeru Yoshida, agitated for an early peace, at least until Yoshida himself was arrested in April 1945. Yoshida, *Memoirs,* 26–29. A fervent voice for ending the war was Prince Konoe, who in February 1945 warned the emperor of a Communist revolution; the emperor listened but continued to defer to the die-hard military. Yellen, "Specter of Revolution," 210–13. The cabinet secretary, Hisatsune Sakomizu, played a key role in the final days leading up to the *seidan,* tricking

the military chiefs into giving their permission for a *seidan* without realizing its true purpose. Butow, *Japan's Decision,* 167. However, in the retelling, Sakomizu may have played up his own role, and he gives too much credit to Suzuki as a master player at *haragei.* "Sakomizu rationalized and obscured the genuine opportunism, vacillation, and incompetence of Suzuki and other members of the wartime government as they shifted from a policy of war to one of surrender." Bix, "Japan's Delayed Surrender," 200.

161 *"gifts from the gods":* Hasegawa, *Racing the Enemy,* 198. Yonai made a similar statement; see Asada, "Shock of the Bomb," 498.

161 *"I curse the emperor":* Yellen, "Specter of Revolution," 209.

162 *Now Hirohito worries:* After the war, Hirohito gave his own reasons for *seidan,* emphasizing that he feared he could no longer protect the sacred jewels that conferred legitimacy on the emperor system and that he feared the entire race might die. Some commentators see Hirohito as a weak vacillator whose spine stiffened only when his own neck was threatened. Drea, *In the Service,* 215. Others say he was willing to die himself to save the imperial house and his people. Kawamura, *Emperor Hirohito,* 185. Hirohito may have been extremely fearful of a Soviet occupation. Hasegawa, *End of Pacific War,* 136; see also Sumio Hatano, "The Atomic Bomb and Soviet Entry into the War," ibid., 95ff. Accounts that record Hirohito saying he was ready to die to save his people were probably confected by propagandists. Roger Brown interview by author; Brown, "Desiring to Inaugurate Great Peace."

162 *One by one the soldiers:* Toll, *Twilight of Gods,* 723–25; Frank, *Downfall,* 293; Butow, *Japan's Decision,* 173–76; Craig, *Fall of Japan,* 114–15.

164 *a ticking time bomb:* Hasegawa, *Racing the Enemy,* 212.

165 *the streets are empty:* Newman, *Truman and the Hiroshima Cult,* 110.

165 *Anyone who disobeys:* Toland, *Rising Sun,* 814, Butow, *Japan's Decision,* 184.

166 *"We are determined":* Toland, *Rising Sun,* 816; Hasegawa, *Racing the Enemy,* 217; Frank, *Downfall,* 299.

166 *Togo's men transmit:* Toland, *Rising Sun,* 816.

Chapter 10: Gambits

Stimson's diaries are in Stimson Papers.

168 *"to save us from":* The death totals in that case would be close to half a million. Frank, *Downfall,* 301.

169 *"When you punish your dog":* Stimson's "Memorandum of Conference with the President" is in his diary for August 8, 1945.

169 *the president regards Hirohito:* Gallicchio, *Unconditional,* 151–53.

169 *mindful of the advice:* Robertson, *Sly and Able,* 434–36; Walter Brown diary, entries for August 10–11, 1945, Doc. 81, NSA. Secretary of the Navy James Forrestal first suggested a compromise approach. Hasegawa, *Racing the Enemy,* 220. Interestingly, according to Hasegawa (218), it was the keep-the-emperor crowd at State that first spotted the potential trap set by Hiranuma. Joseph Grew warned Byrnes that the United States could not accept a Japanese surrender that allowed the emperor to preserve his prerogatives.

169 *"the most honest horse thief":* Ham, *Hiroshima and Nagasaki,* 386.

169 *"From the moment of surrender":* Butow, *Japan's Decision,* 191.

170 *"They wanted to keep the Emperor":* Truman diary, entry for August 10, 1945, HSTL.

171 *Truman refuses to stop all conventional bombing:* Historians Michael D. Gordin and Tsuyoshi Hasegawa disagree on this point. See Gordin et al., Roundtable on Hasegawa. Gordin notes that there were no bombing raids between August 10 and 13, but that was only because Spaatz canceled a raid.

171 *"He said the thought":* Henry Wallace diary, entry for August 10, 1945, Doc. 78, NSA.

171 *figure of 100,000 deaths:* Frank, *Downfall,* 302, 427.

171 *"Physical or figurative?":* McCullough, *Truman,* 460.

172 *"ready for delivery":* Groves to Marshall, August 10, 1945, Spaatz Papers.

172 *Lt. Gen. Nathan Twining:* Twining to Spaatz, August 14, 1945, Spaatz Papers. The cities proposed on August 14 were Sapporo, Hakodate, Otaru, Yokosuka, Osaka, and Nagoya.

172 *"Strongly recommend that":* Spaatz to Arnold, August 9, 1945, Spaatz Papers. Spaatz revealed his view in Carl Spaatz oral history, February 21, 1962, USAF Oral History Program, Air Force Histori-

cal Research Agency, Maxwell Air Force Base (courtesy Katharine Gresham). In typical Spaatz fashion, he eased into the subject somewhat diffidently. The whole exchange is revealing, in a roundabout way, starting with Spaatz's professed indifference to firebombing, which in fact he was trying to end:

Q. What was your attitude toward the firebombing of the Japanese cities?

A. I had no attitude on that. It was a fait accompli by the time I got over there. I had not too much feeling about it one way or another.

Q. What was your attitude toward the necessity and desirability of dropping the atomic bomb?

A. The idea I had was that if we were not going to have this invasion of Honshu I felt that conventional bombing would do the job.

Q. Do you agree with [Edward] Teller and others that the Japanese should have been given two or three days warning before the bomb was dropped?

A. My reaction was not to tell them about it. If they were aware of what you planned to do, certainly they would oppose. You could not tell them because of your regard for your own people—we would certainly have lost too many men and planes. We had far more regard for our bomber crews during the war than they did. Had it been possible to drop the bomb in the ocean or in some wasteland—where they could see the effect—looking back, maybe it would have been better but no one felt that way at the time and we only had two over there at the time. I thought that if we were going to drop the atomic bomb, drop it on the outskirts—say in Tokyo Bay—so that the effects would not be as devastating to the city and the people. I made this suggestion over the phone between the Hiroshima and Nagasaki bombings and I was told to go ahead with our targets.

173 *almost a thousand B-17s:* For the February 3 raid on Berlin, see Clodfelter, *Beneficial Bombing,* 175. Spaatz was reluctant to order the

raid, and General Doolittle, the Eighth Air Force commander, shifted the targeting toward more military targets rather than make an indiscriminate strike at the city center. Tami Davis and Conrad Crane, interviews by author.

173 **pikadon**: Chieko Taniguchi, "Messages from Hiroshima," *Asahi Shimbun,* n.d., https://www.asahi.com/hibakusha/english /hiroshima/h01-00034e.html.

173 *"at a high level"*: Arnold to Spaatz, August 10, 1945, Spaatz Papers.

173 *"is not to be released"*: Arnold to Spaatz, August 11, 1945, Spaatz Papers.

173 *back to "precision" attacks:* Frank, *Downfall,* 303–7.

174 *"Not knowing the extent"*: Spaatz to Arnold, August 11, 1945, Spaatz Papers.

174 *"You are quoted"*: Marshall to Spaatz ("eyes only"), August 11, 1945, Spaatz Papers.

175 *"Press has no authority"*: Spaatz to Marshall, August 11, 1945, Spaatz Papers.

175 *"Before news came last night"*: Spaatz diary, August 11, 1945, Spaatz Papers.

177 *"The boss remarked"*: Correspondence of Sarah Bagby, courtesy of Martha Johnson.

177 *build a hard-stand:* Spaatz to Arnold, August 10, 1945, Spaatz Papers.

Chapter 11: Plots

178 *Togo is casting about:* Butow, *Japan's Decision,* 193; Hasegawa, *Racing the Enemy,* 228; Hata, *Hirohito,* 62; Kiyotada, *Fifteen Lectures,* 268.

179 *Zealous young army officers:* Hasegawa, *Racing the Enemy,* 230.

180 *"Please let me do it"*: Craig, *Fall of Japan,* 137.

180 *Takeshita boasts that he can deliver:* Forrest, "Eat Grass," 4.

180 *he should commit suicide:* Barrett, *140 Days to Hiroshima,* 212.

181 *his entries are cryptic:* Examining Anami's diary entries, which are preserved in the library of the National Diet, Peter Wetzler saw a man torn between humiliating surrender and honorable death. Wetzler, *Imperial Japan,* 152–58. In the end, Anami chose both. Along the way, he was horribly conflicted. At one point, he came close to working with Col. Okikatsu Arao of the Military Affairs

Bureau to concoct a plot to isolate the emperor and stop him from accepting the Potsdam Declaration stipulating unconditional surrender. But he seemed to know the plot was slipshod and he never took the more direct step of using his power to bring down the government by resigning.

181 ***Like the leaderless samurai:*** Hastings, *Retribution,* 510.

181 ***some personal loyalty:*** Butow, *Japan's Decision,* 186.

181 ***"the Green-Green school":*** Toland, *Rising Sun,* 818–19.

182 ***gently eclipsed:*** Kawamura, *Emperor Hirohito,* 27.

182 ***"protect" the emperor:*** Pacific War Research Society, *Japan's Longest Day,* 45.

182 ***peremptory rebuff by Mikasa:*** Ibid., 49; Brooks, *Behind Japan's Surrender,* 231; Wetzler, *Imperial Japan,* 153.

183 ***sensed a lack of conviction:*** Butow, *Japan's Decision,* 193; Hasegawa, *Racing the Enemy,* 229; Hata, *Hirohito,* 62. The motivations of the main actors at this point are subtle and carefully cloaked. Navy Minister Yonai is a case in point. Although his waffling at Big Six meetings frustrated Togo, a diary entry on August 12 from one of his subordinates, Admiral Takagi, shows Yonai with more backbone—as well as cleverness. The navy minister privately chided Umezu and Toyoda for going to the emperor with their pleas to continue the war. ("They say that I am a wimp," Yonai tells Takagi.) Yonai is astute about the need to save face. He confides to Takagi, "It may be inappropriate to put it in this way, but the atomic bombs and the Soviet entry into the war are, in a sense, God's gifts. Now we can end the war without making it clear that we have to end the war because of the domestic situation." Like Konoe and others, Yonai feared a revolt by Japan's starving people. Admiral Takagi diary, entry for August 12, [1945], Doc. 84, NSA.

183 ***If the people do not want him:*** Hata, *Hirohito,* 168; Kiyotada, *Fifteen Lectures,* 269.

183 ***the prime minister is waffling:*** Craig, *Fall of Japan,* 147.

184 ***"What are you thinking of?":*** Hata, *Hirohito,* 63; Butow, *Japan's Decision,* 195. When Togo expressed his concerns to Marquis Kido, the privy seal recorded in his diary, "I feel extremely anxious." This was a very rare display of emotion by the emperor's chief political adviser in his diary and suggests a high level of stress. Kido, *Diary,* entry for August 12, 1945.

184 *deliberately stamp the documents:* Butow, *Japan's Decision,* 197.

185 *"Kill Lord Kido!":* Ibid., 199.

185 *"fool or a madman":* Ibid., 200

185 *seeking Kido's sympathy:* Toland, *Rising Sun,* 825.

185 *Suzuki is genial:* Craig, *Fall of Japan,* 159. But he is not decisive. He laments the lack of "harmony"—his Taoist wish—and says: "Even with these exhausting deliberations on war and peace, we are still far away from any sort of consensus." "To die is easy, to live is difficult," says one of the ministers at the cabinet meeting. The confusion and struggle are amply illustrated in notes taken by Information Minister Toshiro Shimamura. "Cabinet Meeting over the Reply to the Four Powers," August 13, 1945, Doc. 86, NSA.

185 *"Absurd":* Togo, *Cause of Japan,* 328.

186 *"Sacrilegious!":* Brooks, *Behind Japan's Surrender,* 248.

186 *strange reverie:* Togo, *Cause of Japan,* 329–30.

186 *Sakomizu is dumbfounded:* Wetzler, *Imperial Japan,* 154; Kawamura, *Emperor Hirohito,* 180; Toland, *Rising Sun,* 825.

187 *"If we are resolute":* Butow, *Japan's Decision,* 205; Togo, *Cause of Japan,* 332; Craig, *Fall of Japan,* 164.

188 *military coup plotters:* Craig, *Fall of Japan,* 162–63; Toland, *Rising Sun,* 827–28; Forrest, "Eat Grass"; Hata, *Hirohito,* 71. Anami seems to have plotted with a more senior official, Col. Okikatsu Arao, but the precise nature of their relationship remains unclear. Frank, *Downfall,* 318–19.

Chapter 12: Is Tokyo Next?

Stimson's diaries are in Stimson Papers.

190 *between Henry Stimson and George Patton:* Stimson and Bundy, *On Active Service,* 41, 96, 351, 499, 660.

190 *never let up:* Ibid., 478. See Bonnett, "Jekyll and Hyde," 186–88, for an excellent analysis of Stimson's "psychology of combat." "His first tenet was derived from a proposition he applied to every conflict, from the courtroom to the battlefield: that a partisan's success in conflict was predicated on his or her willingness to seize the initiative and apply unremitting pressure on the opposition until it was persuaded to concede" (186). This philosophy, writes Bonnett, and

not moral hypocrisy, explains Stimson's "mentality" in the summer of 1945.

191 **disturbing cable traffic:** Frank, *Downfall*, 326–27; "Magic"— Diplomatic Summary, War Department, Office of Assistant Chief of Staff, G-2, no. 1236—August 13, 1945, Top Secret Ultra, Doc. 88, NSA. The intercept shows field commanders saying they have received an order from Anami to "push forward—[words uncertain, probably 'to the very end']."

192 **"an ultimatum be issued":** Hasegawa, *Racing the Enemy*, 238–39; McCloy diary, entry for August 13, 1945, McCloy Papers.

192 **Groves should resume the chain:** Gallicchio, "After Nagasaki"; Gen. L. R. Groves to Gen. George C. Marshall (memorandum), August 10, 1945, Top Secret, with a handwritten note by General Marshall, Doc. 82, NSA.

193 **"This man is tottering":** Col. Paul Miles, interview by author. Miles, a former professor of military history at West Point and Princeton, was told this story by his colleague, Brig. Gen. George Lincoln.

193 **"atomic bombs will not have":** Frank, *Downfall*, 312; Maj. Gen. Clayton Bissell, assistant chief of staff, G-2, to chief of staff, "Estimate of Japanese Situation for Next 30 Days" (memorandum), August 12, 1945, Top Secret, Doc. 85, NSA.

193 **"What General Marshall":** Gallicchio, "After Nagasaki," 400; General Hull and Colonel Seaman [sic]—1325, telephone conversation transcript, August 13, 1945, Top Secret, Doc. 87, NSA.

194 **"As I understand it":** Malloy, "'Very Pleasant Way to Die,'" 518. For Groves's real-time denial of the effect of radiation—which he either consciously or unconsciously preserved by his strict compartmentation of information—see P. L. Henshaw and R. R. Coveyou to H. J. Curtis and K. Z. Morgan, "Death from Radiation Burns," August 24, 1945, Confidential, Doc. 92, NSA; and General Groves and Colonel Rea, Oak Ridge Hospital, memorandum of telephone conversation, August 28, 1945, Top Secret, Doc. 93, NSA. See also Nolan, *Atomic Doctors*, passim.

194 **"GI'S IN PACIFIC GO WILD":** Feis, *Japan Subdued*, 126.

194 **"Never have I known time":** Byrnes, *All in One Lifetime*, 306.

195 **"did not contain the message":** Washington Embassy Telegram 5599 to Foreign Office, August 14, 1945, Top Secret, Doc. 91, NSA.

195 *"remarked sadly that"*: Bernstein, "Eclipsed by Hiroshima and Nagasaki," 457.

195 *"Concerning very heavy"*: Marshall to Spaatz, August 13, 1945, Spaatz Papers.

197 *"One look"*: Butow, *Japan's Decision,* 206; Kido, *Diary,* entry for August 14, 1945.

Chapter 13: To Bear the Unbearable

199 *does not want to give the military:* Frank, *Downfall,* 314. Hirohito had become convinced that the Americans intended to preserve the emperorship. Japan's minister to Sweden, Suemasa Okamato, sent a persuasive cable on August 13 arguing that the Americans had convinced their Allies to accept continuation of the emperor system. This also helped bring around the wavering Suzuki. Shoji, "Japanese Termination," 63.

199 *hearing rumors:* Forrest, "Eat Grass," 3.

200 *white clothes serve:* Frank, *Downfall,* 431.

200 *will not support a coup:* Hata, *Hirohito,* 72; Hasegawa, *Racing the Enemy,* 241–43.

200 *opaque and cheerful:* For analysis of Anami's motives, see Wetzler, *Imperial Japan,* 158; Hata, *Hirohito,* 78–81. A Japanese-language biography of Anami by Fusako Tsunoda (read for the author by Hideko Takayama) cites two Anami colleagues, who spoke to Anami on July 31 and August 1, saying that Anami always understood he would have to obey the emperor and surrender. One quotes Anami as saying that "there won't be any battle in *hondo* [on Japanese soil]. The emperor won't allow it."

200 *borrowing neckties:* Togo, *Cause of Japan,* 333.

201 *Suzuki apologizes:* Butow, *Japan's Decision,* 207. A fairly detailed account of the meeting, including scenes of much sobbing, was written about six weeks later by Director of Information Hiroshi Shimomura: "The Second Sacred Judgment," August 14, 1945, Doc. 89, NSA.

201 *"I have listened carefully"*: Ibid. The conference was scheduled for ten-thirty A.M., but the time slipped to about 10:50 or eleven. When it was over, Kido wrote in his diary, "I had an audience with the Throne. . . . I really did not lift my head, as His Majesty related

the circumstances with tearful eyes." Kido, *Diary,* entry for August 14, 1945.

201 *well-rested and robust:* Pacific War Research Society, *Japan's Longest Day,* 94.

202 *his aide, Maj. Saburo Hayashi:* Ibid., 87.

202 *Takeshita is after him:* Hata, *Hirohito,* 73.

202 *"The emperor has spoken":* Pacific War Research Society, *Japan's Longest Day,* 91.

202 *A deep lethargy:* Hata, *Hirohito,* 92; Hasegawa, *Racing the Enemy,* 244.

203 *cabinet members eye him warily:* Pacific War Research Society, *Japan's Longest Day,* 104.

203 *"the war situation has developed":* Ibid., 145–46, 165.

203 *"overly polite":* Togo, *Cause of Japan,* 335.

204 *"Was it all right?"* Pacific War Research Society, *Japan's Longest Day,* 211–12.

204 *locks the bag in a small safe:* Toland, *Rising Sun,* 839.

205 *shoots the startled General Mori:* Hasegawa, *Racing the Enemy,* 245; Pacific War Research Society, *Japan's Longest Day,* 106, 219–30.

205 *"I'm thinking of seppuku":* Forrest, "Eat Grass," 5; Butow, *Japan's Decision,* 219–20; Toland, *Rising Sun,* 846–47.

207 *"a mid-summer's night dream":* Pacific War Research Society, *Japan's Longest Day,* 246.

207 *put a bullet in his head:* Ibid., 324.

207 *"Don't they understand?":* Ibid., 274, 300.

207 *Privy Seal Kido emerges:* Toland, *Rising Sun,* 842. Awakened around three A.M., Kido first took shelter in a room for the chamberlains, then returned to his room to tear up documents and flush them down the toilet. He then hid in what he calls a "vault" of the Household Ministry "to spy privately on the situation." He says he met with the emperor at eight A.M. Kido, *Diary,* entry for August 15, 1945.

208 *never uses the forbidden words:* Wetzler, *Imperial Japan,* 159.

208 *"The enemy has begun":* Butow, *Japan's Decision,* 1–6; Dower, *Embracing Defeat,* 35–39.

209 *"How can we lose the war?":* Hachiya, *Hiroshima Diary,* 82.

209 *send princes of the royal house:* Butow, *Japan's Decision,* 225.

209 *"Yoo hoo!":* Dower, *Embracing Defeat,* 23. Brian Walsh notes that the streets were usually empty of females because of untrue but

widespread rumors of rape. Later, prostitutes were organized by the occupation forces.

209 **over 20 million people have died:** The exact number is unknowable. "In the tens of millions," says Frank, *Tower of Skulls,* 8. An article posted at the website for the National World War II Museum says that "a conservative accounting shows 25 million people died in the Asia Pacific War," including about 6 million combatants, mostly Chinese and Japanese, and 19 million noncombatants. "Excluding Japanese, every single day the war continued between 8,000 and perhaps 14,000 noncombatants were dying." Richard B. Frank, "The Miraculous Deliverance from a Titanic Tragedy," National World War II Museum, August 25, 2020, nationalww2museum.org /war/articles/asia–pacific–war-1945.

209 **he expects, instead:** Togo, *Cause of Japan,* 339; Kazuhiko Togo and Shigehiko Togo, interviews by author.

Chapter 14: No High Ground

Stimson's diaries are in Stimson Papers.

211 **bombs are still falling:** Bernstein, "Perils and Politics of Surrender," 17.

211 **seven from the 509th:** Coster-Mullen, *Atom Bombs,* 84.

211 **they fly back to base:** Landon Jones, interview by author. Jones described the flight of his uncle, Maj. Robert Jones, who was a navigator in the 331st Bomb Group of the Twentieth Air Force. Major Jones's combat records are in the Robert Terry Jones Collection, accession no. 2021.143, National World War II Museum.

212 **"Can Doolittle send":** Special Radio Teletype Conference, August 14, 1945, Spaatz Papers.

212 **Doolittle declined:** Doolittle, *I Could Never,* 422–23.

212 **"Why not Tokyo?":** Gen. Paul Tibbets, "Reflections on Hiroshima" (1989), Voices of the Manhattan Project, National Museum of Nuclear Science & History, AHF.

212 **"These operations have been":** Special Radio Teletype Conference, August 14, 1945, Spaatz Papers.

213 **"High ground will be seized":** Ibid.

213 **"scrambler phone":** Stimson and Bundy, *On Active Service,* 641; Bird, *Chairman,* 261.

213 *hearty cheer goes up:* Stimson diary, entries for August 12–
      September 3. While at the Ausable Club, Stimson gave the first-ever
      speech proposing controls on nuclear weapons.

213 *"verge of an emotional":* Ibid.

214 *"in his pocket, so to speak":* Ibid.; Stimson and Bundy, *On Active
      Service,* 644; McCloy diary, entry for September 2, 1945, McCloy
      Papers; Bird, *Chairman,* 261.

215 *"The chief lesson":* Stimson to Truman, September 11, 1945, and
      Memorandum for the President, September 11, 1945, in Stimson
      and Bundy, *On Active Service,* 642.

215 *"future of world peace":* Morison, *Turmoil and Tradition,* 532.

215 *"the President has decided to follow":* Stimson dairy, entry for Sep-
      tember 21, 1945, Stimson Papers.

216 *already too late:* Malloy, *Atomic Tragedy,* 154–55.

216 *"I have often said":* Stimson and Bundy, *On Active Service,* 649;
      Stimson, "Challenge to Americans."

216 *"my views have become":* Stimson to George Roberts, June 11,
      1947, Stimson Papers.

216 **Tsar Bomba:** Alex Wellerstein, "An Unearthly Spectacle," *Bulletin
      of Atomic Scientists,* October 29, 2021.

217 **USS Henry L. Stimson:** Malloy, *Atomic Tragedy,* 181–82.

217 *Cuban Missile Crisis:* Isaacson and Thomas, *Wise Men,* 624–30. In
      Gambling with Armageddon (2021), Martin Sherwin credited "dumb
      luck" for the avoidance of nuclear war. He was critical of Stimson
      for having been seduced by the temptation of "atomic diplomacy,"
      the evil seed of Cold War nuclear precarity. Sherwin (author of
      World Destroyed and *American Prometheus,* with Kai Bird) was a great
      scholar and analyst, and I think he was correct about the motiva-
      tions of Jimmy Byrnes and, to some extent, Truman, but he under-
      estimated the significance of Stimson's feeling the necessity to shock
      the Japanese into surrender. As I have argued, a close examination
      of the record of Japanese intransigence suggests Stimson was right.
      (For further detail, see Asada, "Shock of the Bomb," 497.) As for the
      Cuban Missile Crisis, I agree with Sherwin that the dovish Adlai
      Stevenson deserves more praise than the hawkish Bundy and Lovett,
      but President Kennedy's ultimate solution—a carrot-and-stick mix-
      ture of realism and idealism—was classically Stimsonian.

218 *"like a merciful rain":* Dower, *Embracing Defeat,* 114, 92–93.

218 *On September 27:* Ibid., 294–95.

219 *Hirohito visits Hiroshima:* Bix, "Japan's Delayed Surrender," 225.
219 *"everlasting friendship":* "Hirohito Extols Japanese-U.S. Ties," *New York Times,* October 3, 1975.
219 *Yasukuni Shrine:* Kawamura, *Emperor Hirohito,* 192.

Epilogue: Reckonings

221 *"The reaction has begun":* Wyden, *Day One,* 290.
221 *Most Americans approved:* Malloy, *Atomic Tragedy,* 221n6, cites a *Fortune* magazine poll that 22.7 percent of Americans believed we should have used more atomic bombs before the Japanese had a chance to surrender.
221 *war correspondent John Hersey:* See Blume, *Fallout,* passim.
222 *mayor of Princeton:* Lifton and Mitchell, *Hiroshima in America,* 87.
222 *Albert Einstein, the scientist:* Ibid., 148.
222 *"There is no one":* Hershberg, *James Conant,* 291–97.
223 *"the least abhorrent choice":* Bird, *Color of Truth,* 90–100.
223 *"HENRY L. STIMSON EXPLAINS":* Bernstein, "Seizing the Contested Terrain."
223 *Conventional wisdom congealed:* Walker, *Prompt and Utter Destruction,* 98–104. Although I disagree with Alperovitz's revisionist thesis that dropping the bomb was avoidable, his "Book Two: The Myth" in *Decision to Use the Bomb* is a deeply sourced and persuasive treatment.
224 *"I have rarely been connected":* Stimson to Frankfurter, December 12, 1946; Frankfurter to Stimson, December 16, 1946, Stimson Papers.
224 *"The atom bomb might never":* Stimson and Bundy, *On Active Service,* 626, 629; Malloy, *Atomic Tragedy,* 166. Grew was indulging in some revisionism on his own behalf. As acting secretary of state, he had ultimately pushed for a harder line on Japan. And as late as May 3, he was arguing against keeping the emperor. *Haragei,* of course, is not unique to the Japanese. Iokibe, "American Policy," 46.
225 *pangs of regret:* Lifton and Mitchell, *Hiroshima in America,* 109; Bird, *Chairman,* 263.
225 *guilt and anxiety justified?:* See especially Frank, *Downfall,* 349–60. See Walker, *Prompt and Utter Destruction,* chap. 7; Newman, *Truman and Hiroshima Cult,* chap. 6. For the scholarly debate over the casu-

alty estimates, see Bernstein, "Truman and the A-Bomb," 551–52. For a direct rebuttal of the revisionists on whether Japan was about to surrender, see Asada, "Shock of the Bomb," 501. Bix's analysis:

> The Japanese "peace" overtures to the Soviets . . . were vague, feeble, and counterproductive, in effect of no importance at all. Those maneuvers certainly did not constitute a serious attempt to end the war. Togo himself conceded as much when he said, on 17 August 1950, that "although I asked the Soviet Union to act as a peace mediator, I was unable to advise her of our peace conditions in any concrete form." (Bix, "Japan's Delayed Surrender," 224)

228 *an opportunity to outlaw war:* For a particularly insightful (and sympathetic) view of Stimson's motivations and character, see Bonnett, "Jekyll and Hyde," 174–212. For Stimson's own views, see Stimson, "Nuremberg Trial."

228 *"crimes against peace":* On flaws in war crimes trials, see Dower, *Embracing Defeat,* 443–84. For the most recent scholarship that takes a more benign view of the trials, see Yumi Totani, *Justice in Asia and the Pacific Region 1945–1952: Allied War Crimes Prosecutions* (New York: Cambridge University Press, 2015).

229 *crying "racism":* For racism on both sides, see Dower, *War Without Mercy,* passim.

229 *"the most formidable fighting insect":* Hastings, *Retribution,* 49.

230 *Togo tried to argue:* Kazuhiko Togo and Shigehiko Togo, interviews by author. The war crimes trial record and Togo's prison records are at NA II. For a compelling argument that Togo's conviction as a war criminal and twenty-year prison sentence represent a miscarriage of justice, see his lawyer Bruce Blakeney's "Petition to the Supreme Commander for the Allied Powers: For Review of the Verdict and Sentence at the International Military Trials for the Far East in the Case of Togo Shigenori," November 19, 1948. Of the eleven judges, at least three voted to acquit. Records of General Headquarters, Far East Command, Supreme Commander Allied Powers, NA II.

231 *On October 20, 1950:* Morison, *Turmoil and Tradition,* 540–42; Eleanor Perkins (Stimson's niece), interview by author.

232 *Spaatz died of a stroke:* Katharine Gresham, interview by author,

and Gresham, *General Tooey.* Spaatz turned down the defense indus-
try jobs because he thought it would be "inappropriate" for him to
be looking for contracts from the air force after serving as its chief.
During the 1950s, he published a column on defense matters for
Newsweek. (The actual writing was done by his friend Champ
Clark, the *Newsweek* Washington bureau chief.)

232 **the temptation of science:** Stimson was not the first to worry that science would outstrip morality. The frontispiece of Martin Sherwin's
Gambling with Armageddon quotes Henry Adams (whom Stimson
surely read), writing in 1862:

> Man has mounted science, and is now run away with. I firmly be-
> lieve that before many centuries more, science will be the master
> of men. The engines he will have invented will be beyond his
> strength to control. Someday science may have the existence of
> mankind in its power, and the human race commit suicide, by
> blowing up the world.

Photograph Credits

Pages iv–v: U.S. warplanes fly over the battleship USS *Missouri* in Tokyo Bay, Japan, September 2, 1945, upon the signing of the surrender documents by Japan. National Archives and Records Administration, College Park, Maryland, Identifier 520775.

Page xi: B-29 bombers flying past Mount Fuji on their way to bomb Tokyo, Japan, 1945. Pictures from History/Universal Images Group/Getty Images.

Page 3: Secretary of War Henry Stimson and Mrs. Stimson, 1945. Harry S. Truman Library & Museum.

Page 27: Dr. J. Robert Oppenheimer and Gen. Leslie Groves at the site where the test atomic bomb was exploded, Alamogordo, New Mexico, September 9, 1945. Associated Press.

Page 60: Japanese foreign minister Shigenori Togo. Sueddeutsche Zeitung Photo/Alamy Stock Photo.

Page 87: President Harry Truman meets with Secretary of War Henry Stimson in the Oval Office. Bettmann/Getty Images.

Page 111: Col. Paul Tibbets in front of the *Enola Gay*, the B-29 bomber that dropped the atomic bomb on Hiroshima. CPA Media Ltd./Alamy Stock Photo.

Page 129 (left): Gen. Curtis LeMay (center left) and Gen. Carl "Tooey" Spaatz (center right) meet with officers on Guam, 1945. Bettmann/Getty Images.

Page 129 (right): Gen. Carl "Tooey" Spaatz, 1945. Thomas D. McAvoy/The LIFE Picture Collection/Shutterstock.

Page 141: Nagasaki, Japan, before and after the atomic bombing of August 9, 1945. National Archives and Records Administration, College Park, Maryland, Identifier 77-MDH-12.3.

Page 152 (left): Portrait of Emperor Hirohito at the time of his enthronement in 1928. Ian Dagnall Computing/Alamy Stock Photo.

Page 152 (right): Emperor Hirohito during World War II, 1945. Photo 12/Alamy Stock Photo.

Page 178: Japanese war minister Gen. Korechika Anami, circa 1945. Bettmann/Getty Images.

Page 198: Japanese surrender ceremony on board the USS *Missouri*, Tokyo Bay, Japan, September 2, 1945. Pictorial Press Ltd./Alamy Stock Photo.

Index

Page numbers of photographs appear in italics.

Acheson, Dean, 168, 266n54
Anami, Gen. Korechika, 70–71, 73–74,
  77, 82, 85, *178*, 230, 269–70n70
  "Big Six" meeting on surrender and,
    156–59, 159n, 281–82n156
  fight-to-the-death position of, 178,
    181, 191, 227, 232
  final "decisive battle" (*hondo kessen*)
    strategy, 71, 73–74, 84, 86, 156,
    188, 290n200
  Hirohito and, 162, 181
  Hiroshima's destruction and, 143,
    280n143
  military coup plot and, 178–89,
    199–202, 286–87n181, 288n188,
    290n200
  Potsdam Declaration and, 153–54
  suicide of, 203, 205–7, 207n
  surrender decision and response to,
    164, 165–66, 202, 203, 282n160
Arao, Col. Okikatsu, 288n188
Arnold, Gen. Henry "Hap," 15, 23, 96,
  114, 261n23, 272–73n96
  A-bomb targets and, 42, 100–101
  American "thousand-plane" grand
    finale against Japan and, 195–96,
    211–12
  Hiroshima casualties, reaction to,
    130
  Lovett and, 15–16
  Spaatz and, 114, 115, 117, 172, 174,
    195–96
  Stimson meeting on civilian
    bombing and, 49–50, 265–66n50
Ashworth, Commander Fred, 149, 151
atomic bomb (A-bomb), 99, 175, 188,
  227
  American nuclear preemptive strike
    against Russia considered, xii,
    216, 231
  American nuclear submarines,
    216–17

American public approval of
  dropping A-bombs on Japan,
  221–22, 294n221
American use of, taken for granted,
  xii, 20, 260n20
America's motivation for dropping,
  xii–xiii, xvi, 223, 225–26,
  251–52nxiii, 252–53nxiii, 258n17
Atomic Bombing Missions map,
  xviii
August 6, 1945: first bomb (Little
  Boy) dropped, Hiroshima, xi, xvi,
  123–24, 138n
August 9, 1945: second bomb (Fat
  Man) dropped, Nagasaki, xi, 136,
  138n, 147–51
blast equivalent of, 44
civilian casualties projected, xiv, 47
civilian deaths and, 100, 175–76,
  222
controversy about dropping, xi–xii,
  222–28, 252–53nxiii
decision to use against Japan, 17–18,
  223, 225–26, 252–53nxiii
development cost, 20
development of (code name S-1),
  16–17, 20, 37, 57, 88, 90, 93,
  95, 97
dropping of, approved, 272–73n96
emotional reactions of pilots and
  plane crews, 124, 150, 253nxiii
Fat Man and Little Boy, 44, 93n,
  138, 138n, 147, 151
flash and quake of, *pikadon,* 173
Germany as target for, 251–52nxiii,
  258n17
Interim Committee of presidential
  advisers and, 45–49, 262–63n33,
  265n47
Japanese and other Asians, lives
  spared by dropping two bombs,
  226–27, 227n, 233

atomic bomb (A-bomb) (*cont.*)
  Japanese cities chosen as targets, 17,
    31–33, 35, 90, 93, 95, 99, 138, 172,
    262–63n33, 284n172
  Manhattan Project, xv, 27, 31–34
  Marshall's proposed use in invasion
    of Japan, 193–94, 194n
  moral dilemma of, 47
  noncombat demonstration proposed,
    46, 97–98, 262–63n33
  number of bombs built, 112
  opposition to use of, 44, 101,
    175–76, 262–63n33, 265n44,
    267n56, 284–85n172
  order to drop on Hiroshima from
    Groves to Spaatz, in writing, 111,
    112, 120, 193, 275n112
  question of mass slaughter and,
    262–63n33
  radiation and, 33–34, 48, 144, 194,
    194n, 222, 262–63n33
  ready for use, 97
  revisionist history of, 223–24, 225,
    260n20, 294–95n225, 294n223
  Russian development of nuclear
    capability, 44, 97, 214, 216
  Spaatz's psychological effect
    rationale, 173
  Stimson and, xv, xvi, 16, 20, 26,
    97–98, 258n17, 272–73n96 (*see also*
    Stimson, Henry L.)
  Stimson's article on the decision to
    use the atomic bomb, 223–24,
    293n217
  third bomb, Tokyo as target, xii, xvi,
    138, 139, 139n, 145, 158, 191–94
  Tibbets and, 251–52nxxiii (*see also*
    Tibbets, Col. Paul)
  Trinity test (July 1945), 20, 89–90,
    93, 95, 138
  Truman and, xiv, xv, 90–91, 95,
    99–101, 112, 133–34, 171,
    253–54nxiv, 260n20, 275n112
  Truman halts A-bomb drops, 171,
    172, 193, 284n171
Atomic Bombing Missions map, *xviii*
Ausable Club, St. Hubert's, NY, 167,
    191, 213, 293n213

B-17 Flying Fortress, 114
  Spaatz's plane, *Boops,* 119, 120
  Tibbets flying *Butcher Shop,* 120

B-29 Superfortress, *xi,* 21–22, 86
  altitude for A-bomb drop, 32
  bombing of Japanese cities by, 47,
    174–75, 195–96, 204, 284n171
  bombing of Tokyo by, xiii, 21–22,
    38, 49, 196
  crews' responses to bombing targets
    after Japan's surrender, 211–12,
    292n211
  flight of the *Bockscar, xviii,* 136,
    147–51
  flight of the *Enola Gay, xviii,* 123–24
  Japanese fear of, 72
  "jet stream" problem, 22
  mechanical/flight problems, 122
  Silverplate planes, 122
  Spaatz's "B-29s are not flying today"
    and bombing cessation, 174–75,
    281n149, 284n171
  Stimson's opposition to civilian
    bombing by, 49–50
  "thousand-plane" grand finale
    against Japan, 195–96, 211–12
  See also Spaatz, Gen. Carl "Tooey"
"Badoglios," 179, 188, 199
Bagby, Maj. Sarah "Sally," 117–18, 177
Bainbridge, Kenneth, 90
Balfour, John, 195
Barnes, Lt. Phil, 148
Beahan, Kermit, 149
Beschloss, Michael, 35n
Beser, Jacob, 124
Biddle, Tami, 13n
Bissell, Maj. Gen. Clayton, 193
Bockscar
  Atomic Bombing Missions map,
    xviii
  bomb dropped on Nagasaki's
    Urakami industrial valley, 149–51,
    154, 281n149
  A-bomb mission flight, 136, 147–51
  crew, 147
  Fat Man bomb and, 147, 148,
    149–50
  flight commander Sweeney, 147–51
  fuel pump problem and bad weather,
    148
  Kokura target abandoned, 149
  low fuel problem, 149, 150–51
  "Mayday" call, 150
  miscommunication with Tinian,
    148, 150
  Nagasaki set as new target, 149

Okinawa as emergency landing, 150–51
visual drop only ordered, 149
Bohr, Niels, 262–63n33
Brewster, Oswald, 264n38
Brooks, Phillips, 18, 258n17
  Muscular Christianity and, 18
Brown, Walter, 134–35
Bundy, Harvey, 16, 17–18, 20, 25, 37, 222, 258n17, 260n20
Bundy, McGeorge, 25, 223, 223n, 224, 293n217
Byrnes, James "Jimmy," 44–45, 53, 88, 88n, 90, 91, 94, 98n, 134–35, 194, 265n44, 293n217
  boasting of nuclear advantage, 214
  Japanese surrender, with condition and, 168–70, 179, 191, 284n169

Cate, James, 273n101
Chaplin, Charlie, 68
Cherwell, Lord, 257n13
China, 72, 105, 106, 168
  Japanese aggression in, 69, 71, 182, 191, 269n69
  Japanese raping and pillaging in, 71
  See also Manchuria
Churchill, Winston, 20, 117, 257n13
Clark, Champ, 295–96n232
Cold War, xii, 171, 216, 222, 293n217
Compton, Arthur B., 262–63n33
Conant, James, 33–34, 34n, 47, 222
Coolidge, Calvin, 4
Crane, Conrad, 137

Doolittle, Gen. Jimmy, 63, 76, 151, 212, 285–86n173
  Spaatz and, 116–17, 212
Dugway Proving Grounds, Utah, 23

Eighth Air Force, 116, 151, 212, 285–86n173
Einstein, Albert, 222
Eisenhower, Gen. Dwight, 101–3, 102n, 113, 115, 116, 117
Eisenhower, John, 102–3
Enola Gay, 111, 218
  armorer "Deak" Parsons on, 253nxiii
  Atomic Bombing Missions map, xviii

crew debriefed, 124–25, 131
drops Little Boy on Hiroshima, 123–24
  See also Hiroshima; Tibbets, Col. Paul

Farrell, Brig. Gen. Thomas, 31–32, 95, 131, 136
  Bockscar bombing mission and, 148, 151
  "Tinian Joint Chiefs" and, 137–38
Fiske, John, 258–59n18
509th Composite Group, 42, 251–52nxiii, 258n17
  B-29 Silverplates for, 122
  base on Tinian Island, 122, 137
  bombing Japan, Aug. 15, 1945, 211–12
  creation of, 112
  Japan monitors radio traffic of, 277n122
  New York Times reporter embedded with, 138
  on Okinawa, 177
  order to drop the A-bomb and, 111
  secrecy and, 122
  Tibbets commands, 121
  trains to drop the A-bomb with "Pumpkins," 121, 122, 277n122
Ford, Gerald, 219
Foreign Affairs magazine, 216
  Stimson article on nuclear arms, 216, 217
Forrestal, James, 58, 168, 284n169
  nuclear arms control, the Russians, and, 215–16
Franck, James, 262–63n33
Frank, Richard, 98n, 226
Frankfurter, Felix, 6, 224

Gallagher, Ray, 147
Germany
  Allied bombing of, 12–13
  Allied bombing of Berlin, 89, 92–93, 172–73, 263–64n36, 275–76n115, 285–86n173
  Allied bombing of Dresden, 12, 13–14, 16, 19, 23, 37, 117, 118
  Americans' desire to punish, 19
  A-bomb development and, 17

Germany (cont.)
  bombing to break morale by
    "dehousing," 13, 257–58n15,
    257n13
  Holocaust and, 34–35, 35n, 228
  Lovett and bombing of, 15
  Morgenthau's "pastoralization"
    plan, 10
  Nuremberg trials, 228
  as possible A-bomb target,
    251–52nxiii, 258n17
  postwar future, 10, 12, 88, 217
  secret weapons and, 19
  Spaatz and bombing of, 114, 115
  surrender of, 34, 72, 118
Goldberg, Alfred, 275–76n115
Gresham, Katharine, 232, 255nxvi,
  295–96n232
Grew, Joseph, 53–54, 91, 224–25,
  266n54, 267n58, 284n169,
  294n224
Groves, Maj. Gen. Leslie, 27, 30–34,
  193, 260n21
  A-bomb against Russia and, 216, 231
  A-bomb dropped on Hiroshima
    and, 129–30
  A-bombs to be delivered, 172,
    284n172
  A-bomb targets and, 31–33, 35,
    39–42, 49, 95, 99
  A-bomb tests (July 1945), 90, 93, 95
  background and character, 30–31
  Hiroshima as A-bomb target and,
    48–49
  Hiroshima casualties, reaction to,
    130
  Hiroshima damage report, 278n131
  Interim Committee and, 48
  Manhattan Project and, 30, 31–34,
    262–63n33
  order to drop the A-bomb given in
    writing to Spaatz, 111–12, 193
  radiation and, 194n, 289n194
  Stimson and, 31, 31n
  Stimson confronts on A-bomb
    targets, 40–42, 95–96
  third atomic bomb and, 192
  on Truman, xiv–xv
Guam, Army Air Forces headquarters,
  56, 121, 129
  LeMay at, 56, 129
  Spaatz at, 119, 121, 129, 131, 136,
    138, 171–73, 211

Hachiya, Michihiko, 144, 209
Handy, Gen. Thomas "Tom," 112,
  275n112
Hansell, Gen. Heywood, 23
Harper's
  Stimson's article on the decision to
    use the atomic bomb, 223–24
Harriman, William Averell, 7, 94
Harris, Gen, Arthur "Bomber," 12–13,
  117
Harrison, George, 37, 90, 93, 95, 130,
  191–92, 260n20, 275n112
Hatanaka, Kenji, 188, 202, 204–5, 207
Hayashi, Col. Saburo, 189, 202
Hersey, John
  Hiroshima, 222
Hiraizumi, Kiyoshi, 181–82
  "the Green-Green school" and, 181,
    188
Hiranuma, Baron Kiichiro, 164, 179,
  183, 284n169
Hirohito, Emperor, xvii, 75–78, 152,
  152–66, 182, 230, 255nxvii
  access to, 85
  American public opinion and, 53, 91
  America's need to preserve, 53, 54
  Anami and, 71, 181
  B-29 leaflets on surrender and, 199
  bomb shelter for, obunko, 77, 78, 145,
    160, 162, 163, 200–201, 204
  character and persona, 76–77, 78,
    162–63
  coup attempt, 1936, and, 68, 70, 77
  coup attempt, 1945, and, xii,
    182–89, 199, 204–5, 207
  desire to end the war, 63, 81, 82, 89,
    145–46, 163, 225
  Fundamental Policy of no surrender
    and, 75, 79, 82
  Hiroshima anniversary visit by,
    218–19
  Hiroshima's destruction and, 145
  Imperial Palace bombing and, 38,
    39, 53, 75, 77, 172
  imperial rescript of surrender, 201,
    202–3, 203n
  the jushin and, 161
  Kido's Russian proposal and, 81
  MacArthur and, 218
  official residence (Kantei), 63
  positions on war, 75–76
  Potsdam Declaration accepted,
    159–60

preservation of the imperial line
(*koto*) and, 160–61
protection of, 77
refusal to leave Tokyo, 78
retention of, as surrender condition,
58, 91, 97–98, 156, 164, 165, 167,
183, 184, 191, 199, 223,
267–68n59, 284n169, 290n199
revolts in the name of, 68
"the Showa Restoration" and, 67
son, Crown Prince Akihito, 76, 77
spared from war crimes trial, 228–29
surrender decision (*seidan*), xvii, 53,
159–65, 183, 231, 282n160,
282–83n161, 283n162
surrender meeting, Aug. 14, 1945,
200–202, 290n200, 290n201
surrender recording by, xii, 204,
208–9, 211
Three Sacred Treasures and, 107,
283n162
Togo and, 63, 107–8, 144–45,
280n145
visits the United States (1975), 219
war criminals added to Yasukuni
Shrine and, 219, 230n
Hiroshima
American reaction to bombing, 134
appearance after bomb hits, 124,
131–32
A-bomb dropped on, xi, xvi, 123–24
casualties, 101, 124, 171, 273n101,
278–79n134
Dr. Hachiya in, 144, 209
extent of destruction, 131, 132, 133,
144, 278n131, 278n134
F-13 crews, cameras, and recording
equipment, 131
Hersey's article on, 222
Japanese army inspection team views
destruction, 143–44
news of bombing reaches Tokyo,
141–42
order to drop the A-bomb on, from
Handy to Spaatz, 111–12, 120,
122–23
photoreconnaissance of, 131
photos, xv, 131, 132, 134
radiation sickness in, 144
rebuilding of, 218–19
selected as A-bomb target, 40,
48–49, 95, 100–101
See also Enola Gay

Hiroshima (Hersey), 222
Stimson reply to, 223–24
Hitler, Adolf, 155
banning of Jewish scientists and
impact on atomic bomb, 16–17
Lebensraum, 69
Hoover, Herbert, 4, 6, 55, 69n, 224
Hull, Cordell, 105, 105n, 274n105
Hull, Lt. Gen. John, 193

Ike's Bluff (Thomas), 102n
Inukai, Tsuyoshi, 67
Interim Committee (secret high-level
group), 42–49, 265n47
"Memorandum on Political and
Social Problems," 262–63n33
terror bombing and, 265n47
Iwo Jima, Battle of, 25, 267n58

Japan
aggressive nationalism and march to
war, 69–70
American bombing of, conventional
and incendiary, 21–22, 35–36, 40,
47, 49–50, 52, 70, 79, 119, 132,
140, 173, 195–96, 204, 261n23,
279n140, 284–85n172
American cessation of bombing, 175
American diplomatic overture to,
58–59, 267–68n59
American invasion (Operation
Downfall), xi, 52, 55, 84, 176, 193,
223, 225–26, 253nxiv
American invasion, projected
casualties, xiii, xiv, xvii, 55, 56–57,
101, 223, 253nxiv, 273n101
American "thousand-plane" grand
finale bombing against, 195–96,
211–12
American vengeance for Pearl
Harbor attack, 19, 70
America's "unconditional surrender"
demand, 52–53, 54, 58, 72, 83–84,
86, 104, 106, 135, 168, 169, 223,
267n59, 286–87n181
atomic bomb to force surrender by,
226–28, 227n, 258n17
atrocities committed by, 19, 69,
259n19, 269n69
attack on Pearl Harbor, 63, 75, 92,
105, 110, 230

Japan (*cont.*)
    attempt to build an A-bomb by, 142,
        227n
    B-29 leaflets dropped on,
        about surrender offer, 196–97,
        198–99
    B-29 leaflets dropped on, warning
        civilians of bombings, 108, 115,
        196
    Bataan Death March and, 130
    as beaten, 63, 64
    citizen armies, xiii
    coup attempt, February 26 Incident
        of 1936, 70, 77, 179–80, 184
    coup attempt, League of Blood
        Incident of 1932, 68
    coup plotted to stop surrender, 1945,
        178–89, 199, 204–5, 207
    economic condition (1945) as dire,
        72, 79–80
    execution of American prisoners,
        19, 76, 259n19
    feelings concealed in, 104
    fight-to-the-death position, xiii,
        74–75, 79, 80, 81, 82, 108–9,
        155–56, 166, 191, 225, 227–28
    final "decisive battle" (*hondo kessen*)
        strategy, 71, 73–74, 76, 84, 86,
        156, 163, 188, 225, 290n200
    first American troops land in, 209,
        291–92n209
    gekokujo or juniors overpowering
        seniors, 67, 68, 70, 79
    giri or obligation, 65–66
    haragei, literally, "the stomach art,"
        65, 81, 109, 164, 166, 186, 207
    Hiroshima's destruction and, 142
    home islands unconquered (1945), 19
    industry dispersed in private homes,
        49–50, 265–66n50
    the *jushin,* advisors to the emperor, 64
    kabuki, stylized dance, 71
    the *kokutai,* the imperial system, 61,
        61n, 80, 92, 145, 154–55, 160, 181,
        188
    Manchuria seized by, 62, 68–69, 182
    Meiji restoration, 78, 188
    military of, and code of *bushido,* 66,
        67, 82, 181–82
    mokusatsu (treat with silent
        contempt), 108, 109, 274n108
    national suicide as a *gyokusai,* a
        "shattered jewel," 158

National Volunteer Corps
    (civilians), 85
occupation of, MacArthur and food
    supplies for, 218, 226–27,
    277n119
*People's Handbook of Resistance
    Combat,* 85
postwar future, 91
Potsdam Declaration and, 98n, 104,
    108–9, 142, 153–59, 274n108
protection of the emperor, 77
revolution threat in, 63, 80,
    161–62, 179, 282–83n161,
    287n183
Russia as intermediary for peace
    and, 74, 80–81, 82–84, 92, 106,
    109–10, 146, 152–53
Russia invades Manchuria, 110, 147,
    152–53, 227, 280n147
Russia invades Sakhalin and Kuril
    Islands, 226
Russo-Japanese War, 69
"the Showa Restoration" or
    "government by assassination,"
    67–69, 68n
shukkettsu, "the bleeding strategy,"
    86, 156
sincerity in, 67
size of military forces, xiii, 25
Soviet Union declares war, xii, 97,
    146
starvation of the people, 226
suicidal *tokko* tactics/*kamikazes,*
    75–76, 76n, 81, 187, 223
suicide in culture of (*seppuku*), 66,
    77, 187n, 188, 206
supply lines bombed, 119, 277n119
surrender, xvi, 208–9
surrender ceremony, xiv, *198*
surrender decision, xvii, 152–66,
    178–89, 196–97, 201, 223, 227–28,
    290–91n201
surrender unacceptable, forbidden,
    xiii, xvi, 52, 53, 53n, 63, 208
Tale of the 47 Ronin, 66–67, 74, 181,
    207
thought police in, 71
war casualty figure, 209, 292n209
war crimes trials in, 228–30, 229n
"Yamato race," 67, 69, 156, 229n,
    281–82n156
See also Hirohito, Emperor;
    Hiroshima; Nagasaki; Tokyo

Japan: Supreme Council for the
    Direction of the War
  "Big Six," 61, 70–71, 75, 80, 105,
    108, 109, 146, 154, 269n70
  "Big Six" informed of Nagasaki
    A-bomb attack, 157–58
  "Big Six" meeting of Aug. 9 on
    surrender, 154–59, 281–82n156
  "Big Six" meeting of Aug. 9 with
    Hirohito on surrender, 162–63
  "Big Six" meeting of Aug. 13 and
    military plotters, 185–89
  "Big Six" meeting of Aug. 14 with
    Hirohito on surrender, 200–202,
    290n200, 290n201
  Decisive Battle (*hondo kessen*), (plan
    for Ketsugo Sakusen), 71, 73–74,
    76, 84, 86, 156, 163, 188, 225,
    290n200
  Fundamental Policy of no surrender,
    74–75, 79, 81, 82, 155–56
  Hiroshima's destruction and, 146,
    280n146
  Kido's "Draft Plan for Controlling
    the Crisis Situation," 80–81
  military coup plot and, 178–89,
    199–200
  military members, 70, 108, 109, 158,
    159n, 183, 185, 186, 186–87
  opposition to surrender, xii, 70, 72,
    74–75, 79, 81, 82, 155–58, 178–89,
    201, 267n58
  Potsdam Declaration and, 108, 109
  Russia proposed as mediator, 73, 74,
    106, 108, 146, 270n72
  secret meetings of, 72
  Togo and seeking peace, surrender,
    xvii, 60, 63, 71–72, 108, 143,
    164–66, 201, 231, 232
Jones, Maj. Robert, 292n211

Kawabe, Lt. Gen. Torashiro, 142,
    153–54
Kennedy, John F., 223n
  Cuban Missile Crisis and, 217, 218,
    293n217
Khrushchev, Nikita, 218
Kido, Marquis Koichi, 78–80, 91, 107,
    161, 163, 179, 183, 282n160,
    287n184
  B-29 leaflets on surrender and, 197,
    198–99

desire for peace, 80
  escapes military coup, 207, 291n207
  surrender decision and, 201,
    290–91n201
  worry about assassins, 185
King, Admiral, 226
Kokura, 96, 111, 139, 148–49, 172
Konoe, Prince, 82, 107, 109, 110, 146,
    161, 282n160, 282–83n161,
    287n183
Kyoto
  Stimson blocks bombing of, 41, 47,
    48, 49, 95, 99, 264n41, 265–66n50
  Target Committee chooses for
    A-bomb drop, 40, 41, 49
Kyushu, 223
  Allied invasion of, 55, 85, 134, 194,
    226
  Allied invasion of, fudged casualty
    projections, xiv, 253nxiv
  Decisive Battle at (*hondo kessen*),
    (plan for, Ketsugo Sakusen),
    84, 86
  Japanese defenders of, 85, 92, 193,
    226

Laurence, William, 138
Leahy, Adm. William, 56, 168, 267n56
Lee, Robert E., 52
LeMay, Maj. Gen. Curtis, 22, 35, 119
  A-bomb targets and, 96
  attitude about A-bomb use, xiii
  chief of XXI Bomber Command,
    xiii
  civilian deaths and, 39, 50n
  cold-blooded statements by, 23, 39
  defeating Japan plan of, 56
  firebombing Japanese cities by,
    35–36, 40, 47, 50, 96, 119, 132,
    149, 173, 265–66n50
  Guam headquarters, 56, *129*
  Hiroshima photos, 131, 132, 134
  press conference on A-bomb, 136
  as Spaatz's chief of staff, 172
  Tokyo bombing and, 22, 23, 36, 38,
    39, 261n23
Lincoln, Brig. Gen. George, 193,
    289n193
Lovett, Robert "Bob," 22, 175,
    257–58n15, 257n15
  air force as a separate service branch
    and, 36

Lovett, Robert "Bob" (*cont.*)
  Arnold's air force duties and, 15–16
  as assistant secretary of war for air,
    14–15, 23, 50, 261n23
  background, 15
  bombing of Japanese cities and, 50
  bombing to break civilian morale, 15
  commanding the "Yale Unit"
    bombing group, 15
  Cuban Missile Crisis and, 217–18,
    293n217
  Hiroshima photos and, 133
  Impact magazine, 36
  Luce and, 131
  rebuilding of Europe and, 217
  Spaatz end-of-war communication
    with, 212–13
  Stimson and, 11, 15, 23, 36, 38, 50,
    217–18
  study on Japan's food supplies,
    277n119
Luce, Henry, 36, 131

MacArthur, Gen. Douglas, 56, 113
  briefed on the A-bomb drop, 120
  Hirohito and, 218, 229
  Japanese invasion and, 226
  occupation of Japan and, 227
  "This changes warfare," 120, 176
MacLeish, Archibald, 168
MAGIC, 7, 7n, 271n83
  intercepts of Hiroshima casualty
    reports, 134–35
  intercepts of Japanese diplomatic
    messages, 92, 275n109
  intercepts of Japanese resistance to
    surrender, 191, 289n191
  intercepts of Togo's mail, 89, 107
  intercepts on Kyushu defense, 226
Malik, Jacob, 82
Manchuria, 62, 68–69, 97, 110, 147,
  182
  Kwantung Army surrenders, 147,
    280n147
  Russia invasion of, 110, 147, 152–53,
    170, 227
Manhattan Project, xv, 27, 222
  air-burst bomb and, 32
  A-bomb test/Trinity test, 20, 89–90,
    93, 95
  Conant and, 33–34, 34n, 222
  Groves and, 31–34

  Los Alamos and, xiv, 31, 32,
    262–63n33
  Los Alamos scientists react to
    Hiroshima bombing, 221
  Met Lab at Chicago and,
    262–63n33
  Oppenheimer and, xiv, 31, 34, 43,
    221
  radiation effects and, 33–34,
    262–63n33
  Russian spies at Los Alamos,
    45, 97
  Stimson not kept informed, 33, 35
  Truman informed about, 28–30
  uneasiness by scientists about civilian
    target, 32
Marshall, Gen. George C., xiv, 112
  A-bomb production by Nov. 1
    query, 193–94
  A-bomb targets and, 41–42, 96
  Allied bombing of Dresden and,
    13–14
  America's moral standing and, 39
  bombing of Japanese cities resumed,
    195
  collusion with MacArthur, 56
  emotional self-restraint, 10, 11
  fudged casualty projections for
    invading Japan, xiv, 253nxiv
  Hiroshima bombing and, 130, 136
  Hiroshima damage report,
    278n131
  Operation Downfall (invasion of
    Japan) and, 55–56, 193, 226
  order to drop the A-bomb, 112,
    275n112
  order to drop the A-bomb on
    Nagasaki, 193
  Spaatz's "B-29s are not flying today"
    and, 174–75
  Stimson and, 10–11, 57, 260n20
  third atomic bomb and, 192–94
  Truman meetings with, 28–30,
    55–57, 253nxiv, 264n37
  war fatigue and, 56
Marshall Plan, 217
Matsumoto, Shunichi, 184
McCloy, Ellen, 6, 9
McCloy, John "Jack"
  as "acting secretary of war,"
    191–92
  background, 6
  bombing of Tokyo and, 37, 38

decision not to bomb German
   concentration camps, 35n
Japanese surrender and, 170
Japan's surrender conveyed to
   Stimson, 213
Marshall meeting, on A-bomb
   targets, 38–39
Potsdam Conference, 88, 94
rebuilding of Europe and, 217
response to A-bomb test (July
   1945), 90
on Russia, 94
Stimson and, 6, 9, 11, 57, 264n41
on Stimson and the A-bomb, 20,
   260n20
Truman meeting, A-bomb use
   proposed by, 57–58
ultimatum for Japan and, 192
McDilda, Lt. Marcus, 158
McNamara, Robert, 21, 260n21
Meade, Gen. George, 52
Meiji, Emperor, 85, 160, 182, 188, 201,
   205
Mikasa, Prince, 182
Molotov, Vyacheslav, 62, 83, 107,
   109–10, 146–47
Mori, Lt. Gen. Takeshi, 204–5
Murphy, Charles, 131–32, 278n131

Nagasaki
   added as A-bomb target, 96
   before/after A-bomb photos, 141
   "Big Six" informed of A-bomb
      attack, 157–58
   A-bomb dropped on, xi, xvi,
      149–50, 151, 154
   Catholic population of, 149
   civilian casualties, 150, 151
   importance of dropping a second
      bomb on, 227, 227n
   Mitsubishi armaments plant at
      ground zero, 150, 151,
      281n149
   order to drop the A-bomb, 111
   See also Bockscar
NATO (North Atlantic Treaty
   Organization), 217
New Yorker magazine
   Hiroshima (Hersey), 222
New York Times
   bombing of Tokyo reported, 22
   editorial of Aug. 11, 1945, 185

"GI's in Pacific Go Wild with Joy,"
   194
Stimson's article on the decision to
   use the atomic bomb and, 223
"Tokyo erased, says LeMay," 39
Niigata, 40, 48, 95, 111, 172
Nimitz, Fleet Adm. Chester, 138
Nishima, Yoshio, 143, 145
Norstad, Gen. Lauris, 36, 42, 122,
   261n23
nuclear arms control, 102n, 254–55nxv
   atomic future and, 44
   hydrogen bombs and, 44
   Interim Committee and, 42–49
   postwar agency for, 18, 31
   Stimson's desire to curtail weaponry,
      214–15, 293n213
   Truman and, 215–16

Okinawa, 212
   American forces waiting on, 134
   Bockscar landing on, 150–51
   509th Composite Group on, 177
Okinawa, Battle of, 54, 79, 267n58
   casualties, 55, 266n55
Olivi, Lt. Fred, 149, 150
On Active Service in Peace and War
   (Stimson), 25, 223n
Onishi, Vice Adm. Takajiro, 187, 187n
Operation Downfall (invasion of
   Japan), xvi, 55, 176, 193
   atomic bomb saving lives and, 223,
      225–26
   casualty estimates, xiii, xiv, xvii, 55,
      56–57, 85, 101, 223, 273n101
   Japan's counterstrategy to, 84, 86
Operation Olympic (invasion of
   Kyushu), 55, 85, 193
   fudged casualty projections, xiv,
      253nxiv
   Japanese reinforcement to repel
      landings, 92
   unlikeliness of happening, 226
Operation Starvation, 119
Oppenheimer, J. Robert, xiv, 27, 31,
   43, 253nxiv
   atomic future described by, 44
   attack on Hiroshima and, 221
   belittles A-bomb as a weapon, 46–47
   "blood on my hands," xiv
   A-bomb test (July 1945), 90
   civilian casualties projected by, 47

Oppenheimer, J. Robert (*cont.*)
　demonstration bomb idea
　　opposed, 46
　favors using the A-bomb, 48
　Interim Committee and, 43–49
　Manhattan Project and, xiv, 31,
　　34, 43
　nuclear weaponry and, 214
　radiation and, 34, 48, 262–63n33
　on Stimson's concern over civilian
　　casualties, 45–46
Ota, Saburo, 158

Page, Arthur, 37–38
Parrish, Noel, 275–76n115
Parsons, Capt. William "Deak," 32,
　137–38, 253nxiii, 277–78n123
Patterson, Robert, 192
Patton, Gen. George S., 52, 190, 190n
Pendergast, Tom, 51, 92, 101
Phillips Academy, Andover, Mass., 5
Potsdam Conference, 87–89, 90–91,
　94, 96–98, 101–3, 112, 133
　Cecilienhof Palace, 94, 96
Potsdam Declaration, 97–98, 98n, 104,
　106
　Japanese response, 108–9, 142,
　　158–60, 274n108
　Japan's acceptance, 153, 165
　Japan's conditions for surrender,
　　154–58, 166, 167
　Togo and, 106, 107, 108, 109
"psychic numbing," xiii, 253nxiii
Purnell, Rear Adm. William, 137–38

Rabi, I. I., 251–52nxiii
Roosevelt, Franklin Delano (FDR),
　xv, 88n
　A-bomb development and, 17
　A-bomb to be used on Japan
　　and, 20
　character and personality, 8, 28,
　　256n8
　death of, 27, 52
　German concentration camps and,
　　35n
　Leahy and, 267n56
　Stimson as secretary of war, 4, 8, 11,
　　28–29, 256n8
　Stimson meeting, March 3, 1945,
　　7–8

Roosevelt, Theodore, 9, 23, 54,
　258–59n18
Royal Air Force (RAF)
　"area bombing," 13, 13n, 23, 115, 172
　Bomber Command under Harris,
　　12–13
　bombing a population, 257–58n15,
　　257n13
　Dresden bombing and, 13
　"terror bombing" and, 117
Russell, Richard, 135

Saigo, Takamori, 188
Sakomizu, Hisatsune, 185–86,
　282–83n161
Sato, Naotake, 82, 83–84, 89, 92, 107,
　109–10, 146–47
Seeman, Col. Lyle, 193, 194
Sherwin, Martin, 293n217
Shigemitsu, Mamoru, 160, *198,*
　282n160
Shimamura, Toshiro, 288n185
Slim, Field Marshal Viscount William,
　229n
Soviet Union (Russia)
　American foreign policy and, 99,
　　214, 216
　American nuclear preemptive strike
　　against considered, 216, 231
　American POWs and, 7
　A-bomb development and, 44, 97,
　　214, 216
　Cuban Missile Crisis and, 218,
　　293n217
　declares war on Japan, xii, 97, 146
　expansionist policies, 83, 96, 97,
　　226–27
　German invasion of, 6n
　invasion of Germany, 7
　Japanese peace overtures and, 74, 80,
　　82–83, 106, 109–10, 270n72,
　　294–95n225
　Japanese surrender and, 170
　Manchuria and Russian ports
　　retaken, 73
　Manchuria invasion, 110, 147,
　　152–53, 170, 280n147
　neutrality pact with Japan, 6n, 62, 73
　as police state, 7
　postwar Europe and, 7
　Potsdam Conference and, 89, 96
　Potsdam Declaration and, 106

Russo-Japanese War, 69
Stimson and U.S. relationship with,
    6, 7, 93–94
Stimson's arms control treaty and,
    215
Togo and, 62, 74, 81, 82–84, 109,
    269n62
U.S. motivation in dropping the
    A-bomb and, xii
Spaatz, Gen. Carl "Tooey," xvi, 112,
    129
    A-bomb, emotional reaction to, xvi,
        118, 232
    A-bomb compromise target
        suggested by, 139–40
    A-bomb concerns, long-term,
        176–77
    A-bomb drop approved, 118, 119,
        272–73n96
    A-bomb dropping as a necessity,
        129, 284–85n172
    A-bomb for Tokyo and, 171–72,
        284–85n172, 284n172
    A-bomb order from Handy, in
        writing, 111, 112, 120, 193,
        275n112
    A-bomb targets and, 138–39, 172,
        284n172
    airpower and changing warfare, 176
    Allied bombing of Berlin and,
        172–73, 275–76n115, 285–86n173
    American "thousand-plane" grand
        finale against Japan, 195–96,
        211–13
    area bombing and, 172–73
    Arnold and, 114, 115, 117, 118, 172
    "B-29s are not flying today" and
        bombing cessation, 174–75,
        281n149, 284n171
    background, military career, 113–14
    Bomber Mafia and, 114, 176
    bombing in Europe and, xvi, 37,
        114–16, 117–18, 120, 172–73, 176,
        263–64n36, 274n114, 275–76n115
    character of, 113, 114, 115
    civilian bombing deaths and, 115,
        117, 118, 137, 139, 151, 174,
        175–76, 232–33, 275–76n115
    conscience and inner conflicts, xvi,
        xvii, 116, 117–18, 176–77, 232,
        233, 276n118
    death of, 232
    described by Eisenhower, xvi

diary accounts, xvi, xvii
Dresden bombing and, 117, 118
firebombing of Japanese cities and,
    173, 195–96, 284–85n172
509th Composite Group and, 112,
    211
Guam headquarters, 119, 131, 136,
    138, 171–73, 211
Hiroshima photos, 131
incendiary bombing and, 119, 140
MacArthur briefed on A-bomb, 120,
    176
Marshall reprimand of, after press
    conference, 136–37
Nagasaki bombing of industrial
    valley and, 151, 281n149
Operation Shatter blocked,
    275–76n115
Pacific strategic air war and, 118
poker playing and, 115, 118, 119, 131,
    174
postwar career and retirement,
    231–32, 295–96n232
"precision" bombing on Japan and,
    173–74
records left by, xvi–xvii, 255nxvi
"the Spaatz way," 116–17, 119–20,
    284–85n172
third A-bomb considered, xvi, 173,
    194, 212
Tibbets and, 121
Tibbets given A-bomb drop order,
    122–23
on Tinian, return of Tibbets and the
    Enola Gay, 124
visual bombing and, 115
wife, Ruth, 116, 117, 118, 276n118
Stalin, Joseph, 44, 62, 73, 169, 253nxiii
    A-bomb knowledge and, 97
    Manchuria invasion and, 110
    Potsdam Conference, 89, 96, 97
    Stimson cable for FDR to, 7–8
Stevenson, Adlai, 293n217
Stimson, Henry L., xv, xvii, 3, 3–26,
    95–96, 258n17
    A-bomb drop approved, 96, 225,
        272–73n96
    A-bomb drop ordered, xvi, 17–18,
        20, 26, 41, 251–52nxiii,
        253–54nxiv, 260n20
    A-bomb drops and stopping of
        firebombing, 279n140
    A-bomb production approved, 112

Stimson, Henry L. (*cont.*)
  A-bomb project (S-1) and, 16, 17,
    37, 51, 88, 90, 93, 95, 97
  A-bomb targets and, 40–42, 47, 48,
    95–96, 262–63n33
  A-bomb tests (July 1945) and,
    90–91, 93
  Air Forces redistribution center
    visited, 24–25
  American cessation of bombing
    Japan, 175
  American war weariness and, 19
  appearance, 5, 10
  Arnold and, 49–50, 265–66n50,
    272–73n96
  Ausable Club, St. Hubert's, NY, and,
    167, 191, 213, 293n213
  background, 5, 9–10, 54, 91
  Berlin tour post-bombing, 92–93, 96
  Bohr refused audience by,
    262–63n33
  Bundy and, 16, 17–18, 20, 25, 37,
    258n17, 260n20
  call for a nuclear freeze, address to
    the full cabinet, 215
  character, 3, 4, 9, 11, 14, 30, 31, 52,
    54, 190, 214, 217n, 251–52nxiii
  as childless, 11
  civilian bombing opposed, 23, 35,
    36, 38, 39, 45–46, 49–50, 51, 96,
    264n38, 265–66n50, 267–68n59
  Civil War history and, 52
  conscience, duty, and, 9, 20, 26
  criticism of, 251–52nxiii, 258–59n18
  death of, 231
  diplomatic overture to Japan, on
    surrender, 58–59, 267–68n59
  Dresden bombing and, 12, 13–14,
    16, 19, 23, 37
  Eisenhower and, 101–3
  emotional self-restraint, 11
  empathy of, 10
  ending the war as quickly as possible
    and, 26, 52
  Europe's and Germany's postwar
    future and, 10, 12, 88, 94, 217
  events of March 1945 and, 5–6
  existential anguish of, xv, 232,
    294–95n225
  FDR and, 7–8, 11, 27–28, 256n8
  final show of force/noncombat
    A-bomb demonstration proposed,
    58, 91, 97–98, 267–68n59, 267n58

  German and Japanese codes broken,
    7, 7n
  Germany surrenders and, 34
  Grew urges Japanese peace offer,
    53–54, 224–25, 267n58, 294n224
  Groves and, 31, 31n, 40–42, 95–96
  Harper's article on the decision to
    use the atomic bomb, 223–24
  health of, xv, 5, 8–9, 24, 167, 191,
    223, 231
  heart attack, August 8, 1945, 132–33
  Hiroshima bombing and, 125,
    130–31
  Hiroshima damage report, 278n131
  Hiroshima photos, 133, 134
  Holocaust and, 34–35, 35n
  home (Woodley) and homelife, 4,
    4n, 6, 9, 20, 22, 52, 190, 191
  horses and, 4, 9, 231
  information withheld from, 49–50
  integrity of, 3, 31, 113
  Interim Committee (secret high-
    level group), 42–49
  internment of Japanese-Americans
    and, 258–59n18
  invasion of Japan, casualty estimates
    and, 56–57
  Japanese, attitudes about, 91, 272n91
  Japanese as "Dr. Jekyll and Mr.
    Hyde," 229
  Japanese atrocities and, 259n19
  Japanese diplomats known to, 54
  Japanese surrender, continuing the
    pressure, 190–92
  Japanese surrender, response to offer,
    167–71, 190–91
  Japan's surrender conveyed to,
    213–14
  Kyoto bombing blocked by, 41, 47,
    48, 49, 264n41, 265–66n50
  Law of Moral Progress and, 228,
    258–59n18
  legacy of, 217–18
  Long Island estate (Highhold) and,
    24, 37, 93, 130, 215, 261n24
  Lovett as assistant, 11, 14–16, 23, 36,
    257n15
  Manhattan Project and, 28–30, 31n,
    33, 35
  marriage to Mabel White, 9, 95
  Marshall and, 10–11, 37, 57, 260n20
  Marshall meeting, March 5, 1945,
    11–12

maxim of, 6
McCloy and, 6, 9, 11, 20, 57, 88,
   170, 191–92, 214, 260n20, 264n41
Miami R&R for, 24–25
military service, 10n, 54
moral gravity of dropping the
   A-bomb and, 20, 45–46, 232,
   260n20
moral position of the U.S. and, 35,
   37–38, 51, 264n38
nuclear arms control and, 17–18, 31,
   43–44, 214–15, 293n213
On Active Service in Peace and War,
   25, 223n
Patton and, 190, 190n
photos of precision bombing and,
   36–37, 263–64n36
politics of, 29
Potsdam Conference, 87–89, 90–91,
   94–95, 101–3, 167–68
"psychology of combat," 190,
   288–89n190
racial issues and, 258–59n18
realism and idealism in American
   foreign policy, xv, 7, 52, 89,
   217–18, 254–55nxv, 293n217
records left by, xvi, 6, 254–55nxv
relationship with Theodore
   Roosevelt, 9
retirement, 215
Russia and, 6, 7, 93–94, 170, 214,
   216, 272n94
as secretary of war, xv, 4, 14, 256n8
service in presidential
   administrations, 4, 6–7, 52, 54,
   224
spiritual revival for America called
   for, 18, 258n17
"the Stimson Doctrine," 69n
stress, fatigue, and, 5, 14, 22, 24, 50
terror bombing or firebombing of
   cities and, 23, 49–50, 261n23,
   265n47
Tokyo bombing and, 21–22, 38,
   258n17
treatment of staff and aides, 11
Truman and, xv, 28–30, 87, 90, 91,
   94, 98–100, 256n8, 260n20
Truman meeting, Aug. 10, 1945, on
   Japanese surrender offer, 168–70,
   175
Truman meeting, June 6, 1945, 51
unconditional surrender

modification and, 58, 91, 97,
   267–68n59
Wall Street, law career, and wealth,
   3–4, 29
worry that science will outstrip
   morality, 18–19, 213–14, 232,
   258–59n18, 296n232
Yale Skull and Bones and, 6, 58,
   58n, 94
Stimson, Mabel, *3,* 6, 8, 9, 11, 20–21,
   95, 191, 213, 231
   "projective identification" and
      husband's stress, 21
Strauss, Lewis, 279n135
Suzuki, Adm. Baron Kantaro, 63–64,
   65, 70, 75, 108, 109
   "Big Six" meeting on surrender and,
      154, 155, 158
   fight-to-the-death position, 74, 80
   gekokujo and assassination attempt
      on, 70, 180, 184
   Hirohito meeting on surrender,
      162–63
   Hirohito's desire to end the war and,
      145–46
   Hiroshima's destruction and, 143,
      280n146
   Kido's Russian proposal and, 80–81
   military coup plotted against,
      179–80
   surrender decision and, 159, 160,
      164, 183–84, 185, 201, 282n160,
      282–83n161, 288n185
Sweeney, Maj. Charles, 147–51,
   281n149
Symington, Stuart, 113
Szilard, Leo, 46, 265n44

Taft, William Howard, 4, 52, 190
Taisho, Emperor, 182
Takagi, Admiral, 287n183
Takamatsu, Prince, 187
Takeshita, Masehiko, 180, 188, 200,
   202, 205–6
Tale of the 47 Ronin, 66–67, 74, 181, 207
Tanaka, Gen. Shizuichi, 207
Target Committee, 17, 31–33, 35, 96,
   262–63n33
   large urban center chosen to bomb,
      31–33, 35, 39–41
   radiation question not considered,
      262–63n33

Teller, Edward, 284–85n172
Third Army, 52, 190
Tibbets, Col. Paul, *111*, 120–25,
   251–52nxiii, 258n17
   Bockscar bombing mission and,
      148
   bombing in Europe and combat
      record, 120–21
   civilian bombing and, 121
   Enola Gay flight and dropping the
      bomb on Hiroshima, 123–24, 148,
      277–78n123
   509th Composite Group command
      and, 121, 148
   flying the B-29 Superfortress, 121
   in *Life* magazine, 121
   order to drop the A-bomb, 122–23
   pilot drops "Pumpkin" near Imperial
      Palace, 122, 277n122
   training to drop the A-bomb, 121,
      122, 277n122
Time-Life, 131
Tinian Island, 121
   B-29 takes off for Kokura/Nagasaki,
      xviii, 136
   509th Composite Group on, 122,
      137
   flight of the *Bockscar, xviii,* 147–51
   flight of the *Enola Gay, xviii,* 123,
      124
   Manhattan Project personnel on,
      138
   "Tinian Joint Chiefs" and, 137–38
   Twentieth Air Force base in, 121–22
Togo, Shigenori, *60,* 60–65, 255nxvii
   Allies' terms for surrender and,
      183–89, 287n184
   American diplomatic overture to
      Japan and, 59
   background, 61–62
   "Big Six" and, 71–72, 108
   "Big Six" surrender meeting and,
      154–59
   cabinet resignation and, 209–10
   character of, 62, 104–5, 210, 268n61
   death of, 231
   desire for war's end, 63, 64, 71–72,
      109, 228, 280n143
   Fundamental Policy of no surrender
      and, 74–75
   German wife, Edith, 61, 63, 230
   Hirohito and, 63, 107–8, 144–45,
      159, 280n145

Hirohito meeting on surrender,
      162–63
   Hirohito's *seidan* (sacred decision)
      and, 160, 161, 163, 183
   Hiroshima's destruction and, 145
   as Japanese Foreign Minister, xvii,
      61, 62, 65
   MAGIC intercepts of mail and
      conversations, 89, 107, 275n109
   memoirs, 230–31
   in Nagano, 63, 64
   positions on war, 62–63, 105–6,
      105n, 225, 274n105
   Potsdam Declaration and, 106, 107,
      108, 109, 153
   request that the Allies allow the
      army to disarm itself, 203
   risks of discussing surrender, 71–72
   Russia as intermediary for peace
      plan and, 74, 81, 82–84, 92, 106,
      109–10, 146, 152–53, 294–95n225
   Russian pacts and, 62, 269n62
   surrender decision and, xvii, 143,
      164–66, 201, 231, 232
   surrender decision and military coup
      plot, 178–89
   surrender papers, ruse of wrong
      stamp, 184–85
   Tokyo bombing, casualties, and, 60
   transmits surrender of Japan to
      Washington and London by
      Morse code, 166
   Truman's address on the Hiroshima
      bombing and, 142–43
   war crimes trial and imprisonment,
      229–31, 230n, 294n230
   Washington's reply to conditional
      surrender offer, 178–79
Tojo, Hideki, 63, 230
Tokyo
   American leaflets dropped on,
      196–97
   bombing casualties, xiii, 22, 38, 60
   bombing of, *xi,* xii, xvi, 21–22, 23,
      36, 38, 49, 172, 196, 258n17,
      261n23
   Doolittle's attack on, 63, 76
   Hiroshima bombing news reaches,
      141–42
   Imperial Palace bombed, 38, 39,
      53, 77
   International Military Tribunal for
      the Far East held in, 228–30, 229n

napalm and fires, 22
proposed drop of third A-bomb on,
    xvi, 138, 139, 139n, 145, 158,
    191–92, 212
reports of bombing in American
    papers, 22
War Ministry, Ichigaya Heights, 153,
    155, 202, 228
Yasukuni Shrine, 219, 230n
Toyoda, Adm. Soemu, 70, 74, 157, 158,
    183, 185, 186, 269n70, 287n183
Truman, Harry, 97, 273n101
    aboard the *Augusta,* 133, 134
    A-bomb drop decision and, xiv, xv,
        100, 112, 253–54nxiv, 260n20,
        275n112
    A-bomb dropped on Hiroshima,
        news of, 133–34
    A-bomb drops halted by, 171, 173,
        193, 284n171
    A-bomb killing of "all those kids"
        and, 171
    A-bomb targets and, 99–101
    A-bomb test (July 1945) and,
        90–91, 95
    address to the nation on A-bomb
        drop, 37, 134–35, 142–43
    background, 51–52, 101
    becomes president, 28
    bombing of Japanese cities resumed,
        195
    Byrnes and, 88, 91, 94, 98n
    civilian bombing issues, 51, 134–35
    described by Maj. Gen. Groves,
        xiv–xv
    evolution of views on the A-bomb,
        279n135
    first address to Congress, 52–53
    first war council, April 30, 1945,
        28–30
    Hirohito and, 92
    Hiroshima casualties and, 134–35,
        171, 278–79n134
    Hiroshima photos, 133, 168, 171
    Interim Committee and, 44
    invasion of Japan and casualty
        estimates, 55–57, 101, 253nxiv,
        273n101
    Japanese surrender, "conditional
        unconditional surrender," 168–71,
        194
    Manhattan Project and S-1,
        28–30, 97

    military service, World War I,
        54–55
    moral ambiguity and, 101, 134
    Nagasaki A-bomb attack, ignorance
        of timing of, 171
    nuclear arms control and, 215–16
    Okinawa casualties and, 55
    as political realist, 51–52
    politics of, 29, 91–92
    Potsdam Conference, 87–89, 91,
        96–98, 133
    reaction to Oppenheimer, xiv,
        253nxiv
    Russia and, 226
    Secretary of War Stimson and, xv,
        28–30, 51, 87, 90, 91, 94, 98–100,
        168, 215, 253–54nxiv, 256n8,
        260n20
    Szilard beseeches not to drop the
        A-bomb, 46
    "terrible responsibility" of
        Hiroshima, 134–35, 171
    third A-bomb considered, xvi,
        194–95
    "unconditional surrender" position
        of, 52–53, 54, 58, 86, 91, 92, 106,
        169
Twentieth Air Force, 42, 172, 213,
    265–66n50, 292n211
    base on Tinian Island, 121–22
    disruption of Japanese supply lines,
        119, 277n119
    XXI Bomber Command, xiii,
        22, 23
    firebombing Japanese cities, 35–36,
        40, 47
    See also LeMay, Maj. Gen. Curtis
Twining, Lt. Gen. Nathan, 172,
    284n172

ULTRA, 7, 7n
    intercepts of Hiroshima death toll,
        171
    intercepts of Japanese military
        communications, 92
    intercepts of Japanese resistance to
        surrender, 191
    intercepts on Kyushu defense,
        226
Umezu, Gen. Yoshijiro, 70, 82, 157,
    158, 183, 185, 186, *198,* 200,
    287n183

U.S. armed services
  integration of, 258–59n18
  manpower shortfall, 19
U.S. Army
  Miami's Biltmore Hotel
    requisitioned, 24
U.S. Army Air Forces, 265n47
  bombing of Japanese cities, 21–22,
    261n23
  civilian bombing issues, 12, 13, 23,
    35, 38, 39, 121, 263–64n36
  Dresden bombing and, 13–14
  Eighth Air Force casualties, 116
  incendiary bombing and, 23, 35–36,
    38, 40, 47, 50, 119
  Lovett and strategic bombing, 15
  napalm used by, 22, 38
  "precision" bombing, 12, 13, 13n,
    21, 22, 23, 35, 36–37, 38, 39, 119,
    120
  as a separate service branch,
    postwar, 36
  Tokyo bombing and, 21–22
  Tokyo bombing as strategy shift, 23
  See also specific units; specific targets
U.S. Congress, 8, 17, 19, 216, 217,
    256n8
  Groves's testimony to, 194n
  nuclear policy and, 43
  Truman's first address to, 52
U.S. Navy
  hospital ships in the Pacific, xiv,
    253nxiv
  Japanese invasion armada, xiv
  Seabees build Marianas airfields, 21
USS Henry L. Stimson, 216–17, 217n
USS Missouri, 198

Vietnam War, 23

Wallace, Henry, 171
Washington, D.C.
  National Cathedral, 8–9
  New War Building, 129
Weckerling, Brig. Gen. John, 89
Wellerstein, Alex, 100
Wetzler, Peter, 281–82n156,
    286–87n181

World War II, 73
  America liberates the Marianas,
    builds airfields, 21
  American armed forces, manpower
    shortfall, 19
  American code breakers, 7, 7n, 89,
    271n83
  American war weariness, 19, 25, 56,
    86, 89
  Atlantic Charter, 98n
  Battle of Iwo Jima, 25, 267n58
  Battle of Okinawa, 54, 55, 79,
    266n55, 267n58
  German concentration camps and
    mass murder, 34–35, 35n, 228
  Germany surrenders, 34
  International Military Tribunal for
    the Far East, 228–30, 229n
  Japan surrenders, 165
  Nuremberg trials, 228
  Potsdam Conference, 87–89, 90–91,
    94, 96–98, 101–3, 112, 133
  Potsdam Declaration, 97–98, 98n,
    104, 106, 108–9, 142, 153, 158–60,
    165, 274n108
  "unconditional surrender" demand
    of Japan and, 52–53, 54, 58, 72,
    83–84, 86, 104, 106, 135, 168, 169,
    223, 267n59, 286–87n181
  war in the Pacific, 19, 25–26, 73, 176
  war in the Pacific, casualties of
    combatants and noncombatants,
    209, 292n209
  winter of 1945 and, 19
  Yalta Conference, 6n, 73, 97
  See also atomic bomb; Germany;
    Japan; specific battles

Yalta Conference, 6n, 73, 97
Yamamato, Isoroku, 63
Yonai, Adm. Mitsumasa, 70, 73, 75,
    80–81, 280n146
  "Big Six" meeting on surrender and,
    154, 155, 156, 158
  surrender decision and, 164, 185,
    287n183
Yoshida, Shigeru, 62, 71
  Anti-War Group, 282–83n161
Yoshizumi, Gen. Masao, 163–64

About the Author

EVAN THOMAS is the author of eleven books, including the *New York Times* bestsellers *John Paul Jones, Sea of Thunder,* and *First: Sandra Day O'Connor.* Thomas was a writer, correspondent, and editor for thirty-three years at *Time* and *Newsweek,* including ten years as Washington bureau chief at *Newsweek,* where, at the time of his retirement in 2010, he was editor at large. He has appeared on many TV and radio talk shows, including *Meet the Press* and *Morning Joe.* Thomas has taught writing and journalism at Harvard and Princeton, where, from 2007 to 2014, he was Ferris Professor of Journalism in Residence.

About the Type

This book was set in Bembo, a typeface based on an old-style Roman face that was used for Cardinal Pietro Bembo's tract *De Aetna* in 1495. Bembo was cut by Francesco Griffo (1450–1518) in the early sixteenth century for Italian Renaissance printer and publisher Aldus Manutius (1449–1515). The Lanston Monotype Company of Philadelphia brought the well-proportioned letterforms of Bembo to the United States in the 1930s.